THE WILD SWIMMER OF KINTAIL

PRAISE FOR KELLAN MACINNES:

'Stylish and experimental' THE COURIER

' …eccentric and off-kilter… Kellan MacInnes has been willing to experiment with form, structure and language… ' ALISTAIR BRAIDWOOD

'He often writes very well… His descriptions of wild mountain scenery are precise and vivid' ALLAN MASSIE

'Fantastic and beautiful writing' JOYCE MACMILLAN

'MacInnes has real talent' THE SCOTSMAN

FOR MUM & ANDREW

Also by Kellan MacInnes

Caleb's List
The Making of Mickey Bell

The Wild Swimmer of Kintail

KELLAN MACINNES

2022

Published 2022
by Rymour Books
45 Needless Road
PERTH
PH2 0LE

https://www.rymour.co.uk

© Kellan MacInnes 2022
ISBN 978-1-7395960-5-7

Cover design by Ian Spring
Printed and bound by
Imprint Digital
Seychelles Farm
Upton Pyne
Exeter

A CIP catalogue record for this book
is available from the British Library

The author acknowledges the support of Creative Scotland
in researching and writing this book

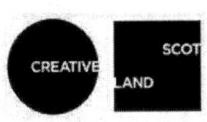

ALBA | CHRUTHACHAIL

All rights reserved. No part of this publication may be reproduced, stored in a retrieval system, or transmitted, in any form or by any means, electronic, mechanical, photocopying, recording or otherwise, without the prior permission of the publishers.

ACKNOWLEDGEMENTS

Special thanks to Lesley Hampshire for permission to use the extracts from 'Kintail Scrapbook' and to Liz Marshall for accompanying me on the 'book' walks and camping with me at Iron Lodge. Also thanks to Sue Collin for her literary critique of the poetry of Brenda G Macrow and to Gillian Zealand, Gareth Dennis and Marcia Pointon. I acknowledge financial support from Creative Scotland. While researching and writing this book I was very grateful for the help I received from the staff of the National Library of Scotland, St. Andrew's University, D C Thomson & Co Ltd. and to Angus and the Loch Mullardoch Ferry. Finally thanks to Ian Spring for having the courage and imagination to publish a book by Kellan MacInnes.

KELLAN MACINNES

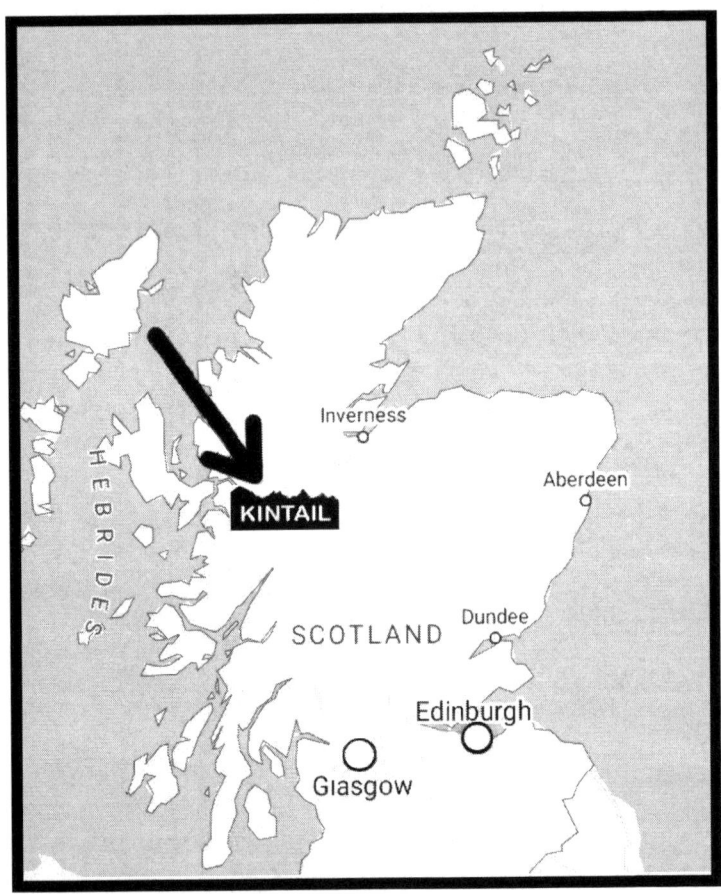

KINTAIL is a mountainous area on the north-west coast of Scotland. Its boundaries are generally taken to be Glen Shiel to the south, the valleys of Strath Croe and Gleann Gaorsaic to the north and An Caorann Mòr to the east. It is one of forty national scenic areas in Scotland. Perhaps its best known feature is the range of peaks known as the Five Sisters of Kintail. Visitors can travel to Kintail by car, by bus from Glasgow or by the scenic Inverness to Kyle of Lochalsh railway line.

Next Page: Brenda G Macrow's sketch map of the hill lochs of Kintail.

ILLUSTRATIONS
(between pages 168 and 177)

Brenda G Macrow and Jeannie, the Skye terrier.

Kellan MacInnes and the Labradoodle.

Photographs from the 1940s: on the hill and wild swimming.

The outflow of Loch Mullardoch photographed by Robert Moyes Adam in 1930.

Blue Remembered Hills: Looking across the mountains of the northwest Highlands to Kintail.

Loch Dubhach.

Loch nan Eun.

Loch Coire nan Dearcag nestles below the summit of Sgurr nan Ceathramhnan.

Loch an t-Sabhail.

Loch a Chlèirich, high on the mountain A'Ghlas bheinn.

Iron Lodge and upper Glen Elchaig.

Glen Affric: hydro-electric development here was carried out more sensitively than at nearby Loch Mullardoch.

The Five Sisters of Kintail.

The lodge under the loch: Benula Lodge where Macrow stayed the night in 1946. It was later submerged by the Loch Mullardoch hydro-electric scheme.

Dornie in 1946 and Dornie now.

All that is gold does not glitter,
Not all those who wander are lost

J R R Tolkien

Ice

The Glen

They said it came from your mother's side, this sense – more a feeling – a fleeting vision in your head of the future. Almost with a shiver you have it now, as you walk along the dusty road between the heather and bog myrtle.

At the foot of the last rise before the lodge the young woman pauses and stands in the road. She can hear sounds, not just the song of the skylarks and the River Cannich tumbling down over the smooth boulders. She can hear noises coming from the lodge. Sounds of hammering and workmen talking and noises like wooden boards being thrown down, and then more hammering.

Drip by clear freezing drip the ice melts. Drip by drip the icy water trickles over the cladonia lichen and purple saxifrage flowering at the edge of the glacier in the short Arctic spring. Drip by clear freezing drip the glacier melts, the strip of gravelly moraine a metre longer now than last summer. Drip by clear freezing drip the ice melts.

Four hundred miles to the south, across the Greenland tundra and the grey sea as the pink-footed geese fly, the young woman walks alone along the dusty road. Close by, the River Cannich flows down from Loch Mullardoch over stones worn smooth by torrents of peaty water. Orange birch leaves float on the surface of the river's steely, blue pools. She, the young woman, is the wife of Archie Chisholm, head stalker on the Glen Cannich estate.

The village of Cannich lies at the eastern end of a remote and beautiful glen cutting a deep trough through the mountains of the north-west Highlands and by the lonely houses at Benula and Iron Lodge to join Glen Elchaig and reach the western seaboard of the Gael near Dornie in Kintail. Kintail, named from the Gaelic *Cean Da Shaill*, the head of the two seas, where the great Atlantic rollers break over the rocky skerries when the storm clouds sweep in from the west.

The young woman turns the bend in the road by the reed beds and marshy edges of Loch a' Bhana where silver birches fringe the loch. A windbreak of Scots pines screens the lodge from sight. The landowner and his acquaintances like to travel north from London each summer to fish Loch Mullardoch for brown trout and the River Cannich for the wild salmon. And as the oaks and birches in the glen tint yellow and then orange they come to stalk the red deer that graze high on Sgurr na Lapaich.

It is the decade before World War Two and each spring, tradesmen, joiners, painters, plasterers and roofers come from Glasgow to get the lodge ready for the gentry. There are missing roof slates lost to the winter storms. Fallen plaster upstairs where the rain came in, rones choked with yellow birch leaves and paint flaked and blistered by the hot sun of a Highland summer. The men stay in the bothy, an old white-washed cottage a hundred yards distant from the lodge and used by the ghillies during the stalking season.

This sunny morning in April 1930, when the fresh westerly wind sweeps the pewter clouds across the sky, the young woman is on her way to open up the bothy and get the place ready for the men coming. She'll struggle to open the sash and case windows. She'll give the stained horsehair mattresses an airing, sweep the dust and cobwebs away and fill the old milk churn with buckets of water from the burn.

Squatting on the dusty cement hearth in the bothy she'll tear pages from *The Inverness Courier* and the greasy, well-thumbed magazines left behind by the ghillies last autumn. She'll glance briefly at the

THE WILD SWIMMER OF KINTAIL

creased pictures of Myrna Loy in a bath of rose petals. Is that all men think about? She'll ponder, not for the first time as she rolls pages from *Life* magazine into knots to light the fire. She'll put candles in the empty whisky bottles that are the bothy's only form of lighting and lay the kindling and coal ready in the grate for the men to put a match to.

They said it came from your mother's side, this sense – more a feeling – a fleeting vision in your head of the future. Almost with a shiver you have it now, as you walk along the dusty road between the heather and bog myrtle. Just at the foot of the last rise before the lodge the young woman pauses and stands in the road. She can hear sounds. Not just the song of the skylarks and the River Cannich tumbling down over the smooth boulders. She can hear noises coming from the lodge. Sounds of hammering and workmen talking and noises like wooden boards being thrown down, and then more hammerinG

The men: they must have arrived early she thinks, and she hesitates a moment before turning back the way she came and heading down the glen, back towards Cannich. She's shy, you see. She doesn't like being at the lodge when the men are there, swearing and undressing her with their eyes. 'Gie us a cuddle darlin' …seein' as ma mammie's no' here.' And yet she likes it too, deep down inside she trembles a little. Dark-haired Glaswegians with tattooed forearms and blue eyes, they'll work bare-chested, shirts off, sun-tanned, brown skin after a week if the weather's kind. So different from Archie's freckles and white skin and red hair, but her man is a good man.

The young woman is peeling spuds from the vegetable plot behind the keeper's house when the barking of the terriers alerts her to Archie's return. He pulls off his muddy boots in the porch and sits down in the chair by the stove watching her cook as she tells him about her wasted journey to the lodge.

'But that canna be,' he says, 'they're no' coming 'til next week.'

In the pale morning Archie wheels his old Raleigh Roadster out from where he keeps it behind the coal shed and pushes it most of the way along the hilly road up Glen Cannich to the lodge.

He finds the place utterly deserted.

No-one has set foot there since last October. A spider has spun an elaborate gossamer-thin web, the work of many weeks, across the padlock on the front door of the bothy.

For the rest of her days, when the peats on the fire burn low and night falls over Sgurr na Lapaich, the young woman will always swear what happened that April morning was a premonition. For that spot in Glen Cannich where she stood still in the road and heard the song of the skylarks drowned out by the noise of hammering and the sound of wooden boards being thrown down is the very same place where today there looms the vast, gloomy, grey, concrete edifice of the giant Mullardoch mass gravity hydro-electric dam.

North

London

Cinntaille! Cinntaille! Air ais!
The witches screamed.
Back to Kintail! Back to Kintail!
                    Gaelic Folklore

'We're going to Soho, number 2 Greek Street,' says my aunt as I struggle to fasten the rear seat belt of the private hire cab. The West End is rammed. The taxi slows as people spill off the pavements. Old Compton Street is thronged with revellers. The driver looks like an extra from the Harlem funeral scene in the Bond movie *Live and Let Die*.

Macrow 1946: *I left London on a night of blue twilight and faint drizzling rain. I had packed up sandwiches to eat on the train, but thought it prudent to go out and have dinner before starting.*

My aunt lives in Camden. Earlier that day, sitting at a desk in my aunt's flat high above Oakley Square I typed Hungarian + restaurant + London into the search box of Google. We order a private hire cab.
'We're going to The Gay Hussar,' my aunt tells the driver.
'Very famous restaurant, you are politician?' he jokes as he presses a button on the meter. He looks like an extra from the Harlem funeral scene in *Live and Let Die*.

Macrow 1946: *My sister and I found a little Hungarian place where we had Wiener schnitzel and salad, with some rather sickly trifle to follow.*

I push open the low wooden doors and enter the little restaurant. A wood panelled room with a yellow, vaulted, plaster ceiling, little wooden tables in two rows, white table cloths, gleaming glasses and shining silver cutlery.

The Polish maître d' in suit and pinkish-red tie greets us.

'Good eevening, sir.'

'Hi. I've booked a table for two?'

'What the name pleese?'

'M-ac-in-ess,' I reply.

He ushers us to a table in the window beside the door. He has to pull the table out for my aunt to get in. This feels like the kind of place Macrow might have come to in 1946 on that night of blue twilight and faint drizzling rain before boarding the night sleeper to Inverness at Euston Station.

A Bangladeshi waiter brings the menu. Macrow wrote that in 1946 they ate: 'Wiener schnitzel and salad followed a by a rather sickly kind of trifle.' I run my eyes down the dishes on the menu. There are six main courses and one of them is Wiener schnitzel, just what Macrow ordered in 1946. Doesn't look like the menu's changed much in the 75 years since then. My aunt orders the mixed Hungarian hors d'oeuvres followed by roast duck with cabbage and potatoes. But I stick to what Macrow ordered 75 years ago. Dessert is more of a challenge. I can hardly ask which item on the dessert menu most closely resembles 'rather sickly trifle' so I swither between layered gateau with caramel topping versus poppyseed strudel before finally opting for mixed berry puddinG We drink Hungarian red house wine. Macrow didn't record what they drank in 1946. In fact she doesn't write about drink much, though when the going gets tough on the banks of the Abhainn Sithidh, she'll produce a flask of medicinal brandy.

> Macrow 1946: *While we were eating, my little Skye terrier, Jeannie, lay under the table, registering strong disapproval.*

'So, what's this new book of yours about?' asks my aunt as we wait for the mixed hors d'ouevres, 'And why are we in a Hungarian restaurant in Soho?'

My aunt's had seven books published, you see. Mainly beautifully produced, laviously illustrated tomes on history of art. She's professor emiritus of history of art at Manchester University.

'I'm retracing the journey of a little known female poet and mountaineer who spent six months visiting the hill lochs of Kintail a remote area of the North West Highlands of Scotland, in the summer of 1946,' I explain.

'Will I have heard of her?'

'No, I don't think so.'

'Try me. What's her name?'

'Brenda G Macrow.'

Silence as my aunt tucks into her plateful of roast duck and cabbage and over dinner I explain to her why we're sitting in a Hungarian restaurant in Soho.

'Basically the idea is a book repeating Macrow's journey to the North West Highlands of Scotland. I'm going to spend the next six months retracing Macrow's travels through Kintail and ticking off all 28 of the hill lochs she visited in the summer of 1946. A bit like Munro bagging, I guess, but swimming hill lochs instead.'

And between mouthfuls I go onto explain how all the hill lochs on Macrow's list lie at an altitude of 1,000 feet or higher. And how in 1946 the Highlands of Scotland stood on the cusp of change in the form of massive hydro-electric development and how many of the remote glens Macrow visited on her travels would never be the same again.

'So what's happening with your flat?' asks my aunt asks a little awkwardly as the waiter clears the plates away.

'Dunno,' I shrug, 'Guess I'll have to try and buy him out... '

'And can you to afford to do that?'

I shrug again.

'I'll just have to, I guess. It wasn't my choice. I don't want to be single. But hey,' I go on, attempting brightness, I don't really feel, 'Shit happens. I do have a plan to make some money though… '

9.30pm: My aunt wants to go home and I've got a train to catch. A train back to 1946, I think to myself. The young Hungarian waiter brings the bill in a leather folder. As I slide my card into the green glow of the chip and pin machine, I see Macrow click open the clasp of her handbaG Macrow lays five coins out on the wooden table. Jeannie stirs and stretches under the table. Stands and sniffs the waiter's trouser leg.

On an April evening in the second decade of the twenty-first century our bill comes to £75.20. I leave a fiver as a tip, the average weekly wage in 1946. I'm a struggling writer after all. It's a Scottish bank note too.

While we're putting our coats on, the waiter asks if this was our first time eating Hungarian food and did we enjoy it?

'Is this the oldest Hungarian restaurant in London?' I ask.

'The restaurant's been here for sixty years,' he replies.

'Would it have been here in 1946?'

The waiter thinks for a moment.

'Maybe round the corner in Frith Street.'

And then I hear the rustle of fabric as Macrow pulls on her coat, straightens her hat and the click of metal as she clips Jeannie onto the lead. The sirens have been silent for almost a year now but sandbags and air raid shelters still stand on every street corner. Outside in the darkness of the Soho of 1946 Macrow hugs her sister and kisses her goodbye. Then with Jeannie following along at her heels she hurries down Frith Street. Past the Anderson shelters and piles of sandbags, past the water dripping from the charred rafters of the bombsite, past the streetlights reflected in the puddles, past the tattered posters warning *Careless Talk Costs Lives* and through the pillars and under the great arch of Euston Station in the blue twilight as a faint drizzling rain begins to fall.

Night Train North

This is the Night Mail crossing the border,
Bringing the cheque and the postal order...
W H Auden, 1936.

Euston Road, 10.15pm on a damp Sunday night in early April. I can hear the tannoy announcements long before I reach the station. Sirens are the sound of twenty-first-century London too. A light drizzle of rain blurs the traffic lights and the red brake lights of the cars. I'm walking in a poet's footsteps, following Macrow down the Euston Road. Yellow London brick glowers down on me, a Scot headed north, headed back to the mountains and the rivers and the rustle of the wind through the pine trees.

Outside a club there's a bit of argy bargy going on. Three lads wanting a late Sunday night drink are being refused entry to the lap-dancing club in Eversholt Street. The bouncers are stopping them going in. The trajectory of their evening changed. The club is next door to the Euston Sauna. It must be that kind of part of town.

London calling: London to where I travel in early spring to start to retrace Macrow's 1946 journey. London calling: to a gay boy from the north, from Scotland, London offering experiences not normally available in the bars of chilly Presbyterian Scotland, round the corner from Kings Cross, south of the river in Vauxhall, Central Station and the Hoist.

There's a young drag queen lives in the street where I'm staying. My aunt says she's never seen him out of makeup. London: city of yellow brick houses and fig trees in front gardens. In a few hours time I'll be leaving London. This morning we walked in Regent's Park. My aunt admiring the tulips while I discretely admire hairy legs and the curve of male buttocks in black cycle shorts.

Over soup and ryebread and cheese we talked about immigration and racism. It's been good being in London, being away from Edinburgh and the trauma of the last twelve months with my ex, but now I'm headed north again. Maybe it's because I'm Scottish but I have this primeval thing that when things get tough I have to take to the hills.

> Macrow 1946: *I only knew that there was a place in Scotland which was calling me back... cunningly weaving its spell from afar... And so—I was going back to Kintail. And, already, sitting in the train at Euston, I could feel the cool mountain wind blowing off the snowfields—smell the sharp tang of peat—*

Today Euston Station lies in the basement of a large 1960s office block. But in 1946 Macrow and Jeannie would have made their way beneath the much lamented and long gone Euston Archway. Demolished to make way for the present day brutalist office block, but promised a resurrection in the architects' plans for the new Euston, destined to be the terminus of High Speed Two, if it ever gets built. My aunt in Camden is much exorcised at the prospect of hundreds of lorries a week, making their way past her flat on the Eversholt Road, on route to what will be one of the biggest construction projects in Europe. The atmosphere in the station's tense too. A big group of drunken youths drinking cans and making a lot of noise. The Labradoodle leans in against my leg.

> Macrow: *Jeannie hates travelling... Some strange phobia about trains has caused her, ever since puppyhood, to break out in a cold sweat at the mere rattle of wheels over sleepers, the distant 'chuff-chuff' of a sleepy engine... Euston Station is her idea of hell; and I knew that even the dose of bromide I had brought for her in my*

THE WILD SWIMMER OF KINTAIL

handbag would do little towards making her relax on this, the first really long train-journey of her life.

Hmmmm? Do dogs sweat? I'm reading this and wondering do dogs sweat? Pretty sure they don't, their main method of losing heat is pantinG But I suppose Macrow is using the phrase 'break into a cold sweat' metaphorically. Still if I were Jeannie I'd be much more worried about Macrow's plans for the bottle of bromide in her handbag than the train journey. Poor Jeannie! Nae wonder she was 'in a cold sweat', she'd probably spotted Macrow buying the bottle of bromide through the window of the chemists's while she was tied to a lamp post in the street outside and was worried about the prospect of being accidentally overdosed by her well meaning, but non-veterinarian trained owner.

The east coast main line from London to Edinburgh: I never can walk though Waverley Station without my scalp tingling at the sound of the station announcements. 'Platform Eleven for the 14.00 to London King's Cross calling at Dunbar, Berwick, Newcastle, Durham, Darlington, York, Doncaster, Peterborough and London King's Cross.'

The Caledonian Sleeper is immensely long. Uniformed conductors wait at every carriage door and, as we walk along the length of platform 15 to reach coach M, we emerge from the covered part of the station and into the night air. Perhaps somewhere past coach M, here in the darkness where the platform ends and the tracks begin, like Harry Potter waiting at Platform 9¾, I'll slip into the night and back to the Euston Station of 1946.

A whistle! The sleeper starts very slowly, pulling out of Euston past the McVitie's factory and graffiti covered carriages in sidings. One carriage is just a skeletal framework, it looks like a bombed out relic of World War Two. In 1948 the McVitie's factory became the first fully automated biscuit factory in the world and Macrow's train too would have passed it. This is like the wartime train journey Charles Ryder takes at the beginning of Evelyn Waugh's novel *Brideshead Revisited*. I've absolutely no idea where we're goinG Past buildings, streets and deserted, brightly lit stations, bridges and girders appear from strange angles as I lie there under the sheet and the scratchy blanket in my underpants.

Macrow 1946: *The train started with a long hiss and clatter of wheels. The lights of Euston went slowly past the window, then faster and faster, until they blended into one long line of wavering gold.*

A fox trots along the tracks outside London while the sleeper is stopped in sidings. Towerblocks and marshalling yards, there's noise from the next compartment and the sound of doors banging around midnight. Folk coming back from the buffet car?

I drift in and out of sleep. I have two dreams. I have this sensation of pressure in my head as the train tilts at every bend. Lying there on my bunk in the sleeper compartment I think of Macrow and Jeannie in 1946. The rattle of the wheels as the lights of London fade, I drift off to sleep thinking about the journey north, out there in the dark. The rythmn of the train wheels singing: Back to Kintail! Back to Kintail! Back to Kintail!

Macrow: *Soon, the warmth of the carriage and the monotonous sing-song of the wheels began to take effect. I took out the bottle of bromide and poured half of it down Jeannie's throat, taking the other half myself.*

Some months earlier: I'm seated on a plastic bucket chair in

THE WILD SWIMMER OF KINTAIL

Hamish's surgery in Queensferry Road. Hamish is the vet for Edinburgh airport, late fifties, beard and glasses, stout and invariably dressed in a short-sleeved, checked shirt. I'm there to ask Hamish what in his expert opinion would be the effect of pouring half a bottle of bromide down the throat of a Skye terrier.

My ex and I used to take the dogs to the vet together. I expect, to the receptionist and nurses, we were that nice gay couple with the old Border collie and the Labradoodle. Now I take the Labradoodle on my own but neither the receptionist nor the vet ever say anything about it. They never ask. Maybe they know to tiptoe around divorce.

I arrived at the surgery ten minutes earlier, carefully slowing the car in the left hand lane of the four lane dual carriageway jammed with traffic roaring out of Edinburgh, slowing right down to make the tight turn between the low stone walls at the entrance to the Elm Tree vet centre. The car park once the garden of the ribbon development thirties style bungalow that now houses the Elm Tree vet centre on this arterial route into Edinburgh from the Forth Road Bridge, gateway to Fife and the A9 north. Crowds of black and gold blazered Royal High school pupils spill out of the school grounds and onto the pedestrian crossings, islands in the tarmac waiting for the green man to momentarily halt the torrent of buses, cars and lorries.

One of Hamish's clients used to live in the bungalow that is now the vet centre and his consulting room was once her daughter's bedroom. A few years back Hamish expanded into the loft, all of which he documented on the surgery's website under the headline 'The Big Build.'

Hamish is one of life's true originals. He's sometimes to be seen peddling along Queensferry Road, buses to the left of him, lorries to the right, with his dogs (two Chesapeake Bay retrievers – a posh kind of Labrador) in a trailer behind his e-bike. Hamish built his electric bike from a kit and all this too is recorded on the surgery's website, making for a diverting read among the more mundane pages about what to expect when your pet is admitted for surgery and advice about kennel cough.

Hamish's knowledge extends well beyond biological mechanics. Once he was late for an appointment and appeared wiping his hands with an oily rag whilst explaining he'd spent his lunch hour adjusting the brakes on one of the vetinary nurse's Ford Fiesta and what a bad job Quik Tyre Fit had made of replacing the brake pads. There's no-one I'd rather entrust the medical care of my dogs to.

Hamish is spraying disinfectant on to the examination table in his surgery having just completed the Labradoodle's annual check-up. He's looked at her teeth, peered into her ears and combed her for fleas. As well as scanning the microchip he inserted in the nape of her neck when she was a puppy before administering her booster vaccinations for parvovirus, distemper and leptospirosis.

Hamish sits down at his desk and starts clacking away on the keyboard below the monitor. A graph of the Labradoodle's weight appears on the screen.

'She's due a worming tablet,' he says.

The Labradoodle puts her paws up on Hamish's lap. He fishes in the jar of dog biscuits on his desk while talking to the Labradoodle in his Johnny Morris dog voice, the one that makes the receptionist and vetinary nurses giggle.

'I'm writing a book,' I say.

The furious typing ceases.

'Researching a book, I should say. I'm retracing the journey of a mid-twentieth century female poet and mountaineer who visited the high-altitude hill lochs of Kintail, er, all 28 of them, during the summer of 1946.'

From my messenger bag I produce the tattered copy of *Kintail Scrapbook* I purchased from Barnados second-hand bookshop,

THE WILD SWIMMER OF KINTAIL

between Cash Generator and the closed down art-deco cinema on Edinburgh's Nicholson Street. Hamish looks at me with polite scepticism over his half-moon specs. It's evidently something he doesn't get asked everyday. He's clearly thinking about the waiting room full of ailing dogs and cats and their anxious owners.

I see Macrow rummaging in her hand bag as the night train rattled north through the darkness as I ask Hamish what in his expert opinion would be the effect of pouring half a bottle of bromide down the throat of a Skye terrier?

Have You Got a Girlfriend Yet?

Back on the sleeper train at dawn, passing pine forests and green fields, I reckon we must be somewhere in Northumberland. I think about all those trips to visit my ex's parents and the time my ex took the train alone down to Newcastle to tell his parents, on my advice, he was gay and his Mum refused to speak to him and ran away out the house. You hang onto a lot of memories from a twenty-year relationship.

I drift back into fitful sleep and awake to a yellow sky through the lower half of the carriage window and a blue sky above. The train is by the sea near Berwick. A Scottish flag flys from a house and then we're passing Torness nuclear power station. Spring is further behind here. The trees are movinG It must be windy. At Craigentinny marshalling yards on the outskirts of Edinburgh there are bluebells out in the ballast amongst the litter. I brush my teeth in the basin I pissed in last night. I feel refreshed. I feel OK.

Since I don't plan on pouring half a bottle of bromide down the Labradoodle's throat, let alone my own, we change trains in Edinburgh leaving the Caledonian Sleeper and taking the morning Scotrail service to Inverness thus giving the Labradoodle time for a quick leg stretch and empty in an quiet corner of Princes Street Gardens. Back on the train again we rattle out past Corstorphine Hill and the red brick Jenners Depository. An easyJet plane waits at the end of the runway, ready for take off, then Dalmeny, the Forth Bridges and North Queensferry.

I risk a glance down to the left through the iron struts of the bridge. One-hundred-and-fifty feet below the piers of the new Queensferry Crossing rise out of the cold grey waters of the Firth. In Macrow's day only the railway bridge spanned the estuary. Now that I think about it though, I reckon Macrow's train took a different route north

THE WILD SWIMMER OF KINTAIL

after crossing the Forth, going to Perth by the old direct line today buried beneath the foundations of the M90 motorway. A Beeching cut that makes the journey by train from Edinburgh to Perth take an hour and 20 minutes compared to around 45 minutes by car.

At Aberdour there's a ruined castle and from Burntisland that view across the Firth of Forth to Edinburgh and Arthur's Seat, all towers and spires, the city on the hill. Bluebells on the railway embankments and the Bass Rock and North Berwick Law again, last seen from the Caledonian sleeper.

The John Haig Company whisky bond in Markinch, tractors in fields, a stand of Scots pines beside the railway, horses graze in a nearby field. Raindrops smatter the window of the carriage as the train crosses the rich farmland of the Howe of Fife. Pheasants peck the stubble in the fields. Roe deer stand on a steep grassy railway embankment. The train runs along by the River Tay. The land is still flat all through Fife. At Perth there are lots of bikes on the train and kids with expensive dental braces.

Macrow 1946: *...there was jolt, and a voice shouted 'Perth!' with that unmistakeable Northern intonation which I had come to love and remember.*

There are Gaelic names as well as English on the station signs now. At Dunkeld there are pine trees. The first woodland of the journey north. The Labradoodle lies under the table, behaving herself, so far. The train speeds past a MacBacPackers minibus in the slow lane of the A9.

'Tea or coffee?' inquires a grey-haired Scotrail employee pushing a trolley rattling with bottles of Britvic orange juice, packets of crisps and chocolate brownies.

Macrow: *A dining-car had been put on at Perth. Later, we went in relays to breakfast, and had porridge and finnan haddie. Indeed, I thought, we had left the South and its customs far behind.*

There are still patches of snow on Ben Vrackie, the speckled mountain. Stone station buildings at Pitlochry and the towers of the Atholl Palace Hotel rise above the town. The A9 sweeps through the Pass of Killiecrankie on concrete stilts and I imagine the twisting single track road in Macrow's time. And then it occurs to me that in a land of footpaths, tracks and roads the A9 is simply the busiest path in Scotland.

1946: *Northward, northward, we sped through the brightening morninG Over the unforgettable Pass of Killiecrankie; between dark folds of pine-forest… across brown moorland where a few stray sea-gulls fluttered like scraps of paper over a mass of tumbled hills.*

Snow and primroses at Drumochter, the A9 Munros streaked with snow. A travelling fair is parked up in a layby at Drumochter and there is fresh snow on the Fara. Scots pines and brown heather as the train rattles downhill to Kingussie. Just outside Aviemore there are chambered cairns close to the railway and I wonder if these are the same chambered cairns Caleb excavated in another life and another book.*

Macrow: *Past Dalwhinnie, Kingussie and Aviemore, where the great, white crests of the Cairngorms leaned against a cold blue sky.*

*Caleb George Cash, the Victorian geographer, archaeologist and mountaineer inspired the author's first book *Caleb's List*.

THE WILD SWIMMER OF KINTAIL

At Tomatin there's a peat stack protected from the elements by a sheet of rusty corrugated iron. At Inverness the Labradoodle and I change trains for Kyle of Lochalsh. At first the train is quite fast across the flat fields by the Beauly Firth. The station at Beauly has been converted into a house and passengers must huddle in a Perspex bus shelter. This is Inverness commuter belt and there is lots of new build housing in what were once fields. At Muir of Ord there is a golf course close to the tracks and then on through douce Dingwall with its fine sandstone buildings.

The railway has a real branch line feel to it now and there are distant glimpses of snowy mountains. I'm seated at a table opposite a gawky, young American student who's writing in his leather bound journal in a fine hand. I'm sure he's gay.

OMG! I can't believe I just wrote that? Aw naw! I'm turning into my mother – speculating on young people's sexual orientation. It happens at work too.

Folk ask me, 'Do you think Lewis might be gay?'

Like when Mum's talking about the neighbours and says, 'Do you think so and so's oldest has a girlfriend?'

She's in the middle of serving up the millet casserole. Her recipes for millet casserole and runner bean curry will go to the grave with her. My mum is a good but erratic cook, sometimes lack of time or a surplus of ingredients from her allotment get in the way. When we were kids, one week we were vegetarians and the next week we weren't, depending on what Mum had managed to get from the shops!

'So and so's girls say so and so's definitely not gay you know, when I ask them,' she goes on, ladling a poached egg onto a pile of spinach on the plate in front of me.

'Help yourself to water from the jug.'

I can see there are smears and fingermarks on the glass and get up to rinse it at the tap.

'You're such a fuss pot,' she says.

I ignore this.

'You know I'll never ask so and so's kids if they've got girlfriends or boyfriends because of when we used to go to Aunt Jenny's.'

I sit down at the table and saw a slice of bread off the homebaked loaf on the cracked wooden board.

'It didn't really rise properly.' She passes me the soya spread. At the age of 77, she's recently become a vegan.

The loaf on the wooden board in front of me is an irregular, roughly rectangular shape, flat and blackened at one end. It looks like something the inhabitants of Skara Brae might have cooked up in a Stone Age oven before bread-making techniques were fully understood. My mother's loaf, the loaf of bread in front of me on the table, it's as if the last 2,000 years of developments in baking technology never happened.

'Oh dear old Aunt Jenny!' she says.

When we were kids and then young teenagers sometimes at weekends my mum drove us in her white Hillman Imp to visit the Aunts, as we called them. They lived in Findlay Gardens and they had a scruffy black dog called Judy that we used to get to walk round the block. Aunt Jenny didnae feed the dog dog food. Oh no. Mum used to complain the dog was better fed than we were.

'I'm just boiling up some chicken breast for Judy,' Aunty Jenny would say.

'It's bloody miles away,' my mum would complain to my stepdad though it was only in Lochend.

The Aunts lived together in an Orlit house in Findlay Gardens. Orlit houses would have been familiar to Macrow. They were a type of pre-fab erected in the years after 1945 in an attempt to solve the post-war housing shortage. Aunt Jenny was tall and straight-backed. Aunt Margaret was tiny and hunched over and my father (my biological one) used to say that after the nuclear holocaust Aunt Margaret would be the only survivor, emerging tiny and hunched into an apocalyptic post-nuclear world. We could hear them bickering in the kitchen like an old married couple while they put the teacups and Penguin biscuits on a floral tray. I think they were my paternal grandfather's aunts by marriage and Mum said we had to visit them because they'd been kind to us when we were little.

In the corner of their tiny front room a yellow budgie flapped about in a cage.

'Oh he's tinkling his bell,' Aunt Jenny would coo.

The next time we visited, the budgie had a huge growth below its winG

'Oh it's not bothering him, the vet says', claimed Aunt Jenny but I couldn't bear to look at the poor creature flapping about in its cage and could hardly choke my Penguin biscuit and orange squash down.

My sister got invited to stay overnight and she told me the Aunts went out to the ice cream van and bought her ice cream at ten o'clock at night. But I was never invited. My mum explained it was because my sister was a girl.

But later when we were young teenagers there was much worse to come. We'd all be sitting there. My sister would be saying something about school and what she did after school with her boyfriend. I don't recall at the distance of 40 years which boyfriend it was. Was it Scott the hairy one, or David the pretty one or Sye the hippy one who dumped her to go to India? It really doesn't matter. The thing was when my sister shut up Aunt Jenny would fix me with a steely eye and say:

'Have *you* got a girlfriend yet?'

Old Aunt Jenny would ask this every time we came to visit. But I never did. I knew I didn't find the girls at school sexually attractive and I wanked about seeing the boys in the showers after football. But I was years away from putting together what it all meant in a world where the only gay person I knew was Mum's friend Phil, who went to the Quaker meeting and was about 40 and even today I would've found deeply unattractive. There were no gay characters in soap operas on the telly. It seems crazy now but I seriously thought I was the only gay teenager in the world. I seriously thought there were no people my age who were gay. But it's difficult to explain because I didn't even know what gay meant back then.

All this agonising and stuff swirling about my head, but it didn't stop Aunt Jenny fixing me with her steely gaze and asking:

'Have *you* got a girlfriend yet?'

So I never ask young people if they've got girlfriends or boyfriends. I'll never put them through that. I'll just mind my own business. In my memory my sister and my mum used to start to giggle when Aunt Jenny asked her inevitable question.

But then suddenly, one day, the tables were turned. My mother's brief, unhappy second marriage to my stepfather had folded and he'd moved out the sunny top flat on the corner of Arden Street taking his Gurkha kukri and his beret and his cartons of Embassy Extra Mild away in his Triumph Herald. The first couple of times we visited the Aunts without my stepdad my mother managed to brush off Aunt Jenny's questions and come up with some excuse for his absence. But then just as I had been, my mother found herself caught in Aunt Jenny's steely gaze.

'Where's Simon?' she'd ask each week and my mother would shift uncomfortably in the orange Parker Knoll chair and fiddle with her hair and make some feeble excuse or invent some reason like he was busy marking exam papers or taking the Triumph Herald to the garage, while we teenagers stared at the carpet.

'Where's Simon?' Aunt Jenny asked again the next time we visited.

The yellow budgie with the malignant growth flapped against the bars of its cage and finally my mother could stand it no more.

'Simon and I are no longer together,' she announced through clenched teeth.

'Oh... I see,' said Aunt Jenny and there was a long awkward silence and after that we never went back. Not ever. We never went back to visit the Aunts and we never saw the budgie and Judy the scruffy black dog again. My mother never took us back after that. Not ever.

And so I will make absolutely no assumptions whatsoever about the sexual orientation of the gawky young man sitting opposite me on the train to Kyle writing in his leather bound journal in a fine hand whilst patting the Labradoodle affectionately. As far as I'm concerned he's a red-blooded heterosexual though from what was about to unfold one thing at least was clear. He must have been born without a sense of smell.

Macrow 1946: *How to describe the remainder of that journey? The thousand-and-one halts... the names that are like a melody once heard and never forgotten. Dingwall, Achanalt, Achnasheen, Achnashellach and, at last, Plockton...*

Seventy-five years on I note down that melody of names from the flickering LED display at the end of coach A: Inverness, Beauly, Muir of Ord, Conon Bridge, Dingwall, Garve, Loch Luichart, Achanalt, Achnasheen, Achnashellach, Strathcarron, Attadale, Strome Ferry, Duncraig, Plockton, Duirinish and Kyle of Lochalsh.

The train passes a little graveyard close by the tracks and remote houses, gable ends stacked with logs. At Achanalt the train is very slow and there are 20mph signs beside the track. There are swallows in Strath Braan and ruined cottages at the foot of Moruisg, the big water. From Achnashellach on I would guess that that the land has changed very little since 1946.

The train picks it way slowly along the shore of Loch Carron. It's like being in a car on a single track road. But then, I suppose, this is a single track railway. This, I reflect, is what the roads would be like if they had had little in the way of investment or upgrading since the 1940s. Today the train journey from Inverness to Kyle of Lochalsh takes 2 hours 35 minutes. According to the RAC website, doing the journey by car takes 1 hour 54 minutes.

In 1946 it took Macrow and Jeannie 16 hours 48 minutes to travel from London to Kyle of Lochalsh. Seventy-five years later it took me 14 hours 2 minutes. So a reduction in journey time by a rather unspectacular two minutes per year since World War Two. One thing became apparent during the 650-mile journey though. These really are two separate countries. Of one thing I have no doubt Kintail is as different from London as Paris is from Stavanger.

A heron stands on the shore, solitary by Loch Carron. And at Strome ferry we come down to the sea. We come down to the shore of the Atlantic Ocean. We've crossed Scotland from the North Sea to the Atlantic. And I overhear two old wifies on the train and how they pronounce the name: Struume Ferry.

The Applecross hills lie behind us now. White cottages beside the sea, lambs and calves in fields, fleeing from the train and there are deer in the heather in Strathcarron.

'We are now approaching Duirinish. This is a request stop,' an electronic voice announces.

The Labradoodle ate something unspeakable off the pavement when we were changing trains in Inverness and now I realise whatever delicious street treat, whatever leftover bit of kebab or fousty bridie it was, is rapidly making its way through the Labradoodle's digestive system. A throat-catching stink of sulphur drifts up from beneath the table where the Labradoodle lies with a smile on her face. I'm hoping no-one will notice. I think we got away with the first Doodle fart but now the Labradoodle is producing noxious, sulphurous Doodle farts at roughly ten-minute intervals. I pretend to be writing something in my moleskine notebook, thinking of Macrow with her notebook stuffed in the pocket of her old raincoat. Soon though, the Doodle farts are making their way throughout the length of the carriage, drifting sneakily up between seats and under tables, wafted upwards by the train carriage's heating system. Aw naw I can't look. I sink deeper into my seat. The group of Italian tourists three tables away are opening the carriage windows with exclamations of 'mamma mia!' and another Italian phrase which I don't need a transalator to understand must mean, 'what's that terrible pong?' Meanwhile the Labradoodle lies contentedly under the table with a smile on its face as I fix the dog with a long, hard stare.

'It's the bromide for you next time,' I mutter.

West

Back to Kintail

*In Kintail everything culminates.
Nothing lacks. It is the epitome of the
West Highland scene.*
           W H Murray 1968

Macrow 1946: *We drove from Kyle of Lochalsh to Dornie in the brilliant sunlight of the April afternoon... Jeannie, who is not nervous of cars, sat contentedly on my lap, looking out of the window.*

I had booked Donnie's Taxi to convey me and the Labradoodle from Kyle to Dornie, having first phoned the eponymous Donnie to check he had no objection to taking a dog in his taxi. Donnie's silver Kia Sedona is waiting for us at the end of the pier as I haul my rucksack and travel bag up from the train.

During the 15 minute drive to Dornie, Donnie points out a shiny new Ford Galaxy in a ditch.

'It was some tourists,' he says, 'they misjudged the bend.'

But I sense the Labradoodle and I are in safe hands with Donnie and Donnie's taxi duly deposits the Labradoodle and me at the doors of the Dornie Hotel.

1946: *We reached Dornie at tea-time. It was quiet, peaceful and friendly, just as I had remembered... The little rows of grey houses, clustered along the water's edge...*

On the desk in my study there's a stack of books about the north-west Highlands. On top of the pile turn is one entitled *A Guide to Eilean Donan Castle.* I turn to the last page and find a card tucked in between the backcover and the dustjacket. The caption on the back of the card reads, 'Loch Long Head, Killilan,' and below it, 'Rudha Sgarbh Bheag Crafts, Dornie.' Now I remember buying this card, casting anxious glances out the window of the shop to where the Labradoodle was tied to a drainpipe outside. I can remember rescuing this card from the wastepaper bin in my flat in Edinburgh. It's a beautiful card, chosen with care but it's what's written inside the card that brings the half tears to my eyes. As I read the words I slip back in time. My ex is going through 'Powered by Our Principles' and having to re-apply for his job and it's all starting to fall apart and I'm thinking what an unlucky year that was. The card is from me and the Labradoodle. Inside it says: 'Good Luck on Wednesday, all our love, we'll be thinking of you.'

Macrow: *I found excellent accommodation at the first place I tried—the Dornie Hotel—whose staff at once provided me with a welcome tea. Afterwards, in the bedroom, I opened a tin of stewed steak for Jeannie, and she ate the lot, with every sign of approval.*

Two weeks earlier: I stand swithering in the aisle of the supermarket, between the tuna fish and the baked beans. The place is a glittering cornucopia of abundance. There is row after row of every variety of tinned food imaginable. Should I get supermarket own brand tinned stewing steak? Hmmm... could be feeding the Doodle horsemeat? My eye lights on a row of blue and red-gold tins: Princes stewing steak. Of course, Princes has been around since 19-oatcake and it's bound to be the brand Macrow bought in 1946.

The single room I've been given at the Dornie Hotel doesn't have an ensuite. The manager was quite apologetic, but I like it. It feels suitably 1940s to walk along the corridor, towel wrapped round my waist, to get to the bathroom. There is a splendid cast iron bath on

THE WILD SWIMMER OF KINTAIL

legs, perfect for a long, hot soak after a day on the hills.

In the evening, after the Labradoodle has wolfed a bowl of Wilsons Original and half the tin of Princes stewing steak, we take a stroll along to the Clachan. Dornie is well provided for with both a pub and a hotel. In Macrow's day there was the Loch Duich Hotel too. Now sadly closed and converted into 'luxury' holiday apartments, gone the way of many a fine Highland hotel.

At the bar of the Clachan a Glaswegian, a red-faced Polish builder working on Eilean Donan Castle and a young local guy who straddles a bar stool in paint smattered workie's trousers. Saturday night. Everyone's drunk in Dornie. At least the young guys are.

Next morning, when I pull open the heavy door of the Dornie Hotel, the raindrops are making big concentric ripples in the puddles on the road outside the white-painted hotel. The Labradoodle pulls at the lead impatiently, smelling the sea air. Across Loch Long the white houses of Camas-longart stand along the kelpy shore. The lower slopes of Beinn Conchra are yellow with whin, higher up the hillside, russet shades of dead bracken in the folds of the hill and the brown of the heather in April.

A burn foaming with white water pours under a grey stone bridge. Mossy rocks and dead bracken line the banks, the smell of damp earth. Thickly matted dead bracken draped over a barbed wire fence, scent of gorse. The road is potholed and patched with asphalt, for this is the old road to Dornie. Buses, cars and motorbikes climbed Carr Brae when this was the main road, then rattled down to Dornie at the foot of the hill by the lochside, giving the motorist of the 1940s a first dramatic view down to Eilean Donan castle. Engineers did not blast the wide sweeping curves of today's A87 along the shore of Loch Duich 200 metres below until 1957 when the Hydro came.

1946: *Far below us now, cars and buses ran along the Glen Shiel* road, their enamel shining as it caught the sun. The noise of their engines filled the whole valley, echoing and re-echoing from the high hills all around.

Glancing down at the Altimax watch on my wrist I see I've gained some height and over the tops of the dripping gorse bushes I can see Eilean Donan Castle on its rock facing the ferry house at Totaig across a rainy Loch Duich. The back of the castle is covered in scaffolding and I realise the young, bearded, flushed with alcohol Eastern European at the bar in the Clachan last night must one of the men in fluorescent yellow jackets I can see working on the scaffolding. In the pub he was complaining about having to work with lime mortar. Now as I pull my hood up against the rain I make the connection.

The hillside is thickly wooded with silver birch, oak and rowan and there are bluebells in the long grass. Daffodils still blooming in April at the foot of a heathery bank and there are creamy yellow primroses among last autumn's leaves.

Where the road drops down and rounds a bend under the beech trees by a low stone wall, through the twenty-first century rain I catch a faint echoing glimpse of Macrow and Jeannie tramping along the road under a blazing sun in 1946.

1946: *The hill-road mounted swiftly up the brown brae. Already, the wayside was starred with a riot of spring flowers—pale-faced primroses, tossing daffodils and windflowers fluttering...*

I can see a grey sheet of water through the trees – Loch Duich. Birch and oak trees climb the hillside on the far shore of the loch above Letterfearn. Some patchy sunshine breaking through the low cloud and mist catches a grassy headland jutting out into the loch.

THE WILD SWIMMER OF KINTAIL

Ten miles to the north-west I can just discern the concrete bow of the Skye Bridge.

A deer fence protects the garden of a bungalow, built on the hillside with a picture window view of Loch Duich at some point in the decades after Macrow left Kintail. A bearded collie wanders out onto the road to greet the Labradoodle.

The clock chimes twelve in the front room of my maindoor tenement flat in Edinburgh. At 12pm, they make public the book festival programme. I won't be in it this year. Make the most of any success that comes your way as a writer they say, for it may not last forever. The year I *was* in it, my ex refused to come and see my event though he did come to the family meal we had at Chez Jules afterwards.

My ex just couldn't cope with me becoming a writer. Couldn't cope with me becoming Kellan, I suppose you could say. He's a really nice, kind, caring person. He was 24 when we met, I was 29. I think we just grew apart. You're not the same person in your late forties as you are in your twenties are you? The hillwalking didn't help either. But it was the writing that finished us, the writing that did for us in the end. He just couldn't bear that I'd published a book and put in print about me being HIV. My ex just couldn't bear me being open about my HIV status and telling people. I guess most folk might feel the same.

But I'm not ashamed of being HIV. It's not a sordid, dirty secret for me. I was just a stupid 23 year old. I didn't do anything different from what all the kids at work do today. I got off my face and had sex. That's all. I was just unlucky and long ago I forgave myself for contracting HIV. And now I'm alone in the world. I'm single after 20 years and I'm going to have to make a go of it.

In my mind Macrow hammers the keys of the dusty typewriter. A smell of inky typewriter ribbon drifts up to her nostrils. 'Hills in

Winter' she types, fingers swollen with arthritis. It seems as if a long age has passed since she stood outside the offices of Oliver and Boyd in sun-drenched Tweeddale Court just off Edinburgh's Royal Mile. Back then she was an up and coming author, new writing talent. Her books sold well. Her publishers loved her. But now the decades have passed and she's dwindled to contributing poems to the pages of *The People's Friend.*

Is that what will happen to me too I wonder gloomily as I stomp along beneath the dripping silver birches? I've already lost my relationship due to my decision to follow my vocation and become a writer. What's gonnae happen to me in the future? Maybe the doom-laden, middle-European poet Czeslaw Milosz was right after all when he famously declared, 'When a writer is born into a family, the family is finished.'

The road has reached the 100-metre contour now. Carr Brae viewpoint is marked on OS Sheet 33, *Loch Alsh, Glen Shiel and Loch Hourn*, as being at a height of 179 metres. Clear of the trees now, on the open hillside the dead bracken lies folded and flattened. At the southern end of Loch Duich the tops of the Five Sisters are white with newly fallen snow. Macrow too arrived in Kintail in April when the peaks were still white with snow.

Legend tells of two Irish princes, washed ashore in Kintail during a storm. The King of Kintail had seven daughters and the princes fell in love with two of the King's daughters. Having promised to send their five brothers for the remaining sisters the princes married the two youngest daughters and returned to Ireland with them. The five sisters waited in vain for them to return and at last in despair, they asked the Grey Magician of Coire Dhuinnid to extend their vigil beyond life itself, whereupon he turned them into mountains.

Six hundred feet below, Loch Duich glistens in the sunshine. New since Macrow's time the radio mast high on the hillside and

THE WILD SWIMMER OF KINTAIL

the electricity cables slung at tree top height across the road. I see the white wake of a small motorboat heading out to a dozen circular cages in Loch Duich, new too since 1946, Marine Harvest's fish farm at Letterfearn.

Sunday morning in Edinburgh: about eleven o'clock, Macrow seems to have managed to make a living from her writing in the 1940s, while here I am, hoover in hand, banging on the door of the boxroom of my flat in Edinburgh.

'You'll have to get up now mate. Checkout time's supposed to be ten o'clock.'

'I have just voken up,' says a groggy Norwegian sounding voice from behind the door.

I turn the Dyson on to full and mutter to myself, 'I'll send the Labradoodle in next, mate.'

Some months earlier: I was standing in Portobello Road in Edinburgh pressing the keys on the cash machine outside the Bank of Scotland while awkwardly trying to shield my pin number with my hand. Your balance is £14.37 flashed up on the screen. Then: Do you want to continue?

'Aw fuck!' The Labradoodle looked up at me. 'What the fuck are we gonnae do dog?'

You'll recall my cunning plan to make some money. I mentioned it to my aunt, when we were sitting in the Hungarian restaurant in Soho, the evening I took the night train north. This then is my masterplan. Airbnb, the saviour of many a starving writer is going to come to my rescue.

Back to Sunday morning in Edinburgh and the Airbnb madness is at its height. Harneet and Jasdeep are due to check in at 4pm but have already been messaging me to ask, since their train from London arrives at Waverley station at 1pm, can they check in early? Nae chance, I think unless I can kick the slumbering Norwegian thespians oot their beds. Or to be more accurate, out of my beds, as it's my flat.

I don't usually accept bookings from theatre companies but Tradfest is one of Edinburgh's more staid festivals. Georgiana the older, grey-haired of the Norwegian storytellers, who was sitting out in the garden in the sunshine, claims not to have known checkout time is 10am despite it being clearly stated on my Airbnb page and in the e-mail I sent them.

'How did your event go?' I ask as I bend over to strip the sheets off the fold down bed in the sitting room. I get the feeling she's looking at my bum.

'Eet is a show about the vild salmon and the farmed salmon,' Georgiana the Norwegian storyteller explains as I shove sheets and towels and a duvet cover into the washing machine.

'Eet is very political. This afternoon ve do another show at Forest Café. You must come Kellan.'

'So is pollution from fish farms a big problem in Norway too?' I ask, scowling at the boxroom door and thinking, come on mate pull yer pants up and get oot.

'Ah yes, ve invented feesh farmeen.'

Five minutes later Martin has emerged from the boxroom and is making his way sleepily down the hall to the bathroom. He's really quite cute. I wish I'd said he'd got time for a shower (maybe I could have cleaned the bath at the same time, offered to wash his back perhaps?) but then again I really want them out of here.

'There's a really nice place just along the road for coffee and breakfast,' I explain to Georgiana, resisiting the temptatation to grab all her stuff off the sitting room floor and start stuffing it into her wheely suitcase.

—47—

THE WILD SWIMMER OF KINTAIL

Like I said, Airbnb is the salvation of many a starving writer today. The other year at *AyeWrite!*, Glasgow's book festival, I was sitting in the audience behind a fairly well-known Scottish poet who was busy telling her pal (another writer most likely) how busy she'd been doing Airbnb all summer.

'Oh but the cleaning, my dear,' she exclaimed at one point, 'Oh but the cleaning!'

And she was right, it's fuckin' hard work like. I'm pedalling hallway across Edinburgh every couple of days to do the changeovers as one group of guest checks out at 10am (or not in the case of the Norwegians) and another group checks in six hours later at 4pm.

Meanwhile I stand at the top of the terrazo steps that lead down to the pavement, a yellow duster in one hand, a can of Mr Sheen in the other, watching Georgiana bump her wheely suitcase down the steps as Martin (still regrettably unshowered) heaves an enormous rucksack complete with Ryanair luggage tags over his shoulder.

'Good luck with the show,' I give them a farewell wave then close the front door with relief.

A few minutes later there is a determined ring on the the doorbell.

Uh oh, what have they forgotten? But it's not Georgiana or cute Martin who didn't have time for a shower. A wizened-faced man in a black hat and a leather coat is lugging a large guitar case up the steps. Another Norwegian storyteller I didn't even know was staying in my flat. He disappears into the back bedroom and re-emerges five minutes later still with the guitar case plus an enormous wheelie suitcase. He refuses my offer of help down the steps with it.

'Good luck with the show!' I give wizened guitar men a wave as he trundles his enormous wheelie suitcase off along Willowbrae Road then close the front door with a sigh of relief.

Back in 1946, I see Robert M Adam parking his car in a lay by on the hill road high above Loch Duich, then opening the boot. He pulls out a camera case and tripod. A cigarette dangles from his lips. Macrow sits on the low wall and crosses her legs and smiles coquettishly.

But it's not true. I later discover to my disappointment, she never met him. No, it never happened, except in my imagination. They never met. It wasn't like that. But I can imagine it. Disappointing though this is it does provide an insight into how the world of books works. The photographs Macrow took herself, of hill lochs in the mist would not have been of publishable quality so Oliver & Boyd used stock photos taken by Adam to illustrate Macrow's books. Macrow wrote the text. Moyes Adam took the photographs and together it was their destiny to inspire a whole generation of Highland holidays.

The old road climbs the grassy hillside to the top of Carr Brae in a sweeping hairpin bend. I notice a milestone in the grass, one mile to Dornie. The line of an over grown stone and turf field boundary wall cuts across the hillside, grass on one side, dead bracken on the other. There are patches of blue sky. I reach the highest point of the road and open the wooden gate to walk the short distance to the grassy top of Carr Brae. The wet tarmac glistens in the sunshine. Not enough blue sky to make a sailor's trousers, I think, but there's enough to put him in a skimpy thong.

Walking back down to Dornie I pause. Above me I can see the pointed snout of Carr Brae projecting out over the loch. There's a bend in the road and a layby and a low wall. I stop and sit on the grey stones and I feel somehow certain it was here Macrow sat and gazed out over Loch Duich to Glen Shiel and Skye that first afternoon in Kintail, after the war, putting time and space and mountains between herself and bomb-cratered London.

1946: We... sat down on a rough, grey wall, looking out across the quiet mirror of Loch Duich far below... the Cuillin rose mistily against the western sky… There was no sound but the quavering bleat of new-born lambs and the crackle of little wild things among the dry heather.

Sitting there on the wall, looking out across Loch Duich to the mountains, I think to myself about my war with HIV, about all the gay guys of my generation who never made it to 30. They never got the chance to be in a civil partnership or to get married. I'm sitting there thinking it's not my place to complain about the situation I find myself in. They never lived to go through a divorce. They never lived to be on treatments that keep you healthy enough to be kicked off benefits and have to find a job. They never got the chance to go back to work. So no, I don't think it's my place to complain about my ex leaving me and having to work in a supermarket and do Airbnb. Because like I say lots of guys of my generation never made it to thirty. And then in my head Macrow sits down next to me. And I think about Brenda sitting there on the wall in 1946. After both our wars, her war and mine.

Macrow's List

My heart's in the Highlands,
my heart is not here;
My heart's in the Highlands
a-chasing the deer.

Robert Burns

Walking in Macrow's footsteps, I set out once more from the Dornie Hotel. Not a bad forecast but cold for the end of April, Skye is a grey blur of rain and the tops of the Five Sisters were white with snow yesterday. Breakfast at the hotel is a bowl of Alpen, coffee, orange juice, sausage, bacon, eggs, black pudding, tomato and toast. Back in my room I fill a glass with tap water from the basin and swallow two tablets of abacavir, one tenofovir, one blue nevirapine prolonged release, one white pravastatin and a small pink lisinopril.

Rucksack on I clump downstairs in my walking boots and out the door of the hotel and set off along the road to Bundalloch, the Labradoodle pulling at the lead. On my right as I walk along the quiet single-track road are the white painted houses of Dornie. On my left behind low, ivy-covered stonewalls and privet hedges are the front gardens of the houses, positioned between the road and the shoreline as they are at Plockton and at Corrie on Arran. There's something special about these seaside gardens.

Macrow: *I had a wild desire to do something extra-ambitious—something no-one in Kintail had thought of doing before. Getting out my map of Central Ross, I lay flat on the floor and brooded delightedly over the lines and contours—the green glen and thin blue streams; the brown mountains, each with its cap of white. At intervals in the high hills, tucked away in the dark curve of a corrie, a tiny blue pool marked a lochan.*

THE WILD SWIMMER OF KINTAIL

It's high tide. As I leave the last of the houses behind, Loch Duich laps at the rocky shoreline beside the road. A green rowing boat is moored close to the shore. On the north side of Loch Long I can see white-painted Conchra House where Macrow spent an afternoon watching the sheep dog trials in 1946. The steep slopes of the eponymous Beinn Conchra are reflected in the smooth surface of Loch LonG No waves, barely a ripple, red-orange clumps of kelp lie among the shingle and white lichen-covered rocks on the shore. On the far side of Loch Long I can hear a cuckoo.

Macrow 1946: *Suddenly, I had it! I would begin an article on 'The Hill-Lochs of Kintail'* visiting each of these little pools in turn, noting its height, surroundings, and the difficulty or otherwise of the ascent. Studying the map again, I realised it would mean weeks of hard work, with even an occasional night on the hills, if I should miss my way...*

Ahead I can see the lumpy, bumpy mass of Beinn a' Mheadhain rising above Loch Long. Like Macrow 75 years ago, my eyes trace a route through the crags to its summit. The Labradoodle is pulling me along on the lead and soon I reach the road end and the sturdy timber bridge over the River Glennan at Bundalloch. A wild-looking farm collie with a broad, white muzzle and thickly matted brown and red hair trots across the bridge to greet us. The Labradoodle rolls submissively on her back. An ancient, unshaven crofter watches suspiciously from a ramshackle barn. As I cross the bridge and take the path by the River Glennan, heading for the lower slopes of Beinn a' Mheadhain he mutters:

'You'll need to keep that dog on a lead.'

Then he adds with a puzzled look,

'Where are you going anyway?'

* Macrow, B G, 'The Hill-lochs of Kintail', *The Scottish Field,* Vol. XCV, No.538, Edinburgh, October 1947, p14-15.

As if to say, there's nothing up there.

Resisting the temptation to ask if he remembers Macrow's visit in 1946 the Labradoodle and I ignore the ancient crofter and his wild farm collie and strike up the grassy hillside.

Macrow: *We tramped along to Bundalloch and crossed the River Glennan by the stout wooden bridge. The sun blazed down on us out of a clear sky.*

It's rough going through deep heather on the lower slopes of Beinn a' Mheadhain but pausing to look back I'm rewarded with a view of sea and mountains. Of Loch Long emptying into Loch Duich at the narrows below Dornie Bridge, framed by the hills of Skye and Lochalsh . Far below me I can see the by-road to Killlilan snaking along the north shore of Loch Long. A pair of wheatears flit across the heather, a slug creeps across a wet cushion of red sphagnum moss. I think it's going to rain.

Macrow: *We began working steadily up the spread-out, lumpy hill with its many hummocks and summits.*

Near the two hundred metre contour line, I reach a line of small heathery crags. I can hear the clack-clack of a stonechat. The Labradoodle and I climb a grassy gully where the bleached grey branches of a dead rowan tree cling to the rock. The first ferns are unfurling amongst the deergrass. Behind me Skye is disappearing in a grey smurr of rain.

1946: *Rain soaked steadily through my boots... Jeannie trotted along demurely at my heels, her long tail trailing in the mud, her coat... sleeked to her steaming sides... wet to the skin...*

THE WILD SWIMMER OF KINTAIL

One thousand feet below me, I can see the A87 and can just make out a white cottage on a little rise at the end of a mile long straight section of the road. I know the name of the white house by the road. It's called Shepherd's Cottage.

I reach the first top of Beinn a' Mheadhain and there 50 metres below me tucked in a fold in the hillside I spot Loch Dubhach, a silver, grey pool among the tawny heather. I take a bearing on the lochan as mist rolls across the higher hills. It's raining when I reach the little burn that trickles out the north-east end of the lochan. The heavy drops of falling rain form concentric circles of ripples on the surface of the dark peaty water.

I've reached my first hill loch.

My first tick on Macrow's List.

Twenty seven to go!

I don't linger though, heading north to the true summit of Beinn a' Mheadhain where the prevailing wind has brushed the flattened tufts of deergrass all in the same direction. A few stones form a tiny cairn. There is a rainbow over Loch Long and now the squally shower has passed, wide views west to Skye and Lochalsh, east to Sgurr nan Ceathramhnan, south to the Five Sisters of Kintail and north towards the mountains of Torridon.

Macrow: *The heather-slope ran steeply down into a hollow—and there was the loch, dark blue and smooth as a sheet of Bristol glass.*

Below me the black waters of Loch Beinn a' Mheadhain beckon and I set off back down the hillside. This lochan, high up on Beinn a' Mheadhain, is less picturesque than in 1946 because today an ugly, barbed-wire fence encircles it and the best view is from a distance. The sunshine has some warmth in it by the time I climb over a gate and walk a few paces down to the lochside. I crouch down and wash my face in the clear peaty water then watch the ripples fan out across the glassy surface of the loch.

From Loch Beinn a' Mheadhain I return to Loch Dubhach, before walking down the steep hillside, back to Bundalloch, revelling all the while in the panorama of sea and mountains stretching to the western horizon. I stop and look down at the Labradoodle. 'We've done our first two hill lochs dog. Two ticks on Macrow's List, 26 to go!' I tell her as she skips off through the heather, headed for home.

Sitting here at the computer, in the IKEA swivel chair, typing, I have the strangest feeling that perhaps I am a writer, maybe this is my life now. I'm sat here in the boxroom, writing on Christmas Eve. It's nearly lunchtime and I'm a wee bit hungover. Last night: in the pub across the road from the supermarket with the other drivers, Paul, Ben and Roman. Halfway through my first pint Roman looked across the table at me and said:

'So what did you do before you worked in the shop?'

So I told him. Only I couldn't get it all out at once. He'd just been asking me about completing the Munros, so I hedged at first, saying something vague like:

'I started climbing the Munros as a challenge because I had a serious physical health problem.' I always say physical health by the way, because else they assume you've got mental health issues.

But then, a few sentences later, I finally managed to spit it out:

'Er... my reason for climbing the Munros was... er... because I've been HIV positive since I was in my early twenties...'

My words hung in the air. Now it was like I was watching myself. I saw the words come out my mouth and float in the air over the formica-topped table. Like a great big cloud, like a plane trailing a banner over the table reading, 'I'M HIV POSITIVE.'

No-one ever says, 'I'm cancer' or: 'I'm motor-neurone disease' but people like me always say, 'I'm HIV'. I dunno why that is. But back to the pub, and my words, still hanging in the air over the faux-wooden surface of the table. But I don't want to reach out and grab my words back. I'm glad I've said it. Now I feel released from the cage of all my half-truths and evasions. You see, telling people you're HIV is a bit like how it was telling folk you were gay in the 1980s. Today the most unlikely people have gay friends. It's not an issue for most people or if it is they shut up and don't say anythinG But back in the eighties there was much more of an edge to telling people you were a friend of Dorothy. It was riskier. It was like that scene in *Prick Up Your Ears* when the playwright Joe Orton is visiting his agent, played in the film by Vanessa Redgrave and he says, 'Can I bring my 'friend' next time?' See that was really edgie back in the sixties. But I still think I'm being quite brave. I had been going to tell Paul and Roman last week when we were in the pub but they were watching the football on the wide-screen telly and my courage failed me.

I'd said it now though. But it was like they were so shocked the conversation just continued. My announcement went whoomph! Straight over their heads, they didn't know how to react.

So I ended up reassuring them,'Probably when you hear HIV/AIDS you think of Princess Diana shaking hands with someone who looks like a skeleton. But it's not the disease it was, guys,' I hear myself say, 'I just take a couple of pills with my cornflakes in the morning and that's me. Gotta be better being myself at work, huh?'

Half-ten on a Friday night in a pub in Morningside Road, when would I ever have thought I'd be having a conversation like this, in a bar like this, when I was a kid and used to go to the library next door? Like I said, I don't think they knew what to say. Roman didn't say anything, Ben who was only twenty-four looked terrified then Paul, bless him said, 'See I lived in London for thirty years mate and HIV disnae bother me. Nothing fazes me mate.'

The conversation moved straight onto something else and I felt like I'd been left hanging. Later, we're in The Waiting Room, so called because it's next door to what was once Morningside railway station and I felt compelled to revisit the subject, saying:

'I've never had a day off sick, you know? About three weeks after I started at the supermarket that Geordie manager, Billy something, what was his name? Disnae matter anyway, he gave me a big long, medical form to complete. I filled it in in shoogly blue biro handwriting, answering all the questions honestly, except when I came to the one that asked, 'Do you take any prescription medication?' I ticked the box for 'YES' but left the space for the answer to the next question blank, 'Please give the names of any medication you have been prescribed.' Then I posted the form to the supermarket's HQ in Bracknell and never heard anymore about it.'

It was just me and Paul now. It must have been nearly last orders.

'See that night I told you about, mate, when I was out with James and someone from the shop gave him a line of coke. We were standing outside LuLu's in George Street at 3 am in the morning and he looked at me and said, 'I don't know anything about you...' So I looked back at him and said, 'I'm HIV positive.' He was the first person in the shop I told.'

And now I've said it again. The world didn't stop. The cars and buses are still grinding up Morningside Road in the rain and the football's still playing on the wide-screen telly above the bar.

Shepherd's Cottage

1946: For six months I lived... tramping and climbing among the Kintail and Lochalsh hills—and I would not exchange those six months for six years in the finest city in the world!

I press the buttons on the phone to dial the number for Shepherd's Cottage. The number starts 01599, the code for Kyle of Lochalsh. The little cottage I'd glimpsed from the slopes of Beinn a' Mheadhain and described by Macrow as 'a shepherd's bothy on a little rise overlooking Nostie' is today a bed and breakfast named Shepherd's Cottage. A sign at the gate depicts a shepherd with a crook, a collie and four sheep silhouetted in front of a garish, orange, setting sun. On the website I read Shepherd's Cottage is where 'Brenda Macrow, the well-known Highland travel writer of the 1940's, actually stayed whilst writing her book *Kintail Scrapbook.*'

Clicking on 'Accommodation' on the website brings up photos of pine double beds and wardrobes, basket chairs, lots of beige and light colours and natural wood. It looks very clean. There are tartan rugs in tasteful shades of mauve neatly folded at the foot of the carefully made beds with their white linen sheets and pillows. All ready to be photographed for the website. The house will be warm and centrally heated. The double room has a kingsize bed and is called 'The Isle of Skye' room. I think I've booked twin-bedded 'Eilean Donan' with its dormer windows.

Macrow 1946: *And then, quite suddenly, in the middle of our third week in Dornie, we found it! A shepherd's bothy on a little rise overlooking Nostie, with two good front rooms, a kitchen and water laid on indoors! We were told... we* might *get it as temporary accommodation if we went and saw the landlord personally.*

The phone rings distantly. A pleasant sounding woman with an English accent answers. I can hear a TV in the background. In my mind's eye I half expected to hear the distant bleating of lambs and the lornly cries of the gulls and curlews over the brown heather.

'I'd like to make a booking.'

'I'll just put the light on in the study,' the English voice replies.

It's seven o' clock on a Sunday night in February. In Edinburgh, out the bay window, behind the line of Victorian villas across the street, the last blue tinge is fading from the sky. Two hundred miles to the north-west I realise it won't yet be completely dark in the little house beside the A87.

'When would you like to book in for?' The English accent asks again.

Macrow 1946: *I set out at once, found Mr Matheson ploughing a field, and the deal was done in a matter of ten minutes. We could have the cottage he said, for two months anyway. After that, it might be wanted for a shepherd...*

I come down for breakfast bang on eight. In the mornings at Shepherd's Cottage the sunlight on the hills is exactly as Macrow described it. I'm the only guest and a place for me is set at the table in the conservatory. As I chomp my way through sausage, bacon, egg and potato scone I can see what Macrow meant. The redesigned Shepherd's Cottage allows you to gaze upon the ever changing hills from indoors.

1946: *Often, we would emerge from the cottage into a world of shimmering gold, with huge, fluffy clouds clotted over the eastern hills.*

THE WILD SWIMMER OF KINTAIL

Findlay, half-collie half-Akita and the reason I don't have the Labradoodle with me for once, is the latest in the long line of dogs to live at Shepherd's cottage. Most were working dogs, tough border collies that could cover a hundred miles in a day and still chase the deer on the hillside behind the cottage in the evening sunshine. Graham and Alison say Findlay is unsuited for a life up here. He's only eight but he has bone cancer. Not much the vet in Kyle can do they say and fearful of fractures they keep Findlay on the lead now and I watch as Graham walks the dog slowly round the house. I stroke Findlay's head and back and gaze into his brown eyes as he lies curled up the sofa in the conservatory with its floor to ceiling windows looking across to the hills on the far shore of Loch Duich.

Graham and Alison are earnest and helpful. They used to work for the NHS in London until it began to affect their health. They bought Shepherd's Cottage nearly ten years ago and know a poet once wrote a book here. Alison shows me a different edition from my own of *Kintail Scrapbook*, the book Macrow wrote during those six months she lived at Shepherd's cottage in the summer of 1946. But somehow 1946 seems much closer in London than it does in Kintail. Inside the front cover of the book is a photo of the last shepherd to live here, a cheery looking gentleman with a big moustache. A friend predicted they'd have a stream of visitors asking about Brenda G Macrow, but I'm the only guest ever to ask about BGM. I hear laughter from downstairs after I've gone up to my bedroom in the attic.

A cold frosty morning, there was a dusting of white on the rocky summit of Arthur's Seat. I was cycling through Holyrood Park on the cycle track below Salisbury Crags. I pushed my bike up the steep hill past the council flats at Dumbiedykes, as music blared from the window of a flat. A Staffie and an Alsatian sniffed about the litter-strewn bushes beside the fifteenth-century boundary wall of Holyrood Park.

I was headed for the Edinburgh Farmers' Market, held each Saturday morning on top of Castle Terrace Car Park, in the shadow of Edinburgh Castle. Tempted by the smell of roasting pork and stalls piled high with organic vegetables, artisan bread and handmade sausage rolls. But I had another stop to make on the way.

I pushed open the glass door of the second-hand bookshop. My nephew looked shyly up from behind the till where he sat looking at his phone. I remembered cradling him in my arms in the ward of the Simpson Maternity Hospital 15 years before. My sister's oldest. Now he'd got his first Saturday job.

'Hi,' I said, then, 'how you doing?'

Or something like that before I started to browse the book shelves. Handwritten labels marked the categories of books: 'Paperback Fiction,' 'Hardback Fiction,' 'Biography.' Next to 'Rare and Antiquarian' I found 'Books about Scotland.' A clothbound, mossy green-coloured cover drew my eye, the book's title embossed in brown on its frayed spine.

It cost £4. A year or two later I found the receipt my nephew carefully tore off the till roll tucked inside the book. I opened the title page of the book and read, 'Kintail Scrapbook by Brenda G Macrow with photographs by Robert M Adam. Oliver and Boyd, Edinburgh 1948.'

Twenty-first century Shepherd's Cottage: only the trees remain the same. As I sit in the garden a heron flies overhead, level with the tops of the silver birches. Just as Macrow recorded 75 years ago there is still plenty of birdlife around Shepherd's cottage. But the road is busy.

Macrow loved life at Shepherd's Cottage but I have a sense the climate of the West Highlands is getting to Alison.

'How's your day been?' I ask when I get back from cycling to the Falls of Glomach.

'Oh you know,' she answers, 'I did the ironing.'

In the conservatory the place setting for tomorrow's breakfast, my breakfast, is already set. Perhaps six months in Kintail is long enough.

Macrow: *After a while, Jeannie and I went into the cottage. The two front rooms were, as we had been told, in very good condition apart from the fireplaces. These we mended with pieces of iron off the salvage-heap. Our living-room had dark polished wood walls and a wooden floor, while in the other room, our bedroom, the walls were papered and the floor concrete.*

The only place I feel Macrow's presence, the Kintail of 1946 around Shepherd's Cottage today, is in the garden. I'm sitting on a bench, reading *Gateway to Skye* by Duncan Macpherson (the renowned Highland photographer who ran the pharmacy in Kyle of Lochalsh) and Macrow's choice of holiday reading back in 1946. I can hear a TV from somewhere in the house and the sound of passing traffic on the A87 momentarily drowns out the birdsong. I count 24 elephants before a Wild and Sexy Haggis Tours yellow minibus hurtles past. The sun is a round shining little disc in the clouds. Little tears of grey black cloud. The wind is rising all the time.

Macrow must have known the tall Douglas fir on the hillside above the cottage. The tree is a landmark for miles around and can be seen from Totaig on the far side of Loch Duich. The byre at Shepherd's

Cottage is still painted red. The house looks old from the outside. But indoors it's as if Shepherd's Cottage 1946 has been gutted and fitted with a bright, glowing twenty-first-century interior full of shiny kitchen units, wide screen TVs and ensuite bathrooms.

> 1946: *There was a splendid sink in the big kitchen—but no sanitation of any description! ...In the afternoon, I wrote... to a hardware shop... for a Primus stove and one of those admirable contrivances which advertises itself boldly as an "Elsan Chemical Closet.".*

I remember as a kid on holiday in the 1970s, in an old caravan on a croft in Argyll, my father pitching the canvas toilet tent. It was tall and green and looked a bit like a knight's tent from the movie *Ivanhoe*. Inside sat the Elsan chemical toilet. I right click the spell checker but I see Microsoft Word doesn't have Elsan in its vocabulary. It prompts me the word I want: else, elan, Elsa, Elson or eland. Eland?

The Elsan was a grey, metal bucket with a black plastic toilet seat on top. At the bottom of the bucket a couple of inches of strong smelling blue chemical liquid sloshed about. At first when I was very young my feet didn't touch the grass as I perched on the Elsan. It was a lot higher than an ordinary toilet. You had to make sure the ties on the flapping tent door were securely tied. It was cold and draughty on a wet day.

My father donned an ancient bomber jacket from the wardrobe in the old caravan. He had a very bushy 1970s style beard and friends said he looked like Lenin. One evening towards the end of the holiday he'd take his bike and pedal along to the Black Crofts and gaze across Loch Etive to Ben Cruachan. If the top was clear of mist it would be a good year. If the summit was wreathed in cloud it would be a bad year, he told us on his return via the Falls of Lora

THE WILD SWIMMER OF KINTAIL

Hotel. The public bar just a hatch in the wall, sawdust on the floor, only cans of MacEwan's Export to drink and a hundred plus varieties of malt whisky. I heard him tell my mother when he got back to the caravan, just as the sun dipped yellow then orange and red into the sea behind the hills around Loch Creran.

Despite my mother's admonishments to pee behind the fence at the foot of the field the Elsan filled up rapidly. When the bucket was full my father took the sharp-pointed, folding shovel he called the Commando spade and walked to the next field where the yellow tansies grew. Surrounded by curious cattle, he dug a (to childish eyes) very deep hole. Beyond the field lay the beach. Lochnell Castle rose out of the trees on the heavily wooded headland of Rubha Garbh-àird. The bay was guarded on the other side by the hillfort of Beregonium, once home to Deidre and the sons of Uisneach.

Then my father tied a thick layer of newspaper around the top of the Elsan. I had to help carry the stinking, heavy bucket while the blue liquid, brown floaters and clumps of toilet paper sploshed about in imminent danger of splashing through the newspaper lid. My arms were going to fall off they felt so sore. The smell of formaldehyde and methanol from the Elsan fluid was making me dizzy and I just knew at any moment I was gonnae get a jobbie down my wellie!

Aching arms and a welcome rest as my father put the Elsan bucket down on the bridge of railway sleepers over the burn while he untied the bailer twine that kept the gate to the cows' field closed. No Scottish Environmental Agency back then to worry about emptying a chemical toilet near a watercourse. We stood by the freshly dug hole hands clutched to our noses as my father untied the newspaper lid and dropped it into the hole before carefully tipping the contents of the Elsan into the sandy soil. The blue Elsan fluid stained the yellow sand. My father threw the first few spadefuls of soil in. Then, once the splashy bit was over, we children were allowed to fill up the hole with the pile of sandy soil he'd dug out. When the hole had been completely filled in my father carefully replaced the turfs he'd removed before digging the hole and we all jumped up and down on it to flatten the ground while the cattle grazed peacefully and the ferry to Mull moved slowly across the horizon beyond the headland of Rubha Garbh-àird.

Upstairs, alone in my room at Shepherd's Cottage, I open the pine-framed window. There are pigs in the field across the road and I see a black and white collie. There are chickens scratting about and just as Macrow did I can hear a cock crowing.

> Macrow: *Sometimes, a black-and-white collie was racing up and down across the blown grass and bog-cotton, full of the joy of living.*

I guess the white cottage, drifting smoke from its chimney, I can see across the road must have been here in 1946, but not the ugly modern bungalow with the polytunnel standing next to it.

Alison cleans my room while I'm out. Making the bed and carefully folding the black T-shirt I wear as a pyjama top under the pillow. She even folds the roll of toilet paper to a point, the way they do in hotels. The room is clean, immaculate and modern. There is, it seems no trace left of the Shepherd's Cottage of 1946 (Macrow just calls it the cottage) with its coal fires, dusty concrete floors and dark, wood polished walls. It's only when darkness closes in around the house and I turn off the lights and gaze out the window at the blue hills and the stars that I sense the Kintail of 1946. Then a car, headlights on full beam roars along the road outside and it's gone. It's the second decade of the twenty-first-century again.

THE WILD SWIMMER OF KINTAIL

Macrow climbs the wooden steps up to the attic. Turns the paint encrusted brass catch on the three foot high door. It opens in the way. Dust motes shimmer, caught in a shaft of sunlight that illuminates the splintered wooden floorboards of the attic. At the edge of the darkness rusty serrated iron catches Macrow's eye. Outside the sun moves behind a cloud and the cool sea breeze from Loch Duich freshens.

I turn the dial on the heater in the bedroom. It's not that warm. There's still snow on the hills. I press the start button on the Hewlett Packard laptop, wondering if HP were around in Macrow's day. I think they were. Later I'll check and find the company started out in a garage in California in 1939 making cash registers before they moved into computers. The screen lights up with the Windows 10 logo.

Today like most homes, Shepherd's Cottage glows with its PC, printer, wide screen TV, iPad, assorted radios, tablets and phones. But in 1946 not so much as a Bakelite wireless graced the mantelpiece in the front room of Shepherd's Cottage. There is more technology in Shepherd's Cottage today than was available to Winston Churchill in 1940. Never mind Shepherd's Cottage: on my wrist, my ten-year-old Altimax watch has more computing power than Churchill had to fight World War Two.

I close the lid of my laptop and sit on the edge of the bed at the open window listening to the chaffinches. I'd rather listen to the birdsong of Kintail.

Macrow: *And so to bed, for our first sleep in our new home, with the fire burning merrily and the little room full of the tang of pine-smoke. Outside the hill-wind was howling on a long, eerie note... We turned out the lamp... nestled into the deep and well-sprung sofa, and pulled the Army blankets over the two of us. Outside, no doubt, the quiet hills were watching us…*

I sit on the bed in the upstairs room in Shepherd's Cottage. I look around me and think the height of the roof must have been raised since Macrow's day. Shepherd's Cottage didn't have an upstairs in 1946. I'm pretty sure I don't recall Macrow mentioning upstairs. Then the realisation begins to dawn. This used to be the attic. They've put me in the attic. They've put me in the attic where Macrow found the gin traps.

Man on a Bike

The magnificent motor-car, immense, breath-snatching, passionate, with its pilot tense and hugging his wheel, possessed all earth and air for the fraction of a second... 'Glorious, stirring sight!' murmured Toad...'The poetry of motion! The real way to travel The only way to travel!'
Kenneth Grahame, *The Wind in the Willows*, 1908.

'For fuck's sake could you go any fuckin' faster that was fuckin' close!' I shout. It's the white van man in my coming oot, too much time spent working in Deliver in the supermarket. I inhale a lungfull of warm nitrogen oxide from the exhaust of the rapidly disappearing white Rabbie's Tours minibus.It just flew past me at about 85 miles per hour on the long straight stretch of the A87 that leads from Ardelve to Nostie where Shepherd's Cottage stands on a little rise above what today is the main trunk road to Skye.

Macrow 1946: *After waiting until one-thirty for the weather to decide what it was going to do, I took a chance, packed up some tea, and got out my long-suffering cycle.*

Graham and Alison had looked a bit dubious when I outlined my plans over breakfast, explaining I intended to cycle from Shepherd's Cottage to Loch Lòn Mhurchaidh just as Macrow had in 1946.
'The road's very busy now you know. Stuff goes very fast on that straight bit with things trying to overtake. Graham's had a couple of near misses just trying to get the car out the drive...'

1946: *The yellow shooting-brake came up the long, straight road, going into Kyle. The sun glistened on its polished woodwork and chromium fittings. A sparrow was twittering on top of my chimney... There was a faint blue haze over the hills...*

Six German motorcyclists led by a well-built man of maybe 70 years of age with an impressive handlebar moustache scream past me. I'm beginning to think Graham and Alison may have had a point after all. A flatbed truck laden with red canisters of butane hurtles past rather too close for my likinG Definitely a lot closer than in the advert on the back of the buses in Edinburgh, the one with the traffic cop demonstrating how you should give a bike the same space as you would a car, still I console myself, only half a mile to go.

But then the doom mongering starts in my head again and I start to visualise the newspaper headlines. Not front page of course, probably be about page seven of something obscure like *The Ross-shire Journal*, 'Little Known Scottish Writer Killed in Accident on A87.' 'We tried to stop him,' say owners of bed and breakfast where Kellan MacInnes, a little known Scottish writer, had been staying before embarking on his fateful journey. 'Police Scotland Warn Highland Roads Much Busier Than In 1946.' Author of book currently ranked 903,467 on Amazon dies in 'Highland Horror Crash.' Heartbroken fans (total: three men and a dug) gather outside MacInnes's home in Edinburgh. 'He survived AIDS only to go under a truck' goes through my mind a I signal left rather shoogily and thanking God I'm still alive bump down off the A87 and onto the tree lined road to Killilan. The birches, rowans and oaks form a canopy overhanging the road, dimming the light level and muffling the roar of passing traffic on the A87. Suddenly I'm back in 1946.

I'm cycling a 1994 Raleigh Nitro inherited from my ex or rather left behind in the wake of the divorce settlement. Much as in 1940 the British Army left vast piles of supplies behind after Dunkirk.

THE WILD SWIMMER OF KINTAIL

Where the Wehrmacht acquired right-hand drive lorries and jeeps I inherited Italian leather shoes, CDs and the bike which had been my ex's Christmas present to himself back in 1994. He can only have been about 25 and I remember he took it out for a ride around Leith on Christmas morning. Just him and the other eleven and twelve year olds all out on their new bikes they'd got for Christmas.

I did some work on the rear brake last summer, the Bowden cable had seized inside its sheathing and front brake only made for some perilous trips to the shop in Roy Bridge. This year I've retrofitted the bike with Armadillo Kevlar puncture proof tyres like we use on the bike tours and now it's a case of the tyres being worth more than the bike.

It's my caravan bike I keep up in Lochaber, I like to wheel it out when it's the weekend of the Mountain Biking World Cup. When there are all these cool, young dudes dripping lycra staying at the campsite with their Giants and Muddy Foxs, all front and rear suspension and hydraulic brakes. My old Raleigh Nitro gets some strange looks. TBH it looks as if it belongs in the late 1980s/early-90s section of a museum of style and design: 'An example of an early mountain bike, note upright seating position and cable cantilever brakes.'

Then suddenly I'm out of the trees and pedalling along beside the shore of the sea loch. A glance down at my wrist, my Garmin satnav says I'm doing 16 kilometres an hour. There's a great pile of telegraph poles by the side of the road, the old kind with white ceramic insulators. Just the kind of telegraph poles Macrow would have wired to the south on. I stop for a neb, wondering if these telegraph poles were here in 1946. Few homes had telephones, only the better off could afford them. Mr Wills the local landowner no doubt had one in the long gone Killilan House at the foot of Glen Elchaig. But all of Macrow's communication seems to have involved a walk to the post office in Nostie to send a telegram.

Reflecting on this and wondering if the vast array of methods of electronic communication available to us today has made the world a happier place (Donald Trump's tweets didnae for sure) I swing a lycra clad leg over the frame of the bike and set off along the road again. See that's something else that's changed too since the 1940s. We've all got to have the right gear for everything. Baggy mountain bike shorts for mountain biking. Classic black Lycra cycling shorts for road biking, Paramo and Montane jackets and Rab trousers for on the hill. Yet Macrow did all her cycling and hillwalking without any specialist gear. She did have a 'long-suffering' pair of walking boots and an old overcoat. Reading her descriptions of long stravaigs over remote Scottish peaks, there's no indication she even carried a rucksack, just her crowdie sandwiches in one pocket and her notebook and pencil in the other, her doughty Skye terrier Jeannie at her heel.

And the distances she covered! In her ability to walk a long, long way, Macrow was much closer to Hugh Munro and the Victorian mountaineers than to today's Munroists with their fancy streak of lightning cars and Goretex and satnavs and i-phones.

Macrow: *We walked slowly along the Killilan road in the blazing sunshine, having not yet decided where to go…*

I'm pedalling along and thinking, all this stuff swirling about in my head, like you do when you're out on your own in the wilds. Ben Killilan and the Corbett Sguman Còinntich guard the head of the sea loch, leading me on along the tarmac, following Macrow and Jeannie on the road through Conchra and Sallachy and Allt-nan-sùgh.

THE WILD SWIMMER OF KINTAIL

It was around midnight. My ex had been drinking. Whether in the flat we jointly owned or after work I don't now recall. But he was dressed in his work suit. Of that I'm sure. He was sitting in the little armchair in the kitchen that came from his Granny's house in Northumberland. The one I spent months re-upholstering when I was on health-related benefits. Upholstery being almost as time consuming a task as writing, I had plenty of time for it back in the dole days. The little armchair sat beside the Rayburn and was the warmest seat in the house, the seat where I put guests who were cold or wet in the winter. On the other side of the Rayburn was the dogbasket with its checked woollen blanket.

My ex was sitting in his suit in the little armchair and he was in the middle of a diatribe (which I was not allowed to interrupt) about our relationship. He was going on and on about something that happened on a beach in Spain almost twenty years and he'd drunk a lot as usual and he was getting angry. As his voice grew louder our two dogs moved closer to me, the older dog lay across my feet, the younger one leaned into my chair. My ex was drunk and hadn't notice the dogs were behaving like pack animals, closing around me, frightened by the raised voices, the pack closing together in the face of a threat.

Suddenly my ex tore his wedding ring off his finger. I wore a matching one on my ring finger. It's in a wooden box in the hall cupboard now. The two rings were Orkney silver with runes carved in them like the elven rings of power in J R R Tolkein's *The Lord of the Rings*. My ex put his ring down on the greenish-grey slate hearth then picked up the foot long cast iron handle used for emptying the ash draw on the Rayburn. The dogs cowered into me and I looked on aghast as my ex picked up the iron handle and with a terrible banging I was sure must awaken the whole tenement, hammered his silver wedding ring flat then slumped back and not long after fell asleep in the armchair beside the Rayburn. I could see his anguish. I knew I was the cause of his suffering. I didn't want another human being to feel like that. But I didn't know what to do. So I just sat there in the armchair stroking the Labradoodle's head again and again and again.

Macrow: *It was... a cool, breezy day, with the sunlight winking over the blown grasses by the wayside. I pedalled steadily along the shore of Loch Long, with clouds of dust spurting up from my wheels.*

At the houses at Allt-nan-Sùgh and Sallochy a collie in the garden races out to bark at me as I cycle along by the shore of Long LonG At a sharp bend below the steep slopes of Ben Killilan a signpost reads: 'Camas–luinie 1½ miles.' I keep straight on through a pair of white-painted iron gates. The triangular peak of Carnan Cruithneach stands out, black against the snow-streaked Munros at the head of Glen Elchaig as I bump over a yellow and red speed hump between stone gateposts, each bearing a notice 'Inverinate Estate No Vehicle Access.'

The buildings here stand on the site of the old township of Killilan which was absorbed into a sporting estate during the nineteenth century. Opposite the graveyard and the stables is a large green barn. Nearby on a little rise stands the bungalow that was once the chauffeur's cottage. I found the thirties style bungalow and cream-coloured village hall dated 1933 with short steeple and leaded windows oddly out of context in a remote West Highland glen until I came across photos of Killilan House prior to its demolition circa 1995. In 1946 when Macrow passed this way the art nouveau Killilan House still stood where the barn stands today. The art nouveau house explains the presence of the remaining thirties buildings, a sort of model village built by the landowner. Photos of Killilan House taken

THE WILD SWIMMER OF KINTAIL

in the 1990s show an attractive, two-storey building in the style of Charles Rennie MacKintosh with gatehouse, inner courtyard and corner tower with steeple and weathervane. But the house looks down at heel, the white harling is crumbling and moss has spread across the slate roof tiles.

A Colonel Wills owned the house. Wills made his money in tobacco of course. The family firm W D and H O Wills first started out in the tobacco business in the 16th century. Today the company is part of Imperial Tobacco, one of the largest cigarette manufacturers on the planet. In the twentieth century, their most famous brands were Woodbine and Capstan Full Strength. In the 1950s the firm also made Strand, a brand famously marketed with the slogan: 'You're never alone with a Strand.' So true when I sat at the bar of The Laughing Duck the last time I was single back in the 1990s I was never alone when I lit up a Marlboro Gold. Today it's like you're never alone with your phone.

The tarmac ends. The road dwindles to a track. Ahead a herd of cattle cluster around a feeding trough by a green shed beside the track. Then a pickup truck and a collie appear driving a flock of sheep down the track. The flat grassland and fields of lower Glen Elchaig behind me now, sweat drips down the inside of my bike helmet as I cycle uphill towards the snow-streaked hills at the head of the glen.

I get off the bike at a red-painted deer gate. Red seems to be the Inverinate estate colour. Suddenly one, no two, no three deer on the track, I cycle on and round a bend and suddenly I'm in the midst of a whole herd of deer. I stop and slowly get off the bike. There are hinds and stags and hummels. I smell the strange disinfectant-like aroma of their scent. They are hungry. The cattle and sheep in Glen Elchaig are fed from feeding troughs. The deer are hungry. Their coats are moultinG They are wild. They are hungry. But they are free.

An ancient landslide has left giant, moss-covered boulders piled on the hillside. Silver birches claw the gaps between the rocks. I'm pushing the bike again as the track, grass growing down the middle of it now, steepens to the high point of the glen. A single, gravestone-like slab stands by the path. As the days shorten and the birch leaves turn from orange to yellow I see a man and a pony waiting here ready to haul a deer carcass down to Killilan.

A couple of hundred metres away from the track a well-engineered two span timber bridge crosses the River Elchaig where it foams down between black rocks. This is the start of one route to the Falls of Glomach. In 1946 Macrow scrambled along the gorge here and felt as if she was clinging on: 'by her eyebrows'. The legendary Scottish climber W H Murray described the route as: 'exposed and dangerous' in places and to be avoided in wet weather. Walkhighlands website says: 'some scrambling is necessary in places.' Despite the bridge and National Trust for Scotland signpost then, the Glen Elchaig approach to the Falls is less a walk, more an easy scramble.*

I cycle on along the track beside the stony shore of Loch na Leitreach. In my mind Macrow is pedalling towards me down the glen, hair streaming in the wind, bumping along the track from Iron Lodge one breezy morning in 1946, Mrs M's crowdie sandwiches wrapped in greaseproof paper in her saddlebag.

A few drops of rain have appeared on the caravan windows as I sit and write this. Aonach Mor has disappeared into cloud, the smell of calor evoking childhood as I light the gas under the kettle. Time passes, the clock hand moves from ten to the hour to five to. Now I can hear the sound of rain drumming on the roof. Another minute and the rain has ceased. An hour later I hear the first cuckoo of spring. I leave my bike where Macrow left her bike and continue on foot down the track to the house at Carnach. Half-a-dozen old pines stand

---

*See page 330 for an easy route to the Falls of Glomach.

THE WILD SWIMMER OF KINTAIL

guard over it and the turf is strewn with lichen-encrusted boulders. In Gaelic Carnach means a stony place.

I pass the house and cross the bridge over the Allt na Doire Gairbhe. On the far side, there are ruins and a lonely chimney and gable end. Who lived here, I wonder? Did children wave across the river in the bright morning of a distant century?

I hide my cycle panniers among the boulders at the edge of the river. The stones used to build the drystone walls that encircle Carnach must have come from the riverbank here, carried one by one by men in white shirts, sleeves rolled up on a hot July day a century-and-a-half ago. I see them pausing to drink from a clay stoppered bottle. A horse and cart stand nearby.

Macrow: *the two bridges at Carnach made light of the turbulent yellow streams, and I was soon tramping steadily up the track to the left of the lacy waterfall...*

On the skyline ahead a white torrent cascades over the lip of the hillside, a little sister of the Falls of Glomach. The stalkers' path makes an easy-angled, rising traverse across the steep, grassy hillside. In 1921 a young estate worker from Killilan was walking here alone, near the waterfall, when suddenly he heard music coming from the stream. Classical music like you'd hear at a concert at the Usher Hall in Edinburgh. Amazed, the young man hurried back down Glen Elchaig to tell his pals. But though many people at different times climbed the path up to the falls the strange music was never heard again. It must have been the fairies...

In two places little landslides have swept the old path away and torn open the grassy hillside exposing craters of ochre and yellow sand, grey boulders and gravel. Then suddenly the hardwork is over. The path climbs the lip of the hillside onto a flat plateau of heather moorland surrounded by snow-capped mountains.

1946: *Once on the top of the brae, I found myself tramping over a green, waterlogged plateau bounded by a semi-circle of cloud-capped hills.*

Up here in the heather, the path is faint and hard to follow. No sign of Macrow's two hill lochs but the cloud cover is high and there are blinks of sunshine so I don't need to fish map and compass from rucksack. The snow-streaked ridges of Sgurr nan Ceathramhnan reach down to the rock-studded plateau. I follow the path as it winds on across the heather, then a glimpse of blue, a shimmer of sunlight on water, Loch Lòn Mhurchaidh. And I feel an echo of the excitement Macrow felt as she lay on the floor of Shepherd's Cottage pouring over Bartholomew's maps of Kintail, imagining the hill lochs as diamonds set in the mountainside.

Macrow 1946: *Crossing a hectic burn, I came to Loch a'Mhurachaidh* [sic]... *an irregular, sun-spangled pool bounded by a fringe of light reeds.*

I leave my rucksack and walk down to a second satellite lochan, 100 metres away. Clouds and sky are reflected in its still waters. There's a small island of heather and moss and lichen-crusted rocks and one bush-like tree, just as Macrow describes. Rocks and reeds in the shallow waters, the bed of the lochan is peaty and muddy, a peaceful place in among the mountains. I crouch down and splash the cold peaty water on to my face.

I pull my Lumix camera out my rucksack and photograph the lochan. The GPS on my wrist connects to signals travelling at the speed of light from a satellite spinning in orbit 20,000 kilometres

THE WILD SWIMMER OF KINTAIL

above the planet. I press the keys on the GPS to record the lochan's grid reference, altitude and position then walk back across the moorland to Loch Lòn Mhurchaidh.

The heather reaches down to the clear waters of the loch. Near the path there's a six foot long strip of sand where blobs of white froth tremble in the strong breeze. Rocks break the surface of the peaty water. I've reached my third hill loch. At this rate it'll not be long til I'm into double figures.

The wind is cold though there's some warmth in the sun. The cool air from the snowfields Macrow could already feel as the train pulled out of Euston in to the darkness 75 years ago. The sun appears from behind a cloud. Patches of sunlight dapple the little waves on the surface of the loch. I take off my rucksack. Bend down and unlace my boots then take my socks off, feeling cold sand under my bare feet. I want to swim in the hill lochs of Kintail. The repeated immersion in cold water is going to be like a baptism of my new life, a baptism of my rebirth as a single person.

I peel my paramo fleece and wickable top off. Unbuckle then step out of my walking trousers and pull down my black Calvin Kleins. I stand there naked under the snow-streaked ridges of Sgurr nan Ceathramhnan. I walk into the water. It's too cold to swim but I crouch down and splash cold peaty water on my body and face then run up and down the strip of sand before drying myself with my fleece. Refreshed, rejuvenated, sweat washed away. My skin tingles. As I pull my clothes back on again a cloud covers up the sun and the breeze from the snowfields strengthens.

The Day the Circus Left Town

'Scots words to tell to your heart...
English words so sharp and clean and true.'
Lewis Grassic Gibbon, 1932

I'd been working in the supermarket all day. In the dying stages of my relationship with my ex, after *Caleb's List* had been published, but neither advance nor royalties had materialised, I thought it might help things at home if I got a job with the same company my ex worked for. He'd always had the nine-to-five paying the mortgage job. I'd always been a free spirit. It didn't work. We split up anyway. But I'm still working as a supermarket delivery driver and we both still work for the same company.

It was a Sunday night in August, festival time, the city swarming with tourists. I was buddied up with Grant the bodybuilder who was filling the cab of the van with his BO. Our second last delivery of the evening was to a Mrs Ollero-Pierce in Spottiswoode Road, one of the canyon-like streets of high tenements in the Marchmont area of Edinburgh. As we drove along, looking for a parking space that would allow us to get the back of the van as close to the customer's front door as possible, I noticed there was something grey and white flapping on the cobbles in the middle of the road. It wasn't a burst open rubbish bag or an item of clothing discarded by a drunk student shambling home late at night. It was a juvenile herring gull, one wing limp and broken, flapping helplessly on the greasy cobbles. We stopped the van across the road from Mrs Ollero-Pierce's first floor flat. Frozen with indecision Grant the bodybuilder with the BO and I sat in the front of the van wondering what to do. It was all just a bit much after ten deliveries mainly to second and third floor flats. I had a brief fleeting vision in my head of a photo of the pair of us, in our yellow High-Vis gilets and stripey blue shirts and black nylon trousers in the *Supermarket Chronicle* under the headline 'Van Hero Grant looked at me. I looked at Grant. He looked back at me. Then I opened the van door and got out. But just as I did so a door opened on the other side of the street and a man and a young girl emerged holding a blanket and a cardboard box. They approached the injured herring gull and rather skilfully, I thought, wrapped the bird up in the blanket and put it in the cardboard box and took it indoors. Grant and I were saved. We didnae need to be hero van drivers that night.

Later, after work I stopped by the book festival in Charlotte Square Gardens. As I rounded the corner of Queen Street and North Charlotte Street I saw, in the windows of Knight Frank, there was an island, an entire island no less, for sale. Only in Scotland, I thought to myself as I waited for the green man at the lights in Charlotte Square, only in Scotland.

I took my pint of Heineken to one of the booths near the stage in the Spiegel Tent. There was a rather glam blonde sat opposite me. She bought me a drink at the interval and I slid one of my business cards I had printed at Prontaprint in Howe Street (over the road from where the legendary gay bar The Laughing Duck used to be) across the formica-topped table to her. Maybe she's a journalist, I thought.

Since my break up with my ex, one of several part-time jobs I do to fund my writing career (until I manage to publish that elusive best seller, the one about the boy magician at boarding school) is working as a bike tour guide. One of the stops on the tour is St Andrew's Square. We wheel across the grass then I prop my bike up against a tree. 'August is a great time to come to Edinburgh,' I tell the assorted group of Americans, Spanish and Brits, 'there's a real buzz to the city with the Festival going on all around. Thousands of actors, writers, opera singers, ballet dancers, amateur theatre companies, comedians, kids' theatre groups, people off the telly, they all come to Edinburgh in August for what is now the biggest arts festival in the world.'

'The Edinburgh International Arts Festival started in 1947 as a way of promoting peace and reconciliation in Europe after World War Two,' I continue, directing my gaze at the middle-aged English couple on the tour who I suspect may have voted for Brexit. Before going onto to tell them about how Rudolph Bing, an Austrian Jew who fled Nazi persecution, became the first director of the Edinburgh International Arts Festival. And how in 1950 the Berlin Philharmonic came to perform in Edinburgh in August, the very same year the Festival was nominated for the Nobel Peace Prize.

If they're not glazing over or yawning (which happens quite often on bike tours despite my best efforts to keep our trip through Edinburgh's history and culture as light and snappy as I can) I'll maybe go on to tell them about how the sombre Scottish capital was chosen for the Festival because of its beautiful settinG If they seem interested I'll tell them the Festival was intended to reinsate civilised values after six years of the barbarities of war. About how the idea of the Festival was quite revolutionary at the time and was part of the new world order post-1945. And how the development of the welfare state was linked to funding of the arts by government. And how the Arts Council was set up at the same time as the National Health Service.

I might even tell them about how in the past the Scottish Kirk suppressed theatre in a long tradition that went right back to the fifteenth-century Protestant firebrand John Knox. And that the opening ceremony of the 1947 Edinburgh Festival took place in St Giles Cathedral, in the very church where John Knox had once preached against the wickedness of the arts. Sometimes they ask about the Fringe and I'll explain that in 1971 there were 78 companies on the Fringe, by 2014 there were thousands. I'll tell them there were 120,000 visitors to 1947 festival. And in 2019 there were 2.5 million

THE WILD SWIMMER OF KINTAIL

visitors to the Fringe alone.

By now though someone's yawning at the back, time to move things alonG Time to deliver my punchline:

'But don't worry,' I say with a cheeky grin, 'if art and culture's not your thing and shopping is, just over there we have the Edinburgh branch of Harvey Nichols, a really top end store. And for a more traditional shopping experience head to the big stone building on the corner with the gold letters on it. I'm sure you've heard of Harrods in London, well Jenners is a bit like Harrods in Scotland.'

And there we go I've got their attention again.

Meanwhile on stage in the Spiegel Tent at the book festival, a bad poet called Andrea was standing at the microphone in a flowery dress reading her 'poetry' aloud in a strong Mexican accent:

'Hees engorged meember,' she recited, 'Like a goreella.'

After an evening spent humping mineral water and cat litter up to top floor flats it all seemed just a little bit self indulgent.

Outside a cute young guy in denim shorts sat in a deckchair in Charlotte Square Gardens reading, just looked so sexy. He made me think about something the novelist Howard Jacobson said once, 'Often people from other countries… will tell me how much they like my work. I'm always surprised by who reads me, because at literary festivals you get the sense you're only writing for people who are retired.' Later, in the porta-cabin toilets round the back of the Spiegel tent, the cute young guy in denim shorts is stood at the urinals pissinG I couldn't see his cock, I was tempted to look but didn't, it was the book festival after all.

My first book *Caleb's List* was published in the December and the following August I appeared at the Edinburgh International Book Festival. I had a pass on a halyard with *Kellan MacInnes: Writer* printed on it and access to the Authors' Yurt with it's free buffet and wine. I keep the pass together with my notices in an old wooden box.

I didn't really start to get nervous until we were walking up the aisle to the stage in the Baillie Gifford tent. Then I spotted my mum and sister sitting there in the audience just as the chair of the event was saying into his microphone, 'Welcome to the Edinburgh International Book Festival. Will you please give a very warm welcome to Kellan MacInnes!'

For those three magical weeks in August it was as if I had drawn the curtain aside and looked into a wonderful, colourful world of imagination and creativity. And I knew in that instant my life had changed and could never be the same again. Like drawing aside the curtain on a toy theatre and entering a world populated by colourful, successful writers and handsome, aspiring poets. But then the book festival ended. It was like the day the circus left town. The curtain swept back and the world became a drabber, dimmer, duller place again.

As I walked out of the book festival at midnight, two security guards stood chatting in the deserted foyer. There was a crescent moon over George Street as I walked through Charlotte Square and down to Princes Street to get the number 44 bus back to reality and the wee guy in a blue tracksuit top with a carrier bag asking, 'Is this the bus to Penicuik?

MisterBnb

Macrow: *There came a day when there was hardly a breath of wind. We sat out in the sun, letting the drowsy warmth sink into our bones. Every sound came, sharp and distinct, across the golden air, even the 'chip-chop' of a spade where a woman was digging in a neighbouring field... I felt lazy, lying in the sunlight... 'Jeannie,' I said, putting away my papers, 'This is too good a day to waste. We're going out!'*

A cool, overcast Sunday morning in July, I'm cycling along the shore of Loch Long again, marvelling once more at the distance Macrow and a Skye terrier walked. The only reason I'm biking it along here is because I dinnae fancy a seven mile trek along Loch Long before I even start the walk up to the hill loch. I stop and prop my bike up against the rusting steel handrail on the parapet of the bridge over the River Elchaig and eat one of the 1940s style sandwiches I made the night before with crowdie purchased from the shop in Dornie. OKish but not a patch on mature cheddar.

1946: *There was no bridge over the Elchaig... and I had to ford it on foot. It was wide, shallow and very stony. Part of the time Jeannie was almost swimming... A shower of silver drops fell on to the grass as she shook the gleaming waters of the Elchaig from her shaggy coat.*

The deck of the bridge is supported by steel girders and carried across the Elchaig by three sturdy, moss-coated, concrete piers. Constructed in the 50s or 60s, I reckon, as I wander onto the bridge and look over the side. It's been here for decades. Something once new grown old in the decades gone by since Macrow and Jeannie walked this road. Just like Macrow said the Elchaig here is wide, shallow and very stony. And I can almost see Jeannie splashing over the brown, weedy stones that line the riverbed, that summer afternoon 75 years before me and my bike came this way.

Macrow: *After a short rest, I put on my thick socks and boots, and we rambled on to Camas Linne* [sic], *a cluster of little grey houses at the foot of brown braes.*

A rusty sign pokes out of the bracken at the side of the road: *Camas-luinie*. I lock my bike to a fencepost next to a flatbed trailer. A hand-written sign *Bothy* points towards a one-storey, white-painted cottage.

Pedalling through Sallachy, I remembered I'd forgotten to fill my water bottle. I could drink out the streams but it's probably best not to, given my CD4 count (a measure of the relative health of the body's immune system) ranges between 300 and 500 (in a healthy adult CD4 is normally in the range 800-1200). A person with HIV and a CD4 count below 200 is the point when doctors make an AIDS diagnosis. Probably my CD4 count is high enough to avoid suffering any illness if I was unlucky enough to drink water contaminated with something like cryptosporidium from animal droppings but like I say, probably best not to chance it.

There's no-one about. I push open the door of the bothy and go inside, breathing in a familiar smell of stale woodsmoke and damp teatowels. I find my way past a wood burning stove and armchairs to a sink and tap where I fill my water bottle.

Boots on, rucksack on my back, bike locked. I set off, over a wooden bridge, stepping between the puddles, headed up Glen Elchaig again. Where the tarmac ends a track continues. A pair of vintage tractors, with grass sprouting up through crumbling tyres and rusty sumps, look ancient enough to have been in use when Macrow was here. Behind a low wall a black pig with a white snout snuffles contentedly in the grass and I feel guilty about the Scotch egg in my rucksack.

Macrow 1946: *...two bare-footed children played among piles of fresh-cut logs in the yard. They... laughed at the site of Jeannie trotting along with her ' kilt ' swinging and long tail trailing in the dust.*

The floor of the glen is carpeted with green arable fields, while the hillsides are all brown heather and scattered birch trees. A buzzard flaps over the treetops. Carnan Cruithneachd is a black triangle to the east. I walk through a field of sheep and reach the last inhabited house in Glen Elchaig. The gate scrapes across the stony track and somewhere at the back of the house a dog barks.

A Thursday afternoon, about twenty-five-past-two, I'd just chained my bike up at the top of Chalmers Street in Edinburgh. Back in the 1990s, there was a row of falling down Victorian houses along one side of Chalmers Street and an old school on the other. Behind the Victorian houses (that long ago succumbed to the wrecking ball of Dalton's demolition) stood the Royal Infirmary. Victorian gothic with crowsteps and turrets and a high clock tower, and from the upper deck of the number 23 bus as it rattled round the corner into Forest Road, I always read the verse in gold letters over the main entrance in Lauriston Place with a tingle: 'I was sick and ye visited me. I was homeless and ye took me in.'

It was in the genito-urinary medicine department of the old Royal Infirmary that, on a bleak Monday afternoon 25 years ago, I was diagnosed with AIDS. I wrote about it in *Caleb's List*. Today the hospital has gone. Decamped to Little France where the French courtiers who accompanied Mary Queen of Scots once pitched their tents in the shadow of Craigmillar Castle.

Nowadays the old Royal Infirmary site is known as the Quarter Mile. Black glass skyscrapers tower above the slate roofs of the old grey stone wards and in my evening job as a supermarket van driver I frequently deliver to the flats there. It's always a crates on the sack-trolley job and there are lifts for which we poor van drivers are duly grateful. The eight-storey, black, glass tower-blocks make for lifeless, canyon-like streets and the development seems set apart from from bustling Lauriston Place. The worst feature is the locked gates blocking access to the Meadows. Had access through the Quarter Mile to the Meadows been allowed it would have made the development less soulless and the Meadows a safer place at night.

I wouldn't fancy having a flat here, though some of the penthouses do have spectacular views south across the Meadows to the Pentland Hills. But a flat in one of the grey, stone buildings that were once hospital wards? The bit at the top of Middle Meadow Walk where you used to see the blue flashing lights of the ambulances as they stretchered dying car crash victims into Accident and Emergency. A flat in there? No thanks. In the oldest parts of the hospital legs were sawn off without anaesthetic. The screams of the patients absorbed into the walls, a faint echo of the screams lingering still. Blood splatters on the plaster beneath the fresh white paint. A flat in there? No thanks.

Back to the present where I'd just chained my bike up outside the Chalmers Centre. I was there for my six monthly check-up. The Chalmers Centre for Sexual Health moved into its brand, spanking, new building a few years back. It used to be that HIV patients like me had to attend the clinic every three months. A nurse would take my bloods and then after an anxious two week wait I'd return a fortnight later to see the doctor, always a consultant, for The Results.

Today, with most folk doing so well on modern HIV treatments, you only have to go the the clinic once every six months. Inside, the smart, new building made me think this is what it must be like going to a hospital clinic in Germany, only the twenty-minute wait to see the nurse is NHS.

Usually I just see a nurse practitioner who weighs me, asks me how I've been keeping, asks me a couple of questions about my mental health and if I think I need a sexual health screening and then does my bloods and issues a repeat prescription. If there's a problem with the results the clinic will phone me.

Around once a year though, you still see a doctor for a review and on this Thursday afternoon I saw the consultant who, as a registrar 25 years ago was the young doctor who first diagnosed me as HIV positive. This must, I think, be a unique situation in the NHS. To be seeing the same doctor who diagnosed me with HIV some 25 years ago. The doctor also happens to be gay and likes hillwalking. He glanced at briefly at the figures on the computer screen in front of him then turned towards me.

'Your bloods are fine. What have you been up to?'

'Aw I've been really busy. I've been letting my flat on Airbnb, for the festival like.'

A smile appeared on the doctor's face. Then he said:

'I've got several friends and patients who are letting their flats through an online platform called MisterBnb. It's a gay version of Airbnb and they've had all these cute guys staying with them.'

He paused before delivering the punchline. I glanced up at the poster on the wall warning of the dangers of needlestick injury.

'It's all the same rates and money you get on Airbnb but I think there's a lot more emphasis on orientation and welcome!'

We both laughed. Afterwards, cycling back across the Meadows on my way to work at the supermarket, I thought how, I just could never have imagined on that bleak Monday morning in 1997 when I was first diagnosed with HIV, that twenty-five years later I'd be sitting in a room with the very same doctor having a ridiculous conversation about making all this money from something that back then in the early days of the internet hadn't even been invented yet. Things change, huh?

At a copse of alders and rowan beside a bridge I leave the unsurfaced road and follow an old stalkers' path along beside a stream. Ten minutes walking brings me to a stand of half-a-dozen ancient, hoary birches. Macrow must have stood beneath these trees. I gaze across Glen Elchaig. Far below me the grey road gleams in the green glen and the Allt an Daimh, the stream of the deer flows down the hillside out of Loch nan Ealachan. Then movement, on the floor of the glen 800 feet below, catches my eye. Deer, running in the glen, a big herd, dozens of beasts, running fast, something has spooked them. In a long line they charge across the flat grassland and as I watch the leading beast plunges down through the birch trees and across the Allt an Daimh. I stand and watch transfixed as stags and hinds with calves at their heels splash through the water and emerge in a shower of crystal droplets on the far bank before disappearing out of sight behind the next fold in the hillside. This line of deer, crossing the burn as they have done for centuries and so I think, as I shoulder my rucksack and walk on up the hill path, the Allt an Daimh must have got its name.

1946: *Lying among dark grey hills, calm, quiet and sheltered from*

THE WILD SWIMMER OF KINTAIL

the wind, Loch nan Ealachan might, indeed, have been a refuge for the wild swans after which it was named.

I sit on a rock above the loch and eat a sandwich and then the Scotch egg. The green reeds sway gently as the wind ruffles the surface of Loch nan Ealachan. I wonder if anyone else read Macrow's book and then set out to visit the hill lochs as I am doing. Number 4 on Macrow's list ticked off, I say to myself, as I take a last look at Loch nan Ealachan and pick my rucksack up.

Macrow: *We reached Bundalloch at sunset—and the longest part of the whole journey seemed to be that three mile tramp back to Nostie, where the little cottage stood waiting for us in the dusk.*

The Starbucks Scribblers

He took his laptop to the hospital on the day of his diagnosis, and started writing. Wannabes, dabblers, hobbyists, Sunday painters and Starbucks-scribblers, take note.
  Ian Samson, *London Review of Books*, 2013.

Macrow sits with notebook and fountain pen at a wooden table. Jeannie lies curled up on the bare floorboards, gazing up through her long grey fringe. Outside the hawthorn bush is a mass of white flowers. A smell of seaweed drifts in through the open window and across the fields, out in the bay, porpoises flash black shiny fins in the sunlight on Loch Duich.

'I think you should read this, dear,' my Mum said, as she handed me the latest issue of the *London Review of Books*. It contained an article by Ian Samson about the best-selling Scottish novelist Iain Banks. The piece had the title 'Banksability' and was all about what it takes to be a successful writer. Three paragraphs in, it described how, on the day he was diagnosed with cancer, Iain Banks sat up in his hospital bed in Kirkcaldy with his laptop and started writing. I put the LRB down and thought, 'I'm just not made of the right stuff. I'm just not tough enough. I don't have what it takes. I'm clearly destined to be a Starbucks Scribbler forever.' These then are a few random thoughts and anecdotes of a true Starbucks Scribbler.

Saturday 1 June, white clouds flit across a blue sky brightened with bursts of sunshine. I'm in Roy Bridge, packing the caravan up, getting it ready for towing to Dornie. It's the world's smallest caravan but I'm nervous about towing it. However since I don't plan on becoming a long term guest of Graham and Alison at twenty-first-century Shepherd's Cottage (and my flat in Edinburgh is occupied by Airbnb guests from South Korea until Thursday when a young

German couple from Mannheim arrive for three days) I need an alternative form of accommodation. I guess Macrow and Jeannie would have checked straight into the Dornie Hotel but for me it's the caravan.

Like I said it's the world's smallest caravan.

When folk ask:

'What's your caravan like?'

First I say (deadpan like):

'It's a Tammy Wynette style chrome Winnebago I bought with the royalties from *Caleb's List*.'

Silence (usually follows).

Then:

'Just kiddin' haha!'

Then:

'Do you remember the episode of *Father Ted* Graham Norton was in? The one when Father Ted and Dougal and Father Jack went to stay in a caravan. Well it's like the caravan in *Father Ted*, only smaller.'

You see, caravans are like Marmite. The Marmite things a cliché now and as a writer I should be avoiding clichés. Not rubbing salt in a wound or banging my head against a brick wall. Still just this once we'll let it past. As I was saying, caravans are like marmite. You either love them or you hate them. Snooty, queeny friends tend to fall into the hating caravans category.

'Sounds ghastly,' said Chris's ex-TV presenter other half.

'Isn't it damp all the time?'

Well no, or at least it's a lot less damp than a tent, the alternative accommodation for the starving writer when not confined to his freezing garret. Two days in a tent with a wet mutt I can thole but if it's still raining on day three then I'm bundling soaking flysheet, damp sleeping bag and soggy pillows into the hire car. I would also point out in passing that the no less a person than the erstwhile machar, Liz Lochhead has a caravan at Glenuig in Moidart.

So you are not rich writer? So you are not successful? Nope. Or I wouldnae be driving a van for a supermarket four nights a week. Nah, like I said, I'm a Starbucks-scribbler, me. This then might be an appropriate place to pause for a moment and hear from a successful Scottish writer.

Near the beginning of his best-selling book *At the Loch of the Green Corrie*, the successful Scottish writer Andrew Greig described: 'barrelling along Loch Broom' in his Audi 'the gear change smooth as political tongues.' He concluded the paragraph by stating, 'And a good story can buy a motor car.' I turned the page and concluded that as one of The Independent Scottish Publisher's writers you'd be lucky to be able to buy a second-hand bike with your royalties.

I was sitting at the kitchen table reading *The Author* magazine. As I turned the page, I heard the reassuring creak of the wicker dog basket as the Labradoodle shifted position. I was reading a piece by Jad Adams: 'Time was,' he wrote, 'when I would visit publishers they always seemed to be located up stairs lined with boxes. The offices smelled of old books and nicotine, grey cigarette ash lay on piles of manuscripts... '

Hmm, I reflected, the Independent Scottish Publisher is definitely of the backstairs variety.

Quite literally.

A Highland village somewhere west of the A9: It snowed in the night. Spring snow: March snow. The dogs raced around in ecstatic circles in the inch of snow that covered the field. March snow. It melted quickly in the spring sunshine. I was on my bike, cycling

THE WILD SWIMMER OF KINTAIL

along a single track road to post the manuscript of my first book from a Highland post office. I pressed the latch down and pushed open the black-painted, wooden door of the post office, the manuscript of *Caleb's List* tucked under my arm. The dimly lit interior of the post office felt dark after the bright sunshine reflecting off the snowfields of Beinn Chlinaig against the blue sky outside.

Desultory, dusty rolls of sellotape, post it notes and jiffy bags arranged on half-empty shelves. An old man in black jogging bottoms and a brown jumper was sitting on a stool behind the counter. A clear plastic tube attached to his nostrils held in place by a cord around his neck. He was overweight and wheezed as he put the manuscript of *Caleb's List* on the scales.

It was a complicated transaction. Did the package need to be sent special delivery or recorded delivery? And I struggled to fit the manuscript, which filled two cardboard envelope files and a covering letter into the jiffy bag in the manner recommended on page 124 'Do's and Don't's of Approaching a Publisher' of *The Writers and Artists Yearbook*. I had to buy postage for a second, stamped-addressed jiffy bag for the publisher to return the manuscript in. In total the post and packaging came to £27, how many times would I have to do this? Could I afford to do this?

Some publishers accepted electronically submitted manuscripts back then but not all by any means and anyway this felt right, cycling to a Highland post office in the snow to post a manuscript to a publisher with an address in the heart of Edinburgh's old town. Anyway e-mail submissions are boring.I wanted the experience of the manuscript being returned, the polite letter of rejection to stick on the wall above my desk. As the old man put the jiffy bag containing the manuscript of *Caleb's List* on the scales I watched the needle go down to 3.2 kilos and wondered when I'd see the manuscript again. I imagined lying in my bed in my pants hearing it thud onto the tiles of the front porch at home.

But what would happen if the manuscript wasn't returned? The Publisher's website had a grandiose sounding address: 189/2 The Lawnmarket, Edinburgh. How romantic I thought, as the wheezing man with tubes stuck up his nose stuck stamps on the A5 size jiffy bag containing the manuscript of *Caleb's List* in the tiny Highland post office. It was late March and outside an inch of snow covered the fields by the river.

I should have spotted the clue.

I was standing in a courtyard that was really more car park than courtyard, behind the Camera Obscura and opposite The Scotch Whisky Experience. The clue was in the address, I suddenly realised, in the 189/2 bit. I'd been expecting a shiny brassplate on the door. Instead there was a bog standard stair entryphone. My finger hovered over the lowest of six black buttons. The one with the piece of cardboard tucked behind the scratched clear plastic with The Independent Scottish Publisher scrawled on it in blue biro.

Trepidation: a meeting with a publisher, I pushed the buzzer. There was no reply, no answering voice. But the lock buzzed almost immediately and I pushed open the door and climbed the concrete steps past blank front doors. On the second landing, a door opened and a tall thin blond girl said, 'Kellan?' and she led me up another flight of stairs, carpeted this time. A door was open, a double bed neatly made with a checked bed spread, a glimpse of a bathroom with a light blue suite then a kitchen with a wooden sideboard. A copy of that day's *Herald* lay on a table. Then we climbed the stairs to the attic where the Publisher sat in his room high above the city looking out across the spires and towers, like Saruman in Orthanc, wielding a wizard's power over people's dreams.

I perched on the edge of a chair in front of The Independent Scottish Publisher's desk. I glanced nervously around. I'd never seen

THE WILD SWIMMER OF KINTAIL

an office like this before. Every surface including the windowsills and the publisher's desk had been buried beneath an avalanche of books and papers. Very little of the carpet was visible. A narrow path led from the door to the desk between yellowing piles of paper. Forgotten or rejected manuscripts, I wondered? The tall thin blond girl sat behind an elderly looking PC. There was another monitor on the publisher's desk and a keyboard. Both completely surrounded by papers stacked a foot high. The Publisher had to stretch his fingers down into the papery chasm to type on his keyboard.

And that was the next time I saw the manuscript. It was sitting on top of a pile of books on The Independent Scottish Publisher's desk. I recognised the red cardboard file with my handwriting in marker pen on it. The Publisher looked anxiously at its bulk:

'How many words did you say it was?' he asked queasily.

Like I said with The Independent Scottish Publisher you'd be lucky to be able to afford to buy a bike with your royalties. So it's a caravan in Dornie for me. And it's more than ten years old now.

It was the Munros led me to buy a caravan. Like I said, caravans are marmite but me, I like them. When we, for there was a 'we' back then, these days there's just a me and the Labradoodle, The Plan was to buy a second-hand one. I remember how we stood on the tarmac at Knowepark near Livingston looking at yellowing signs in caravan windows. £2,499 *Sold As Seen*. Sold as Seen? What did that mean, we wondered? Someone suggested the small ads in the *Dundee Courier*. Quick Sale — retired couple giving up caravanning.

But then my ex had The Dream.

'I don't think we should buy a second-hand caravan,' he said to me sleepily one Saturday morning.

'Why for no for?'

'I had this dream last night,' he explained, 'we paid cash for a second-hand caravan we bought from this old crone who looked a bit like your granny.'

'A bit like my granny?'

'Well in my dream we got five miles up the road and a wheel fell off and there were like sparks flying off the axle and it was scraping along the tarmac.

My ex's dream seemed to be articulating an unspoken fear we both shared. We didn't know anything about caravans. They had brakes and gas central heating. Did they need MOTs?

That's when the internet came to the rescue.

We discovered you could buy a brand, spanking, new caravan, (imported from Poland) for the almost the same price as a second-hand one. Manufactured in the industrial town of Nieuviadow (one of those Soviet-era factory towns where the town was named after the local factory) and imported by a caravan dealer in Stafford who sold them in the UK under the name Freedom Caravans. When I first saw it, the heavy-duty, galvanised-metal chassis of the caravan reminded me of TV footage I'd seen of military trailers towed behind Soviet lorries during the Red Army's invasion of Afghanistan in 1979.

The new caravan came with a manual translated very literally from the Polish. It made reference to the 'brking' system, the 'colapsible' legs, the 'lehght' of the cabin, the brakes 'sdjudtment' and heaven forbid the brakes 'malfunktion.' The instructions for putting the double bed up were headed 'Preparation for a night rest' and the section on maintenance advised that every six months we should 'press fat through two lubricating nipples into the overrunning brake mechanism.' In the event of getting a puncture the manual stated 'to take caravan's wheel, it should be rested on the hind legs.'

I tell D&G I'm camping at Dornie. That's David and Graham to you btw, not Dolce & Gabbana though they are about the same age but not nearly as rich.

'Does the old wifey still come round for the money?' They ask.

THE WILD SWIMMER OF KINTAIL

I remember her too. Last time I stayed at Dornie campsite, regular as clockwork around five in the afternoon a big silver car would appear and at each caravan a white-haired, elderly lady would get out and collect the money. Make the cheque out to Mhari Macrae she'd say.

This time when I get to Dornie campsite though it's a florid-faced son of Mrs Macrae driving a beat up white Renault Kangoo van collecting the money.

'It's twelve pounds a night for a car and a caravan,' he says.

He doesn't seem too keen to give me a receipt either.

At The Loch of the Birds

She stopped running now, for she was getting breathless. Beside her the burn splashed and gurgled over the white stones. She put the blue pebble into her pocket, and sat for a while staring at the foaming stream.
     BGM, *The Amazing Mr Whisper*, 1958.

I begin where Macrow began, standing on the stone slipway beside the bridge at Dornie. The waters of Loch Duich wash gently over the old, barnacled stones. I begin where Macrow began, standing beside a pile of lobster creels on the slipway at Dornie. The fronds of brown kelp sway gently in the salt seawater. The traffic roars across the bridge above me.

Macrow: *...along the shores of blue Loch Duich, where the great hills lie clustered about the quiet waters, and sea-birds call softly to each other in the dusk.*

I wheel my bike up the slipway and when I reach the A87 pedal along the footpath that leads to the Bridge at Dornie. I ain't cycling on the A87 again that's for sure. It's just too nerve-shredding. The lorries, the mobile homes, the cars and the motorbikes. And think about the animal deaths on the road, what it must be like for the deer and other creatures that happen to stumble upon the deadly strip of tarmac racetrack between the trees. No. I'm on the pavement, keeping close to the parapet of the bridge with the slight but nagging anxiety that, even though I'm not actually on the road, just close to it, I may still be hit on the back of the head by the wing mirror of a passing coach or lorry. I cast a quick glance down to where the black waters of the tidal race swirl under the bridge, as Loch Duich empties into the sea.

At the south end of the bridge I go through the subway and past the painted houses at Dornie. Here it's quieter, more like the Highlands of 1946. More like the quiet of Appin I remember from when I was a kid in the '70s. The quiet of the Highlands you still find today in a few remote, lonely places like at Inverie in Knoydart.

At the Dornie Hotel, where Macrow and Jeannie spent the first two weeks of their summer in Kintail, before they rented Shepherd's Cottage, I take the old hill road that climbs the brae behind the village. Today it's a by-road signposted 'Carr Brae Viewpoint' but in 1946 this was the main road to Skye. It reaches a height of almost 600 feet on the hillside at Keppoch before plunging down to the shoreline of Loch Duich. For centuries before Macrow came to Kintail, to reach Dornie you had to make the steep climb up Carr Brae. But your reward was a dramatic view down to Eilean Donan castle, one of the most romantic views in the Highlands, rivalled only by the view of Castle Stalker in Appin in Argyll.

I end up pushing my bike most of the way up Carr Brae. There are horses in a field beside the tumbledown sheds at the highest point on the old hill road. Robert Moyes Adam, who took the photos for *Kintail Scrapbook*, Macrow's book about the six months she spent in Kintail, must have stopped his car along here, some time in the 1940s. In the picture he took, the hillside less wooded, more open back then, sweeps down to a cottage by the shore of Loch Duich. Twenty years later civil engineers dynamited their way through the rock, blasting a cutting to carry the new trunk road in sweeping curves along the loch side. And I think of the otters and seabirds that lived among the boulders on the shore before the new road came.

Macrow: *Loch Duich flashed and winked in the sunshine... A grey heron flew with slow, heavy wing-beats along the near shore.*

Freewheeling and singing (out of tune) to myself in the Highland morning, I rattle down the hill to Inverinate on the shore of Loch Duich. On the twenty-five-year-old Raleigh Nitro my ex got for Christmas when we lived in Great Junction Street in Leith, in another lifetime. I hurtle past the shades of Macrow and Jeannie climbing wearily up the hill in the opposite direction, heading back to Nostie where the little cottage waited for them in the dusk.

Branches of birch and oak shade the road. Then suddenly in the bright sunshine, at the edge of my peripheral vision, at a sharp bend in the hill road, just before the mossy, stone bridge across the An Leth Allt, a black shape flits across the road. Then the black flicker of darkness is gone. It was nothing. A floater in my field of vision and I think no more of it as I freewheel on down to Inverinate in the sunshine of the Highland morning.

Macrow 1946: *We rested at the bridge over An Leth Allt, gazing down at the foaming burn as it rushed over white rocks. I had been told that this part of the road is said to be haunted by the ghost of a black dog... running across the road.*

The Labradoodle's coat is dark brown, almost black. Maybe it was a ghost was from the future, I think, as cantilever brakes and rusty cables sqeaul and I come to a stop on the old stone bridge. The leafy branches shade the road. A deer gate leads invitingly into the woodland lining the sides of the gorge. There's space to park as well. This must be the start of the walk.

As I'm sorting out my rucksack I glance at my phone and notice the date. Monday 3 June. The date of our civil partnership ceremony, just six months after the Labour government brought in the Civil

THE WILD SWIMMER OF KINTAIL

Partnership Act. Six months after Elton and David Furnish, so it's Brenda's birthday and my wedding anniversary today.

> Macrow: *I pedalled through Dornie and over the brae towards Inverinate. On the edge of the village, I left my cycle by a grey stone bridge...*

I squeeze through the deer-gate and follow the grassy path beneath the silver birches. Bluebells, primroses and wood sorrel grow along the steep banks of the stream. The path has wooden handrails – great I think, this will be a good walk to include in the book – nice easy start. The path leads down to a wooden footbridge across the stream. A couple of planks are missing from the bridge and it doesn't look like anyone's walked along here for a while. But a reassuring handrail runs along the far bank and I push on along the path further into the gorge. It's nagging at the back of my mind though that the path wasn't shown as crossing the stream when I looked at the map in the caravan last night. Never mind I expect it'll cross back to the other side soon.

I walk another few minutes through dense woodland then catch site of a bright blue plastic water pipe in the stream. This doesn't feel right. I don't think we're going the right way dog. I get the map out. Careful study of it now, rather than the cursory glance after the pub last night, reveals I haven't even parked in the right place. Duh! I should have parked further up the road near a small building. I retrace my footsteps back across the bridge and under the overhanging branches. Sweat runs down my temples.

> 1946: *I meandered along the course of the stream, looking for the marked path. Several times I thought I had it—only to discover I was on a sheep-track. (I found out later that it is much higher up,*

running along the side of the hill.)

I leave the bike where it is and walk a quarter of a kilometre up the road to find the start of the Coire Dhuinnid stalkers' path beside a small waterworks which explains the blue pipes in the stream. I open a gate and walk past an old stone building once a cottage, then a byre, now deserted. Raspberry canes run wild in what was once a walled garden at the back of the building where a rowan tree still guards the house.

I follow a faint track along the hillside. One hundred and fifty feet below I can see the road and the stone bridge and the wooded gorge. The track rounds a bend and I push open a deergate leading onto the open hillside. I've found the path. It feels right.

I see the first yellow flowers of tormentil that day, heart-shaped petals in the grass at the edge of the track amongst the dog violets and birdsfoot trefoil. The gorge of An Leth allt and the path that traverses the steep sided Coire Dhuinnid are turning out to be a spectacular corner of undiscovered Scotland for me. I've never been here before. The stream cascades down in a series of stepped waterfalls and deep, blue-green (ranging through brown to black depending on the weather and light level) natural rock swimming pools where rowan and birch cling to the mossy rocks. These are faery pools to rival those in Skye and Glen Etive and would reward exploration by (adventurous) wild swimmers prepared to scramble down to the foot of the steep sided glen.

Movement across the boulder-strewn bed of the stream catches my eye. Wild goats! Road signs on the A87 warn drivers about feral goats. With their long, shaggy, matted coats they look ungainly beasts. But as I watch a big, grey billy goat with splendid horns catches the scent of a human and leaps across the gorge. Balancing on a rock in the middle of the stream before jumping onto the crags on the far side where he again balances perfectly while standing sideways on a narrow ledge on a cliff above the gorge. As I stand there on the path, awe-struck, the phrase 'agile as a mountain goat' flashes into my mind and I understand perfectly what it means and it doesn't seem a cliché on a summer's morning in a glen in Kintail.

Higher up, beyond the pools and waterfalls, the path reaches the level moorland of upper Coire Dhuinnid. The An Leth Allt meanders peacefully through rocks and heather, the drama of the gorge and the goats left behind.

> Macrow: *The hills became bleak and bare. I found the ruin of an old shieling, now a tumbled heap of grey stones...*

Mist is sweeping across the top of 631 metre high Boc Mor as I take a compass bearing along the line where the path should be and tramp up through the heather. Slight intuition, a feeling born of experience, a line of dripping iron fenceposts in the mist, flat stones at the edge of a burn and on the far side a thin gravel line edged with heather. I've found the path. At my feet the pink flowers of lousewort brighten the tawny shades of deergrass.

I reach the high point of the path, the place I plan to leave it and walk across a kilometre of heather, peat hag and bog to the summit of Boc Mor. But a high deer fence marches impenetrably across the skyline. I aim to tick off Loch Bhuic Mhoir and then climb to the summit of Boc Mor, Macrow's clenched fist of a mountain, but the deer fence bars the way. I plod along the line of the fence looking for a gate or a stile or a gap to squeeze through. I photograph Loch Bhuic Mor 200 metres away through the wire. But I don't think that counts as a tick on Macrow's list of hill lochs. The sun's come out now so at least we won't get lost up here among the pools and lochans, peat hags and rocky outcrops. Do people ever come here I wonder? We reach the three unnamed lochans to the east of Loch Gorm Mor before I give up. The impenetrable deer fence bars the way back to 1946.

My ex was on the red wine. He was most of the way through the second bottle. We were going on holiday the next day, probably somewhere in the Highlands with lochs and mountains and a beach for the dogs. Only he was making it clear he didn't want to go. He was saying he wanted to go to Greece instead. Clearly the prospect of a wet weekend in Fort William with me and the dogs wasn't floating his boat. When he'd finished the second bottle of red wine he started rifling through the filing cabinet in the boxroom looking for his passport. The Labradoodle shifted uncomfortably in her dogbasket beside the Rayburn. Had I hidden his passport? No. The more sober one, as usual, I found it for him. He shoved the passport and his wallet and his i-phone into his messenger bag along with a pair of sunglasses.

'I'm going to Greece!' he shouted as he banged the front door shut behind him and the dog barked furiously.

Out in the street he flagged down a taxi and got it to take him to Edinburgh airport where he paid £800 on his credit card for a scheduled British airways flight to Athens where he arrived the next day, hungover and with just the messenger bag and the pair of sunglasses. He made it onto the ferry to Naxos before the Royal Bank of Scotland stopped his cards thinking they'd been stolen by a thief who'd jumped on the next flight to Greece. Somehow he sorted it all out with his bank by phone from the Greek island and he would re-appear two weeks later looking sun scorched and sporting a wispy ginger beard flecked with grey.

Meanwhile, next morning I took the dogs to the caravan where I was faced with an unexpected two weeks alone. How to use the time I wondered? I had around 30,000 words of a novel written and a pretty good idea of the rest of the storyline in my head. I had 14 days. I thought if I can write 4000 words a day by the end of the holiday I'll have around 85,000 words, about the right length for a complete novel. Most days I only managed around 3000 words but it was enough. Two years later the novel I wrote in the caravan in the rain while my ex lay on a beach in Greece was published under the title *The Making of Mickey Bell*. My first novel was finished and so it seemed was my relationship.

Back at the high point on the path from Camas-luinie, I munch a sandwich. Maybe I could avoid the deer fence by approaching Boc Mor from the old road from Dornie at the highest point on Carr Brae. I should've bought a 1:25000 map. I chastise myself, but as far as today goes there's still plenty of time to walk to Loch nan Eun two kilometres in the opposite direction. I take a bearing and set off across the rock-studded heather and grass.

Looking back I can see Beinn Sgritheall, the Knoydart peaks and the mountains of Glen Shiel. I reach an unnamed lochan near a point marked 599m on the map. Cloud still covers the top of distant Sgurr nan Ceathramhnan. A sort of flat tundra of peat hags and heather moorland stretches out in all directions. On a rocky outcrop silhouetted against the skyline a deer hind, head tilted to one side, watches me curiously. We crest another fold in the moorland and Loch nan Eun appears, but discouragingly faraway. The sun is beating down now and I'm flagging. But I won't give up on my search for Macrow's hill lochs and walk for another half hour over cushions of red sphagnum moss down to the shore of Loch nan Eun and wash my face in the peaty water. Hill loch number five!

KELLAN MACINNES

Macrow: *Loch nan Eun... is... set in a welter of wild hill-tops... There are some little islands, as bleak and barren as their surroundings. I had hoped to swim out to the nearer, and largest, one—but one look at the water, oily black and full of bright, slimy weeds, made me change my mind.*

A feeling of great isolation and remoteness surrounds me as I stand on the shore of Loch nan Eun, largest of the hill lochs of Kintail. This place hardly visited by man since the ice melted, this expanse of black water and heather-covered islands ringed by distant mountains. Untouched by farming, it escaped the designs of the hydro board surveyors, left alone to the deer, the skylarks and the stonechats. The way it lies in the folds of the low, brown, heather-covered hills, it looks as if a Celtic giant could climb up and tip the blue water out and send it pouring down into Glen Elchaig 1,500 feet below.

Time passes more slowly up here than the way it spins in the great metropolis of London. Seven decades, the skylarks and the stonechats don't count the years. Easy to flutter back to 1946 on the wings of the wheatear perched on a lichen-spattered boulder in the heather. Up here among the mountains it feels like the world has remained unchanged since 1946. Here on the shore of Loch nan Eun, that long ago Highland summer still feels very close. On my way back, at the top of the heathery rise near point 599m, I pause and look back down to Loch nan Eun and its islands, still, deserted. My passing barely a flicker, a grain of sand on the beaches of time, seven decades, time holds her breath on the shores of Loch nan Eun.

The Longest Day

The hills have seen so much, and it has all come to the same end. Ashes and dust, a lament of pipes in the gloaming; and, at last, a shadowed peace broken only by the lingering cry of the whaup over the whitening bones…
BGM, 1946.

They knew it not at the time, but the high tide of Scotland's 300-year-old Union with England had been reached two years earlier on June 6 1944. On a day that defined the modern world, when landing craft carrying Shimi Fraser and a Commando Brigade crunched onto the shingle shallows of a Normandy D day beach.

As a man Shimi Fraser embodied the history of the turbulent relationship between Scotland and England. Aka Simon Fraser, Lord Lovat, the Lovat Frasers were Norman in origin and most likely were henchmen of William the Conqueror. One of his ancestors Sir Alexander Fraser married a sister of Robert the Bruce.

Another Lord Lovat was executed for his part in the 1745 Jacobite uprising led by Bonnie Prince Charlie. According to accounts of the time the executioner, after beheading Lord Lovat: 'lifted the dripping head aloft by scrawny hair and paraded it round the platform to an exultant crowd'.

For 700 years the Lovats had named their eldest boy, the clan chief, in the Gaelic style, son of Simon, MacShimidh. He was known to his friends and family as Shimi. He had been educated at Eton and Oxford before returning north to be laird of his ancestral Highland estate in the fertile farmland, west of Inverness, at the head of the Beauly Firth.

As the ramp of the landing craft banged down on Sword Beach Shimi jumped into the waist-deep, salt water. Shells of high explosive threw up great clouds of sand and the sea air was thick with acrid smoke and machine gun bullets. The dead of the 2nd East York Light Infantry lay stacked on the wet sand. The survivors dug into shallow death traps barely clear of the rising tide.

Crouched down in the bow of the landing craft next to Shimi was 21-year-old Billy Millin in a steel helmet, clutching a set of bagpipes. Billy was wearing a kilt in the traditional Scottish manner (nae pants under it) and was armed only with a sgian-dubh. As they jumped off the landing craft's ramp Shimi ordered Billy to strike up *Blue Bonnets are o'er the Border* and they splashed ashore through knee-deep salt water onto the black oily sand.

And in the words of Iain R Thomson: 'Clear and wild across the water, a stirring cry, down from hill and torrent, the call to battle brought the centuries close… ' and filled the Commandos – English, Irish, Welsh and Scots – cowering in the landing craft with the spirit of the fighting Highland clans of old. They stormed ashore and turned the tide on Sword beach in blood and fought their way off the beach-head and through the lines of poplar trees to Pegasus Bridge and the village of Breville on the road to Paris and all the way to the smouldering ruins of Berlin, that day they turned the tide on Sword Beach in blood.

Scotland and England: two nations that had fought as one in World War Two to save Britain from invasion by a common European foe. But Unionism had reached its high tide in the seaweed of a Normandy beach that June day in 1944. Winston Churchill's Conservative and Unionist Party would take 55 of the 72 Scottish parliamentary seats in the general election of 1952. But just 15 years later a young female candidate would win a shattering victory for the Scottish National Party in the Hamilton constituency near Glasgow and the first cracks would begin to appear in the façade of the Union between Scotland and England.

THE WILD SWIMMER OF KINTAIL

1946: The cottage stands on a little rise on a mile long straight stretch of dusty road. Macrow drifts in her mind from the page. Her fountain pen scratches then pauses, hovers a quarter of an inch over the page while she remembers the first time she came to Kintail. Nightime, heavy lashing rain, the long column of green army lorries and jeeps throwing up a mist of spray and surface water.

Or was that how it happened? Or is it just my writer's imagination working overtime?

Shivering in the back of an open-topped truck, a hundred miles inside the closed militarised zone that was the north-west Highlands of Scotland. She remembers the magisterial disembodied voice over the crackling static on the glowing orange dial of the Bakelite radio: 'This is London... streets and runways... we shall fight them on the beaches ... and men will say this was their finest hour.'

So what was it like? How was it then, this world of 1946? Time to view a highlights reel:

In February 1946 the Bank of England was nationalised and an American dance craze, the Jitterbug, swept the UK. In March, Churchill delivered his Iron Curtain speech in Fulton, Missouri. In April Scotland beat England 1-0 in a Victory International at Hampden and Clement Attlee announced India would be granted independence. In May, George Orwell left London for Barnhill on the Hebridean island of Jura and in June, the TV licence was introduced. In July the first bikinis went on sale in Paris. In August, the Arts Council was set up and in October the BBC Light Programme broadcast the first episode of *Woman's Hour*. The Bush DAC90 bakelite radio went on sale and the HIV virus which originated in the African city of Kinshasa had spread to Brazzaville in the Belgian Congo. *Thomas the Tank Engine* was published, Mervyn Peake's novel *Titus Groan* came out and Hermann Hesse was awarded the Nobel Prize for literature. In October, the Nuremberg Trials were taking place and Lord Haw Haw was hanged for treason. In America, the first mobile phone conversation took place on two phones in cars 150 miles apart. Women had only had the vote for 21 years and then only if they were householders. The coalmines were nationalised and Tupperware went on sale for the first time.

The sailor in Kinshasa with HIV in his blood, the first mobile phone conversation, Turing's computers, bikinis, Tupperware, in 1946 all the pieces were in place, all the pieces to make up the modern world.

And who was Brenda G Macrow, poet and mountaineer? Let's click the mouse and Google her name and see what the world-controlling, long tentacles of the sinister search engine has to say.

Clack clack clack I type B – r – e… line one Brenda G Macrow. Line 2 of Google prompts me with Brenda G Macrow author. I click on her name. I'll go with her name alone. So I click on Brenda G Macrow.

Line one is Amazon (course it would be, wouldn't it?) Brenda G Macrow books. Line 2 is Amazon again but gives a book title this time. *The Amazing Mr Whisper*, not one of Macrow's climbing books then I'm guessing.

The search engine lists 10 results per page. Scrolling down I see at a glance that most of the results are about Macrow's books. For sale on Amazon (mainly) and other online books sellers like Abe books from which I purchased most of the published works of Caleb George Cash when I was writing and researching *Caleb's List*.

The Google monster proudly tells me at the top of the screen it has found 59,300 results for Brenda G Macrow in 0.60 seconds.

The last entry on page one of Google is for *Speyside to Deeside* one of Macrow's books I bought a while back and which sits on the shelves in my study at home.

Line 5 offers a short biography and list of works by Macrow from

THE WILD SWIMMER OF KINTAIL

a site called Biblio which Norton anti-virus says is OK.

Line 6 is a link to someone's wordpress blog which says, 'This little ditty was written by Brenda G Macrow (1916-1911.)' Poor Macrow died before she was born according to this blogger.

Line 7 is a link to the site Goodreads where it tells me there is one review of *The Amazing Mr Whisper.*

There are also quite a lot of references to her (better known) collaborator Robert Moyes Adam who provided the photos for her books. But all there really is, all that survives of us as writers ultimately, I'm forced to conclude from this morning spent digitally stalking Macrow, is the titles of our books on Google offered for sale secondhand.

Line 3 is the most promising though. Prior (Brenda G Macrow the Author) Obituary – Bognor Regis Observer. Bognor Regis May 2011 Abbas Combe Nursing Home Funeral 12 May 2011 Portfield Cemetery. And it is on this link that I click.

Then about page 8 of the 59,300 results Macrow begins to fade. Her books still appear sporadically in the results but now a Brenda G Smith has appeared in the results and a Maryanne Macrow who graduated from the metropolitan school of nursing in 1967. My Macrow is beginning to disappear into the digital mist.

According to volume 3a, page 825 of the register of births in the General Register Office, Brenda Grace Joan Barton was born in the third quarter of 1916 at Edmonton, Oxfordshire as World War One raged all around. Though not I guess, all around number 86 Inderwick Road in Hornsey where her father Joseph William Barton, a company secretary and his wife Grace Barton, née Tabiner lived. Page 52 of volume 4b tells me Brenda G J Macrow married Dennis E Prior sometime between October and December 1949 at Bishop Stortford, Hertfordshire.

There's one more place to look, maybe the best, most obvious place? What does the blurb from her books say about her I wonder? Here's what's printed on the inside of the dust jacket of her best known children's story *The Amazing Mr Whisper*:

'Brenda G Macrow was born in London and of part-Scottish descent she was educated in England and in the USA. She started writing stories at the age of 12 and had her first poem published at the age of eighteen. She admits that she achieved nothing of much consequence until she fell under the spell of the Scottish Highlands about which she has written five books and which she considers her spiritual home. She enjoys mountaineering and classical music – her childhood love of fairytale and fantasy led to this believable fairy-tale.'

Travels with a Labradoodle

The Doodle is stretched out asleep on the grass in front of the caravan. Sitting there in my deck chair at Dornie campsite I realise I'm only a few fields away from Shepherd's Cottage. Only a few fields of yellow whin and marshy clumps of soft rush separate me from Macrow and 1946.

It's Wednesday 5 June, take two climbing Boc Mor and visiting its satellite hill lochs. Rising like a miniature Suilven over the lochan-studded moorland, 2,000 feet above Loch Duich, this 631 metre peak is proving as much of a challenge to summit as many of its mightier Munro cousins. As I'd found out the previous day, the obvious route up from Coire Dhuinnid was barred by a six-foot-high deer fence, unpassable without bolt cutters. Now I do possess a pair of said bolt cutters purchased from Machine Mart in Edinburgh's Portobello Road. They cut through barbed wire nae bother and greatly improved the Labradoodle's woodland walk by the banks of the River Spean after I removed a couple of sections of ancient, fallen down fence. But I find them a bit on the heavy side to carry on hillwalks.

Like I said for me and the Labradoodle it's Boc Mor: take two. Today we're heading for the radio mast. We've had a wee look at the map. Well actually, about an hour long look over a couple of cans of lager while the sun dropped low over Loch Duich. The sky turned yellow behind Eilean Donan Castle and the oystercatchers lined up along the shore and the breeze rustled the wild flowers by the lane where Macrow once wandered the shoreline collecting white sea shells.

As I turn to put the file of newspaper clippings back on the shelf behind my desk, I see the vase of dried flowers I picked along the verges of the lanes at Dornie, and next to them the white seashells I collected along the shoreline at Shiel Bridge. I mean to scatter them on Macrow's grave.

Like I say we've had a good look at the map and I'm reasonably hopeful that by taking the track up to the radio mast we'll be able to avoid the six- foot-high deer fence that has encircled the hill with a necklace of wire since Macrow passed this way.

1946: *Wasting as little time as possible, I started off up the hillside. Behind me, Loch Long fell away into a blue hollow...*

Past the fjord-like twists of the sea loch, past Dornie, Ardelve and Nostie and beyond Glenelg, in the west I can see the twin peaks of Beinn Sgritheall. There is milkwort in the gravel at the edge of the road, its petals an even deeper shade of azure than the blue sky.

To the east, at the head of Loch Duich, the crooked peaks of the Five Sisters guard the approach to Glen Shiel. The road climbs along the gorse-covered hillside to the sound of birdsong and the rustle of the wind in the dry grass.

There's a great view from the radio mast. From up here the motor yacht lying at anchor beside Eilean Donan Castle looks very James Bond. High on the brown, heathery hillside above the road, the radio mast bristles with an array of aerials and satellite dishes and mobile phone masts. In the Kintail of 1946 Macrow had to cycle to the post office just to use the telephone. But then I think, as I stop to mop my brow with my pink and white buff, Macrow was free in the cottage at Nostie. She had no mobile phone, tablet, notepad, laptop, PC, TV or landline, just the creak of the old pines, the song of the skylarks and the lonely cry of the oystercatcher.

I stand below the radio mast, beside the portacabins that surround it, looking across to where Loch Duich opens out to the sea and Skye spikes the skyline. The radio mast is a grand viewpoint, a great place to sit on a summer's night and gaze out into the west, over the mountains and the sea.

The Labradoodle and I can't linger though, we must press on across the scratchy, crisp heather moorland in search of the hill lochs of Kintail. We traverse the rough heathery hillside (following in Macrow's footsteps was rarely easy going) aiming for a narrow defile between the crags and heather slopes. High overhead, a buzzard turns lazily on the thermals, hunting. A faint vehicle track eases our progress across the rough hillside, a green stripe across the brown heather. There are the white and yellow flowers of cloudberries here and I remember when I first found cloudberries on the ridge of An Socach, high above upper Glen Affric on the way to Sgurr nan Ceathramhnan.

I can spell that perfectly every time now.

I typed it right first time.

'Gaelic's coming on, eh MacDoodle?'

The Labradoodle lifts an ear.

'No Master, I dinnae think so,' says the look in her sleepy brown eyes.

1946: *I surmounted the corrie behind Creag Reidh Raineach (The Smooth Crag of the Bracken). From here, I could see as far north as the hills beyond Glen Carron—a wonderful tapestry of grey and gold, splashed with waves of dark blue where the cloud-shadows moved softly over ben and corrie.*

The track climbs promisingly on up the hill, skirting below the crags of Creag Reidh Raineach. We reach another fence but only a low, sheep-type one this time. To the west, the sea glitters blue and every jagged peak of the serrated Cuillin ridge is clear of even a wisp of cloud, like Naxos or Tenerife but on a more northerly latitude than Moscow.

The Skye Bridge leaps the narrow straits of Kyle Akin in a single concrete span. What would Brenda have thought? I wonder as we plod on along the grassy track to reach a gate in the fence where the heathery hillside levels out to a lochan-studded plateau on the far side of which Boc Mor rises like a mini Suilven.

Macrow: *At about 1,500 feet, I attained a stretch of flat peat-bog from which, in every direction, I could see the hills rolling away into the clouds, splashed with great patches of golden light.*

'Hmmm... Labradoodle?'
The dog stops and looks up at me.
'It still looks discouragingly far away and it's very hot again today.'
'Yes master, well this was yer idea so dinnae moan at me,' says the look on the Labradoodle's face as she flops down among the reeds in a peaty pool and drinks deeply of the clear, cold water while the blue hills stand all around.

Macrow: *I tramped on over newly-burnt heather, looking for some of the many small lochans marked on my map.*

We twist our way between boulders, peat hags and tiny lochans, making for the distant whaleback of Boc Mor. A glint of blue among the heathery folds, Loch a'Mhuillin, Loch na Faolaig and Loch na Craoibhe-caoruinn. Macrow's hill lochs, like blue gem stones, set in the green plateau.

1946: *I was now entering a wilderness of desolate grey crags and precipices... On the fringe of this upheaved and tortured land, I found Loch Gorm, the Blue Loch.*

THE WILD SWIMMER OF KINTAIL

On across the heather and rocks, who was the last person to walk across here? There can't be many folk come up here, I think.

1946: *Suddenly I came upon a small herd of deer, quite close by. I stopped dead, and we stared at each other... My note-book flickered, and they moved off.*

Macrow with her notebook, me with my digital camera, only the hills remain the same.

Boc Mor looms ahead. It's a surprisingly rocky wee hill and I look for a route up the south-east ridge.

Macrow: *Before me, the bulk of the Big Roebuck rose like a huge clenched fist against the sky... I climbed up its round, ugly face to the tiny pimple of the cairn. I was now 2,064 feet up, the highest I had been so far in my search for the hill lochs of Kintail.*

Break a leg up here, Doodle, and we'll never be found, I mutter, as we tramp on across a flat, spongey, heathery bog, and then climb another low fence to reach the foot of Boc Mor. From below the cairn looks very much the pimple Macrow described. I pick a line and climb a rake of heather between little crags. The cairn looks bigger than Macrow described. From the top the crags sweep down to Loch Long and I have a glimpse of Loch Bhuic Mhoir tucked in a green fold among the crags.

1946: *Below me, on the far side of the hill, Loch Bhuic Mhoir, completely devoid of islands or trees, lay dark and still in a dark brown hollow.*

Publishers Oliver and Boyd used Robert Moyes Adam's photos to illustrate *Kintail Scrapbook*, Brenda G Macrow's account of the six months she spent in Kintail in 1946. Moyes Adam was an archivist and botanist at the Royal Botanical Gardens in Edinburgh, an 'amateur' photographer with a great love of the Scottish landscape, the heir to a long tradition of landscape photography. His archive of 15,000 glass-plate negatives of Scottish landscapes would eventually become the stock holding of D C Thomson of Dundee.

Tom Normand, writing in 2007 described: ' ...the topographical romance of Robert Moyes Adam.' Moyes Adam's photos were very widely used in *The Scots Magazine* and in innumerable and multifarious books, in Normand's words: ' ...becoming ubiquitous in the literature of Scotland and indeed something of an embedded motif in the Scottish psyche.' Mainly Adam's photos illustrated travel books, often books with a romantic and/or sentimental flavour: '... while occasionally the photographs would accompany poetry and a kind of wistful prose reverie as in Brenda G Macrow's *Unto the Hills* (1947) [sic]*.'Adam's work, Normand argued: ' ...fed a hunger for wild panoramic views in a period of (rapid) urban expansion.' **

It's very hot as I walk back across the flat, red-with-sphagnum moss plateau of Creag Reidh Rainich, the smooth crag of the bracken. The sun beats down from an azure sky and I think of Macrow giving herself up: 'to the caresses of Apollo' and I'm feeling like I want to do the same.

I'd wanted to do the same on Beinn a' Mheadhain but I would probably have got hypothermia. To cut a long story short, it wasn't a day for sunbathing or for exposing any bare flesh at all. I might have got away with a quick moonie at a low flying RAF tornado but naw,

---

* *Unto the Hills* was first published in 1946.

** Normand,T 'The Book and Photography' in *The Edinburgh History of the Book in Scotland*, Vol. 4, 1880-2000, ed. Finkelstein & McCleery, Edinburgh University Press, 2007.

not a day for taking yer claes aff. The weather, blatters of rain off the Atlantic, wasn't conducive to sunbathing shall we say. Today is though, so I stop beside a mossy ruin next to the track.

Macrow: *The sun fell warmly on my face and shoulders. I scanned the landscape. Not a soul in sight… I undressed, and lay flat on the warm rock, giving myself up to the caresses of Apollo.*

I take off my rucksack, unlace my boots, pull my socks off and peel my sweaty, BO smelling, blue Jack Wolfskin top over my head. Heart thumping I unzip my Mountain Warehouse shorts and stand there in the Superman pants I bought for a laugh from H&M on Princes Street for climbing the Skye Munros.

I pull my pants down. I'm a bit of an exhibitionist, you see. My cock twitches and gets a bit bigger with the excitement of being naked in the great outdoors, under the blue sky and the heathery hills, feeling the breeze around my bare bum. Then, like Macrow, I stretch out naked and give myself up to the caressing rays of Apollo.

But, there's a problem. It's not that I'm not worried about anyone coming up along the track and seeing me. Macrow's hill lochs make even the Corbetts look busy. So I dinnae think there's much chance of someone coming this way and anyway I don't care who sees my willy. Naw, the problem is that although I've spread my Paramo jacket and overtrousers and fleece out on the long grass to lie on, there are still blades of grass poking up through the gaps. I shift uncomfortably as a blade of deer grass brushes my bare thigh. In my mind's eye I see a sheep tick poised on the end of the blade of grass just waiting to sink its mouth-parts into my testicles dangling there in the heather.

Aw fuck! Think how many ticks I removed from the Labradoodle last summer. I wince at the thought of having to remove a tick from my balls or my cock or even worse – I'm sitting upright now, a drop of sweat drips down my temple – getting a tick in my arse crack. I think of it lurking there among the black hairs waiting to retract its *capitulum* and sink its mouthparts into the puckering skin around my anus. Aw fuck! Would I even notice it down there? Could I distinguish it from a mole? I imagine myself feeling my skin for rogue bumps in the shower back at Dornie campsite, squatting naked over a mirror in the caravan, clutching the Labradoodle's tick picker.

Like that time old Dr MacMillan at the genito-urinary-medicine clinic prescribed self-treatment with a bottle of acid and a mirror for a bad case of anal warts. Jeans and pants round my ankles I would bend over the kitchen table holding my cheeks apart while my ex applied acid from a dropper bottle.

'Hello bottom,' my ex would say as I bent over the kitchen table. It was another nail in the coffin of our romance.

I quickly realised I was much happier making the half-hour bus journey to the clinic in Lauriston Place where I'd lie on my side on a hospital trolley in the clinic with my pants and jeans round my knees while a nurse gently parted my cheeks and dabbed acid on the miniature cauliflower-like warts that had sprouted around my bumhole.

I shift again, my Paramo jacket moves and I can feel heather scratching my balls. It's too much. I can't do it. I love nude sunbathing, but the thought of the ticks. I stand up, momentarily naked under the mountain, then reach for my Superman pants and reluctantly pull my clothes back on.

Macrow: *I felt I could have stayed forever... Regretfully, I shouldered my pack and began the long descent, trudging steadily down through gathering shadows towards the gleam of white houses below.*

Jock Macrow

Let's not quarrel,' he said, 'I want you to tell me what you've done with the blue stone.'

The sun suddenly dipped beyond the western hills, and a breath of cold air stirred the pines.

'You will know me,' he said, 'and you will not know me. For you are of the world; and I am a wraith, a fleeting shadow, the whisper of the wind across the grass.'

                        BGM, *The Amazing Mr Whisper*, 1959.

The A87, the main road north, is a blight on Dornie. That's what I'm thinking as I lean over the parapet of Dornie Bridge watching a small motorboat nose its way through the tidal swirls and eddies of black water that surge beneath the bridge. A grey muzzled Staffie sits upright in the prow watching the shoreline intently as the black tidal race swirls under Dornie Bridge.

Macrow: *Sometimes, at evening, I have fished from the bridge; and the surging current sweeping round the stone pillars has made me quite dizzy.*

The long hot spell of weather ended at Tuesday lunchtime. The sun boring a hole through a high, thin layer of cloud, little grey tears, rents of cloud over the Five Sisters. The rain fell on and off all afternoon. The white motor yacht sailed out of the bay. As dusk falls I walk across Dornie Bridge. The tide is high. The air warm and humid, midges brush my face, the whine of a mosquito in my ear. I stand in the middle of Dornie Bridge gazing down, watching the ripples spread across the smooth surface of Loch Duich. Then I remember what Macrow wrote about her Chicago friends and the smooth surface of my synapses flicker, making the connection. A thought bubbles to the surface of my brain while the kelp sways under Dornie Bridge.

The tide races, swirling in black eddies and currents like my mind. Macrow said her Chicago friends. How did Macrow have friends in Chicago? Then I remember Lesley's voice, crackly with static, phoning from Chichester. I stood in the caravan, mobile pressed to my ear gazing across at the Ferryman's house at Totaig, white against the green birch and pine-clad slopes. There's a questioning voice in my head. And the voice is asking: what did you do in the war, Mummy?

Lesley Hampshire, Macrow's only daughter had told me Macrow worked at an American airbase during World War Two. Then words sound in my head, flying off the page, set in 12 point Garamond. Words Macrow wrote, 'so sad—the days that are no more. So strange—the beautiful things in the world that are always the shortest lived.'

> 1946: *The apple-blossoms were scattering on the grass. A few warm, heady days, and they had opened from waxen buds into a cloud of white wings... They were blowing into the cottage; but, somehow, I had not the heart to sweep them up. By the morrow, they would be crinkled and withered on the polished floor. Until then, let them lie in their strange, forsaken loveliness, a memory of one enchanted hour. So sad—the days that are no more. So strange—the beautiful things of the world, that are always the shortest-lived...*

I wonder who Macrow was writing about in this heart-felt, wistful passage. A short-lived romance with a handsome USAF pilot suddenly cut short when his Liberator bomber was shot down over

THE WILD SWIMMER OF KINTAIL

Berlin? Nostalgia, a melancholy feeling of lost love pervades this section of *Kintail Scrapbook*, the book Macrow wrote about the six months she spent in Dornie in the summer of 1946. In one of the big hit tunes of World War Two, The Andrews Sisters sang about apple blossom time and this passage would have been very evocative to the reader of the late 1940s.

Already my writer's imagination is working crazy double overtime. Why did Macrow go to Kintail in 1946? Standing there looking over the parapet at the sea I imagine Jeannie (a gift from Macrow's handsome USAF pilot lover?) at a USAF base. Like the dog in the war movie *Memphis Belle*. I see Jeannie sitting at the end of the runway beside the Nissen huts, ears cocked, listening for the distant sound of the planes returning.

I see USAF Flying Fortresses queueing at the end of the runway, awaiting clearance from the control tower to take off. Just like today at Gatwick when the Easyjet Boeing 737s queue up at the end of the runway awaiting clearance from the control tower to take off for Spain, the Greek Islands and Tenerife. The roar of the propellors of the Flying Fortress, the wings droop, heavy with fuel and 100lb bombs, Lesley on the phone saying:

'I don't know what my mother did in the war. It was before I came along.'

Brenda G Macrow was born plain Brenda Barton in 1916. She was 23 when war broke out in 1939. She'd just turned 30 when she came to spend six months in Kintail in the summer of 1946. She would marry in 1949 aged 33. So she had at least ten years for previous relationships and it was wartime. In the 1940s age 30 was more like 40 today. You see, even as I write it, I'm still unpeeling new layers of story.

Like I say, I knew Macrow had worked for the Red Cross during the war and had also been the librarian on a USAF base. Then I discover in the course of my research that Brenda Barton had married a Herbert John Macrow, an Englishman of Scottish descent known as Jock in May 1941. Naturally I order Jock's birth certificate from the General Register Office. A couple of days later I spot an e-mail in my inbox. The pdf of Jock's birth certificate is available to download. At least I hope it's Jock Macrow's birth certificate. I had to use a bit of guesswork and might possibly have got the wrong Herbert John Macrow. But he's three years older than Brenda so it seems he's likely to be the one. I can cross-reference him on the copy of their marriage certificate when it comes through the post. Meanwhile the pdf icon winks intriguingly from the foot of the screen. Open me, open me, it says. I click the mouse.

Herbert John Macrow aka Jock was born 15 July 1913. His father, also Herbert, worked as a carpet salesman for a furniture dealer's. There was no space provided on the birth certificates of the time for his mother Ethel's occupation. The family lived at 13 Sherard Road in Eltham, South London.

When I went to Foulis and interviewed Gillian Zealand from the Grampian Hillwalking Club (her father, the journalist and artist Colin Gibson, illustrated some of Macrow's articles for D C Thomson and corresponded with the poet in 1980s) she'd said: 'It would have been one of those short-lived wartime marriages.'

But now it looks like Macrow was married to Jock for four or five years. It seems Jock introduced Macrow to the Scottish Highlands and mountaineering, in the Cairngorms in 1941. Indeed Macrow once wrote: 'The Cairngorms were my first love.'

Could this have been the newly wedded couple's honeymoon I wonder? But the mystery of this mountaineer's tale is what happened to Jock? I spend time carefully checking through Macrow's published works, reading between the lines of her poetry and prose, trying to build up a picture, a timeline of her life in the 1940s. On occasions, I work backwards. For example, I'm curious to know, as a dog owner myself, when Macrow acquired Jeannie the Skye terrier who accompanied her on her travels and is a big character in *Kintail Scrapbook*.

> Macrow 1946: *At evening, the homing birds flew slowly across a quiet sky, their wings beating in time to some sweet, sad sweet rhythm of earth and sea... Across the road, beyond the greystone wall of my garden, the long, dry, cream-coloured reeds would tap out a message on the evening air... I would gather my papers together and go in, leaving Jeannie to play contentedly with an old shoe in the grass. Jeannie is the Peter Pan of all dogs—though, if she were human, she would be roughly the same age as myself.*

Ah, that 1940s punctuation, who uses em dashes today? Who today knows the difference between an em dash and an en dash? Macrow uses so many em dashes. Who the heck uses them today, I wonder as I keep having to click through Insert, Symbol, More Symbols to finally reach Special Characters, that remote, forgotten corner of Microsoft Word where they keep the Em Dashes? How does the function of an em dash vary from an ordinary dash or en dash as it's properly known? There's a lot of them in Jane Austen and Dickens, I seem to recall. It seems the copy editor who worked on Macrow's book was closer to the Victorian era than our own twenty-first century with all its acres of text on screens. What future for the em dash in the world of Snapchat and WhatsApp?

But I digress. As I was saying, I already knew Brenda Grace Joan Barton was born in 1916 which made Macrow 30 years old when she came to Kintail in 1946. Since one dog year is held to be equal to seven human years then Jeannie must have been roughly four-and-a-half in the summer of 1946. So if Macrow acquired her as a puppy, a lover's gift from Jock perhaps, she must have got the dog in 1942.

Like I say, Macrow's books and other published work were my starting point when doing the detective work needed to build up a picture of Macrow's early life. I opened *Unto the Hills*, Macrow's first book, an anthology of poems illustrated with the black and white photographs of Robert Moyes Adam. Here on page vii, the foreword, written by one HJM. Who could HJM be? I wondered for a few seconds, before the realisation quickly dawned HJM must be Herbert John Macrow, BJM's first husband, known as Jock because of his Scottish ancestry. But what the heck was he doing writing the foreword for her first book published in 1948 when I'd assumed the marriage had been a shortlived wartime affair? The plot thickens, terrible cliché, I know, but by April 1946 Macrow was on the night train north with Jeannie headed for six months in Kintail alone. So what happened to Jock? He seems to have just vanished.

Eventually by post this time, rather than pdf download, Brenda and Jock's marriage certificate is waiting for me on the tiles of the front porch when I go down to the apartment, as I now think of it, to get the place ready for the next group of Airbnb guests. First thing I do is cross reference Herbert John Macrow's age on his marriage certicate, 27 with his date of birth, 1913 on the birth certificate. Phew! I've got the right Herbert 'Jock' Macrow then.

Brenda Grace Joan Barton married Jock Macrow on 14 May 1941 in the parish church at Bray in the county of Berkshire. According to the certificate, he was a bachelor, she was a spinster, he was 27, she was 24. Prior to his marriage, Jock was living in Bishop Stortford and he worked as a railway clerk, a reserved occupation during World War Two. So he would have been exempt from military service, shooting down in flames my romantic theory of a wartime marriage between Macrow and a handsome young pilot, cut tragically short. Brenda Barton, soon to be Brenda G Macrow the writer, has recorded her occupation, her day job we'd call it today, as a saleswoman. Brenda's father and Jock's mother, Ethel Mary Macrow were the witnesses for the marriage certicate. Herbert Macrow Senior is marked as decd (deceased) in the abbrieviation of the clerk's spidery handwriting.

Jock had some experience of hillwalking and it was he who introduced Macrow to the Scottish mountains*. He had climbed Ben Tirran,** describing it as an easy climb (correct) and accurately describing the view from the summit. The marriage seems to have lasted around five years, from 1941-1946. What is certain however is that during the war years Macrow fell in love with the Scottish mountains and out of love with her first husband Jock.

Maybe they fell out over the foreword he wrote for *Unto the Hills* Macrow's first book, beginning as it does: 'A great deal has been written about the Scottish Highlands and it is perhaps with a certain amount of apprehension that one realises that yet another book has been added to the list.' Well, gee thanks Jock! Talk about damning with faint praise. Maybe Macrow read the foreword then packed her suitcase on the spot, bought her one-way rail ticket and flounced off to Kintail in the huff.

Then I sense the parallels of the past and present, as I remember climbing Arthur's Seat with my ex and the Labradoodle one summer evening after work. My ex wasn't keen on going all the way to the

*Macrow, H J, 'These Things Endure', *Scotland's SMT Magazine and Scottish Country Life*, Edinburgh, Vol. XXX, No.3, September 1942, pp 18-21.

**Macrow, H J, 'The Heart of the Braes of Angus', *Scotland's SMT Magazine and Scottish Country Lif*e, Vol. XXXIII, No.4, Edinburgh, April 1944, pp 26-31.

top of Arthur's Seat, preferring to make more of a circumnavigation of the hill with several fag breaks, sorry, stops to play ball with the Labradoodle. On this occasion though, I'd nagged my poor ex, just back from a long day in the department store, to come up to the top of Arthur's Seat with me because the Independent Scottish Publisher had asked me to e-mail them an author photo.

One of the photos my ex took that evening of me and the Labradoodle standing at the summit of Arthur's Seat, was used by the publisher on the cover of *Caleb's List*. The dog and I stand silhouetted against the sunset. It's a striking image. When the book came out, the publisher commented it was the best book cover they'd ever done and they didn't even take the picture. The relationship was falling apart big style by then but my ex still took the cover photo for my first book (though he refused to be credited in print for it). So down through the years I seem to have ended up in a similar situation to Macrow and Jock in 1948.

'It is a long time since many of us were able to wander among the hills,' wrote Jock in the foreword to *Unto the Hills*. Intriguingly he goes on to say he was: 'present during most of the moments' described in the book. So Brenda's first marriage ain't looking like some six month, ill-judged, wartime, fling anymore and then there's that paragraph Macrow wrote about sweeping up the fallen blossom. 'To Jock who has heard the song of the hills and the call of the isles, and will therefore understand,' so reads the dedication on page 3 of *Unto the Hills*. Now dedications in books can be tricky things. My ex point blank refused to have *Caleb's List* dedicated to him. There's a lot of emotion goes into them, I guess they're a bit like memorial plaques on park benches or inscriptions on gravestones in a cemetery.

Jock Macrow comes across as a strong character, even from the distance of 75 years. A tough guy who, during one epic in the hills above Glen Clova in 1945 tied his bike to Macrow's and hauled her over the Capel Mounth track. Comfortably seated in the National Library of Scotland, I read an entertaining account of this gruelling 36-mile-round trip by bike from the Glen Clova Hotel to Ballater in gale force winds, rain and mist. Written by Brenda G Macrow under the title 'Over the Hills to Ballater' the piece appeared in *Scotland's SMT Magazine*, which was published by the Scottish Motor Traction Company to promote travel by long distance coach in Scotland.

For reasons best known to themselves Macrow and Jock had chosen to cycle the high altitude Capel Mounth track in order to go to the shops in Ballater. I've not done it, but I would reckon that even on a state of the art twenty-first century mountain bike equipped with front and rear suspension and Kevlar puncture resistant tyres, the peat bogs and boulder fields of the Capel Mounth track would make for a tough day out. Quite what it must have been like on a heavy 1940s bike in adverse weather conditions doesn't bear thinking about. But it must have made for purgatorial progress as Macrow and the taciturn Jock hauled their bikes up to 3,000 feet. The tension in the relationship still seeps through pages penned 75 years ago. Of their struggle over the peat bogs and boulders of the Capel Mounth path Macrow would later write: 'Jock, my husband and companion, said little except to remark that it was easier if one put the right hand under the carrier at the back and guided with the left… ' Though Macrow records they did do some singing ('as is often our habit among high hills') during the earlier part of the day. To make matters much, much worse when they at last got to Ballater it was a bank holiday and all the shops were closed!

Jock comes across as a man's man. When I first began writing about Macrow, Jock was just a shadow, ' …one of those wartime flings.' But now here's Jock emerging from the pages of the *Scotland's SMT Magazine*. He's a strong character pushing apart the pages on his way out of the musty volumes of the *Scotland's SMT Magazine* and *Chambers Journal*. Jostling his way to the front of our story, a man with a pivotal role in our tale, for as Macrow herself acknowledged, decades later in the 1980s, it was Jock Macrow made her fall in love with Scotland.

Clearly an educated, intelligent man, he writes well, if a little formally. The mention in an article about Glenfinnan of knee trouble due to an old 'rugger' injury hints at education at a minor English public school.* His only poem I've come across so far is good, but in prose Macrow is by far the better writer.**

Like most men of his time I guess, he comes across as sexist. Writing about ghostly bagpipes sometimes to be heard at Cortachy Castle in the Braes of Angus, Jock concluded that: 'The cynical merely point out that the majority of those who have heard the music are of the fair sex, and leave it at that.'

Intelligent and educated he may have been, but Jock Macrow comes across as pompous and lacking a sense of humour, writing of his young wife of barely a year: 'I amused her vastly by unwittingly taking, a seat on a wood-ants nest! (Incidentally why *do* women laugh at such things?)' He moans? But of course it's funny… ants in your pants. I'd have been laughing too Jock.

Macrow seems rapidly to have eclipsed Jock in the writing world. As success came her way Jock was left behind and in the end all she took with her was his surname.

The A87 is a blight on Dornie. That's what I'm thinking. And it's

*Macrow, H J, 'A Memory of Glenfinna', *Chamber's Journal*, W & R Chambers, Edinburgh, Eighth Series, Vol. XIII, January-December 1944, pp 385-387.

**Macrow, H J, 'Nocturne', *Chamber's Journal*, W & R Chambers, Edinburgh, Eighth Series, Vol. XII, January-December 1943, pp 154.

THE WILD SWIMMER OF KINTAIL

difficult to cross. At the end of the bridge by Eilean Donan Castle, the firm of civil engineers who designed and built the trunk road also provided a subway below the A87. I walk through the subway while the traffic roars by overhead. Peeling paint and like all subways the world over: urban graffiti. A fat cock ejaculating globules of spunk and scratched on the wall next to it the words: *squeeze me*.

I think to myself, the bit in *Kintail Scrapbook* where Macrow nude sunbathes is a crucial scene. Both she and I are sexually experienced people. Both Macrow and I had lovers in the past. Now we're both alone by a Highland lochan. Now we're both alone in a remote Highland village. Our secrets lie spilled across the pages. Set in twelve point Garamond by the publisher in his tower high above the city on the hill. The floodlights on Eilean Donan Castle have come on now. Rain and darkness fall on the hills. The midges swirl around the streetlights like ideas. The words are written. The page is printed.

Tug of Love Dog

Edinburgh: five-to-eight on a Monday morning in July. I've got the Labradoodle on the lead. We're walking to the park. My ex was supposed to pick her up at 7.45 but I guess he must be stuck in traffic or have got up late and well, the Labradoodle is needing out. Since the divorce we share the doG These days the Labradoodle spends half her time with me and half her time with my ex. It's usually a week with me and then a week with my ex and his new partner in Corstorphine.

'She's a tug of love dog,' I tell friends jokingly. 'You'll see her picture on the front of the *Daily Record* if my ex dognaps her and takes her off to Spain.'

The grass in the park is soaking wet and glistens in the morning sunshine. Every blade of grass in the park shines with water from the heavy rain over the last two days. A July monsoon, but now the sun is shining from an azure blue sky. Just as I let the Labradoodle off the lead and she skips off through the wet grass I see the blue Toyota Avensis pull up and double park in the road. My ex bangs the car door shut.

'Mornin',' I say.

Then:

'At least it's not raining for once.'

Which is good because I'm been playing tennis in the afternoon at the municipal courts at the Meadows with the trolley boy from work. My ex tells me it's costing him and his new partner £700 to join a tennis club in Corstorphine.

Five decades after she left Kintail, Macrow wrote a poem called 'Dog for a Day,' a poem about looking after someone else's pooch. I think of Macrow and that poem now as, a little reluctantly, the Labradoodle jumps up into the boot of the Avensis and my ex drives

THE WILD SWIMMER OF KINTAIL

away with his dog for a day. I walk back from the park in the July sunshine, my baseball boots damp from the wetgrass, wondering if 150 miles to the north, the sun is shining on Loch Duich.

> Macrow: *Jeannie and I left Dornie early, and set off along the hill-road by the shores of Loch Duich, rejoicing in our youth and strength and the beauty of the morning...*

The rain beats down on the roof of the caravan as I open the old linen-bound book at page 68 and read how on a sunny morning 75 years ago Macrow and Jeannie set out to walk from the Dornie Hotel to the Falls of Glomach. I count the blue kilometre squares on the map and work out it's a 34-kilometre-round trip with around 900 metres of ascent. As I've said previously, Macrow shared with Hugh Munro, A E Robertson, Caleb George Cash and the rest of the Victorian mountaineers, a propensity for covering (by today's standards) vast distances on foot. I stroke the Labradoodle's furry head and decide we'll start the walk from the graveyard at Clachan Duich and take the dirt track road from Ruarach to the clearing in the forest marked on the Ordnanace Survey maps of the 1940s as Dorusduain.

Next morning high white clouds drift across a sky of resin blue and the sunlight glints on the waters of Loch Duich. The weather Macrow and Jeannie had 75 years ago. L has come up from Edinburgh for the weekend to do some of the 'book' walks with me. I open the boot of her black VW Golf and haul my rucksack out. The Labradoodle has her nose pushed out the window of the car, watching me anxiously.

> 1946: *I was carrying a vast parcel of sandwiches in my pack, and the binoculars over my shoulder; for we had a day's hard work ahead of us, and would be tramping over completely strange ground.*

We lesser twenty-first-century mortals have just driven the six miles from Dornie. How did you do it Macrow? Brenda you were tough, I'm thinking, as I lace up my climbing boots.

In 1946 the old graveyard at Clachan Duich stood quietly beside the shore of Loch Duich as it had for centuries past, the place where the folk of Kintail buried their dead. For Clachan Duich lies at the end of a 'coffin road' that runs from Glenstrathfarrar to Kintail over the Bealach na Sroine. The gravestones huddled around the ruined kirk, daubed with white and grey and orange lichen. On the little hill beside Clachan Duich a bare-headed, kilted Scottish soldier guarded the war memorial with its inscription *Sgur Uran!* the Clan MacRae battle cry, the name of the highest peak of the Five Sisters.

1946: *I opened the iron gate, and we went softly in among the moss-grown stones.*

Today the kilted soldier looks down on the A87, carried over the narrows on a bridge of concrete stilts while the old road does a two-mile loop around the head of Loch Duich. There's a big carpark, a wide strip of gravel, at the start of the path to the graveyard. Must be for when there's a funeral. The days of Highlanders carrying a coffin for miles, over the hills from Glenstrathfarrar, a tradition that has long gone the way of blackhouses and crusie oil lamps. I open the iron gate and follow Macrow along the narrow path to the old graveyard.

We're not alone. A couple of American tourists are wandering among the graves.

'Could this be Grandpa Macrae's tomb?' I overhear a man in a bright yellow, waterproof jacket ask.

I'm holding a tattered copy of *Kintail Scrapbook* in my hands, and stepping carefully over the gravestones. I sense Macrow standing beside me in her brown overcoat, notebook in hand. Never imagining years later, another writer would return to Clachan Duich to follow in her footsteps. And I see Gillian Zealand in the dining room of the Factor's house at Foulis. The table strewn with her father's typewritten letters and Macrow's poems on looseleaf sheets, as she turned to me and said, 'I'm just glad someone's doing something about it all at last.'

The sea breeze off Loch Duich flicks the pages of Macrow's book. The book published decades ago, the book forgotten, as I turned to chapter XIII.

1946: *The earliest grave… I could find was that of 'Captain John Stewart, of the Sloop,* Hawke of Rothesay, *accidentally drowned in 1805.'*

We walk round and round the graveyard. I push back the wild, white roses and brambles that grow over the gravestones. I screw up my eyes, the better to see the words carved in stone beneath the ochre lichen. But we cannot find the grave of Captain John Stewart, of the Sloop, *Hawke of Rothesay*, 'accidentally drowned in 1805.'

We're running out of time. We still have a hill loch to bag. I even return myself on a later occasion and drag a puzzled Labradoodle round the graveyard on the lead. She didn't seem that comfortable. Perhaps it was the smell of old bones beneath the turf. But I never do find Captain Stewart's grave. I conclude that in the 75 years since Macrow came to Kintail the inscription on the gravestone has faded to illegibility. Lichen has spread its grey web over the stone carved letters and hidden them from my eyes.

I was seated in the swivel chair in the boxroom of my tenement flat in Edinburgh. I was phoning round independent bookshops. Marketing my book, it's called. I picked up the Panasonic landline handset from where it sat on its charger and entered the number 01875, the code for Sutherland.

Two hundred miles away, in the far north-west, in Achins bookshop by the seashore at Inverkirkaig, the phone rang with a strange echoey sound. As I pressed the phone to my ear, I saw the stony footpath leading up beside the burn, through the rowans and silver birches, to the white falls of Kirkaig roaring down to a deep black peaty pool below the steep slopes of Suilven.

In the bookshop beside the sea loch the bookseller of Assynt answered the telephone.

'Is that Achins bookshop?' I asked.

I explained I was following up an e-mail sent to independent bookshops across Scotland.

'Do you have a copy of a book called *Caleb's List*?' I continued, feeling a bit like J R Hartley phoning round second-hand book shops, to ask if they had a copy of 'Fly Fishing' by JR Hartley in the famous 1983 Yellow Pages advert in the days before search engines and Google.

'Ah now, I saw that one at a bookfair the other week,' said the Sutherland accent at the end of the phone. 'What's his name? The chap from the publisher's showed me a copy. There's a picture of you and a dog on the cover.'

I explained I'd just been talking to a lady at the Ceilidh Place in Ullapool who, having initially dismissed the book as being about Arthur's Seat and therefore too faraway from north-west Scotland, was now going to order a copy from Bertrams, the book distribution company. Also there was a lot in it about the Victorian mountaineer Caleb George Cash exploring the Cairngorm Mountains which weren't so far from Ullapool after all were they? Building up to the crux of my sales pitch I continued:

'And there's some local interest in the book too,' I explained, 'there's a chapter about how I got my old dog from Allan MacRae, one of the leaders of the Assynt Crofters, when she was a puppy.'

At the mention of Allan Macrae the voice on the other end of the phone paused and then said, 'Well, it must have been a bloody badly behaved dog then!'

There was laughter at both ends of the phone.

'Those were a wild bunch those dogs of Allan Macrae's,' he went on and I felt Cuilean beside me, smelt the damp rainwater smell of her coat on a wet day and remembered the wild look in her eyes as she raced in joyful circles through the heather.

Macrow: *I passed wave upon wave of infant trees, all clothed in vivid green... young plantations of larch and pine.*

Past the buildings at Ruarach the green conifers close in, grown tall in the 75 years since Macrow and Jeannie came this way. After a two kilometres we come to a clearing in the forest, a flat meadow of long grass and unfurling bracken. We've reached the place where the 'white lodge' of Dorusduain once stood. Of the house I can see no trace, just the meadow and two immensely tall, old Scots pines. All that remains are the kennels. The slate roof's still on but twelve foot high birches grow out between rusty iron railings where the keepers' dogs once slept on the cement floor.

1946: *At Ruarach, we branched off up the rough road to... the white lodge of Dorusduain. Here, several shaggy collies came bounding out to meet us, but they allowed us to pass after loud barks of greeting and approving tail-wags at Jeannie, who finds the Highland dogs very amiable on the whole.*

Where are the collies of Dorusduain now? No dogs rush out to greet the Labradoodle at Dorusduain today. I peer through the rusted railings at the pens behind the derelict kennels and mourn the collies that ran out to meet Macrow. And I lament the fall of the house of Dorusduain. No dogs run out to greet us as we reach the clearing in the forest where the house once stood. Only the rustle of the leaves on the birch trees, only the wind in the long grass. I walk on and I miss the shaggy collies of Dorusduain that rushed out to greet Jeannie and Macrow on that sunny Highland morning one summer long ago.

Macrow: *The forest thinned and was lost, and our path meandered through bare, riven hills, away from the music of the stream.*

The June sun is high in the sky, the path dry and dusty, the Labradoodle panting, tongue hanging out.

'Go on, drink your water,' I tell her and she jumps down off the path, drinks deeply from the stream then stretches her front legs out and lies down in the clear, cold water. Back on the path she shakes herself and a myriad of droplets of water sparkle in the sunlight. I bend down and run my hand over the Labradoodle's cool, wet fur. Somewhere from across the years Macrow bends down to pat Jeannie.

Macrow: *We walked on over peat, boulders, and brown heather; and there was no sound anywhere but the far-off crying of gulls*

THE WILD SWIMMER OF KINTAIL

flying inland from the sea.'

I'm walking a coffin road. It ends at the mossy gravestones by the roofless church at Clachan Duich in the sunshine by the sea-loch. In the pictures I click through as I type, the Kintail summer is blazing from a blue sky. The fading vapour trails of jets in the stratosphere make a saltire cross in the sky. L is wearing a sunhat and a skort, shorts that unzip to become a skirt. I quite fancy getting one to wear myself, I tell her.

The path is well maintained, this is National Trust land purchased for the nation as part of the post-war settlement. I click the mouse onto the next picture. Think of Macrow crouched down by a boulder in the rain, the stubby pencil on damp paper, the drops of rain falling on the open pages of her notebook.

In the narrow pass at the high point of the bealach the track is fainter, the way marked with stone cairns and behind me I feel Macrow's footsteps on the path.

1946: *A cold wind sweeping along the narrow gulley opening out over the Bealach na Sroine told us we were approaching the summit plateau.*

There is a photograph in the April 1985 edition of the *Scots Magazine*: in the little cottage in Chichester, Macrow sits uncomfortably upright in an armchair. A long necklace and a white polo neck, her lips parted in a thin smile, a book open on her lap. One of her own, I wonder? Her hair a touch unkempt and windblown on the back of the chair as if she'd just stepped off the summit of one of those West Highland peaks she wrote about and so loved.

Interviewing her, the journalist David Foster asked her how she recorded her walks in the hills. He'd always been 'tremendously impressed' by her way of describing a view as if it were there before her eyes. The poet's answer was simple: 'I've a photographic memory,' she replied.

1946: *At last, we surmounted a rise. There, spread out before us, stretching away into dim distance, lay a land of enchantment and desolation, the untouched fastnesses of the high hills.*

The sun beats down, the path leads on. There are streaks of snow on the hills and pink orchids in the long grass by a fallen down drystone wall at the head of the bealach.

Macrow: *In a deep glen below and to our right, the Amhainn Gaorsaic* [sic] *flowed from Loch a' Bhealaich, Loch Gaorsaic and Loch Thuill Easaich, so that the three pools of water had the appearance of pendants strung onto a silver chain. In passing, we added these to our collection of hill-lochs, as they are set at a height of around, 1242 feet...*

As the Labradoodle trots along the path beside me I run through the rules of Macrow's game of collecting hill lochs, such as I know them to be:

1. Each hill-loch must lie within the boundaries of the Parish of Kintail.
2. Each hill-loch must be above 1000 feet. (I know this because in a letter to Colin Gibson dated 12/10/93: Macrow wrote: 'While

THE WILD SWIMMER OF KINTAIL

working on 'Kintail Scrapbook' I had a wonderful time visiting every hill-loch over 1,000ft.')

3. Each hill-loch must have a name. (But then I'm not sure about this last one because I think she visited some unnamed lochans. I'll need to check.)

And now there's a new one:

4. A sighting of a hill loch (even from a distance) is enough to add it to the collection, to tick it off the list.

The path begins to zig-zag down the far side of the bealach. Below me the Abhainn Gaorsaic is a blue seam in the floor of the glen. And then we're there: down beside the river following its shallow pools and banks of shingle, Carnan Cruithneachd looming over the Falls of Glomach like a witch's hat. L is braver than me (plus I've got 23 kilos of Labradoodle attached to my wrist) and she scrambles down a gravelly path by the side of the Falls to try and catch a glimpse of the waterfall. That's the thing about the Falls of Glomach, you see. It's really difficult to get a good view of them. They're not called the hidden falls for nothing.

Macrow: *...a dull, throbbing roar... The stream began to leap and wrestle with itself... Then it leapt two or three steps—and disappeared in clouds of flying foam, falling three hundred and 70 feet in to the abyss...*

I'm terrible with heights. No really, I am. You've no idea what a battle I had with the Skye Munros. L holds the Labradoodle and I force myself to take a few steps down the steep path that leads along the edge of the cliff.

Macrow: *I turned away, feeling that if I stayed any longer I should be dazed by the noise and drawn down into the black chasm below.*

I stop and look over the edge. The sun moves behind a cloud. The gorge is dark. A spindly rowan clings to a ledge. Wet ferns glisten on slimy rock. The roar of white water fills my head. My testicles tighten, then I realise I'm touching my willy like a wee boy.

The Writing Time of Brenda G Macrow

I have no excuses for this book. It was just one of those things I had to do.
                        BGM 1948.

The ten years from 1945-55 were a golden age for Brenda G Macrow. As far as writing and climbing were concerned, she was in her prime. She was a free spirit. Tellingly, Macrow's favourite movie (she went to see it three times) was Powell and Pressburger's *I Know Where I'm GoinG* Released in 1945 the film tells the story of a determined young woman who finds romance while stranded on the Hebridean Island of Mull. Though Macrow would live a long life, on into the twenty-first century, the decade following the end of World War Two was her purple patch. Never again would find again the writing form of those Highland summers just after the war.

During this period Macrow wrote her best known and arguably finest poem 'Climb in Torridon Liathach, 1947,' published two poetry anthologies plus numerous articles for widely read periodicals and magazines of the time. She also wrote *Kintail Scrapbook* and followed it up with her most successful and best-remembered book *Torridon Highlands*. Reviewing *Unto the Hills* (on sale for 15/- in 1946 or £25 in today's money) *The Scotsman* described Macrow's first poetry anthology as: 'a book to treasure, a book to recall glorious days spent in the open air, a book to set your feet itching for the old hill-paths again.'

And what was the literary world of 1946 like? Neil Gunn and Maurice Walsh wrote about the blue Cairngorms, Jessie Kesson like the women Macrow saw working in the fields around Dornie. While Gunn and Walsh (of whose books Macrow was a huge fan), were getting all the plaudits, quietly disappointed but stoical, Nan

Shephard shoved the returned manuscript of *The Living Mountain* into a drawer and left it there until the 1970s.

BGM's articles and poetry appeared in *The Scots Magazine* alongside the photographs of Robert Moyes Adam and the drawings of Colin Gibson. *The Scots Magazine* was an altogether more literary publication in the 1940s than it is today. Its pages featured short stories by the likes of Neil Gunn and Jessie Kesson. Leafing through the yellowing pages of *The Scots Magazine* in the reading room of the National Library of Scotland, as sleet falls on George IV Bridge and the buses splash through slushy puddles, I guess that much of the material published in the journals and magazines of the 1940s would appear on the internet today.

Macrow published her early poetry in the now defunct *Chamber's Journal*, a literary and scientific magazine produced by Edinburgh publishers W & J Chambers at 11 Thistle Street from 1832-1956. Her name jumps out at me from the index page. The Journal appears, to contemporary eyes anyway, a strange mix of literature, short stories, poems and science. Stories by Naomi Mitchison, DK Broster, Ben Humble and Seton Gordon share the pages with articles on 'Cement for Sticking Rubber Soles to Boots and Shoes', 'Electric Hammers for Minor Building Jobs', 'Wind Dynamos' and 'Easier Crack-Finding in Metal Parts.' After World War Two started the index became increasingly full of articles with titles like 'Demonstrating the Efficiency of the Gas-Mask' and 'Blitzed Areas, District Heating for'. The wartime flavour is also conveyed in articles like 'Snow Soldiers: The Men who Fight on Skis.'

BGM's prose and poetry also appeared in *The Scottish Annual and Braemar Gathering Book,* a rather obscure journal still published today. In the 1940s and 1950s it included articles by Ben Humble ('The Lost Road' and 'The Queen Goes Through Glen Tilt'), Tom Weir ('The Cairngorms Nature Reserve') as well as 'Landseer;

THE WILD SWIMMER OF KINTAIL

Painter-Stalker of the Royal Forest' by D C Thomson's very own Colin Gibson. The 1952 edition included a piece with splendid accompanying photos entitled 'The Golden Eagle' by one Seton Gordon. More surprisingly, among the heather and mountains, was an article by the Scottish Nationalist, Moultrie B Kelsall, calling for the establishment of a Scottish Parliament.

If Macrow was writing today her work would be called nature writing. Writing about the Cairngorms at the same time as Nan Shepherd, Macrow was a prolific writer who crossed the path of many a better-remembered figure in the world of post-war Scottish mountaineering: Ben Humble, Rennie McOwan, Tom Weir and Syd Scroggie among them. According to David Foster: 'Tom Weir recalls the powerful impression her books made on him at an early stage in his career.' Rennie McOwan regarded BGM as one of his heroines. *Kintail Scrapbook* McOwan said included a passage on the signs of spring which in his words: 'make anyone want to get out of his armchair and seize a rucksack.'

Macrow 1946: *There is something about the Western Highlands which gets into your blood... you will be amazed at the change in yourself after only a few weeks among these lovely hills and glens. You were weary, and tired of life and living? Somehow, you have found rest and a new outlook. Your nerves were ragged, shattered by the war? Somehow they are calmed, and your heart is quiet and steady...*

Macrow first came to Scotland at the age of 24 and like Caleb George Cash all those years before it was to Aviemore she came, arriving by train in a snow storm in May 1941. 75 years before my Airbnb summer she and her new husband Jock spent their honeymoon at Mrs Mac's B&B in the nearby village of Coylumbridge.

During that holiday Macrow and Jock walked to the highest point of the Lairig Ghru as well as visiting Ryvoan Pass and An Lochan Uaine. The couple climbed Cairngorm on a Wednesday in May by the route taken by the funicular railway today. From Jock's description, it might as well have been Kajenjunga. This was Macrow's first ascent of a Scottish mountain and it was one of two life changing events that both happened to her in the Cairngorms.

In 1955 Macrow wrote that, 'Among the Scottish hills, the Cairngorms were my first love.' They are her 'blue-remembered hills… your peace a charm that will not let me go.' In her mountain writing and poetry Macrow gets right to the heart of why it is we climb mountains. She expresses with a poet's skill why we go to the hills.

Macrow once wrote of her childhood: 'Always, colour fascinated me… I loved snails for the stripes on their shells, and the neighbour's big tabby cat who had a sugar-pink nose and twin emeralds for eyes.' Gillian Zealand, writing in 2006, drew attention also to Macrow's 'ability to capture a scene with both the language of a poet and the eye of a painter.' And she continued: 'Her perception of colour is particularily striking. The Pools of Dee, set in the stark landscape of boulder-fields at the head of the Lairig Ghru, are 'copper-coloured at the edges and a deep greenish-blue in the centre, as if oil had been spilled on the water.''

Though she would live on into her nineties, Macrow would never again find the writing form, the purple patch, the spike in creativity and artisitic endeavour of those Highland summers after the end of World War Two.

1946: *I picked up the portable typewriter and a suitcase and started off down the steep hillside, Jeannie slithering delightedly ahead.*

THE WILD SWIMMER OF KINTAIL

Though Macrow continued to write all her life, by the dawn of the twenty-first century her output had dwindled to contributions to *The People's Friend*. Some of these later poems, in the words of one of her sterner critics were 'little better than the twee rhymes in greetings card.' Poor Brenda! How did it come to this?

What happened? How did the promising and widely published young poet of the 1940s, ' …who is already well known' according to the back cover of *Speyside to Deeside* (1956) finish up writing rhyming couplets for *The People's Friend*. Part of the answer is to be found in the said rhyming couplets. Significantly, they are absent from Macrow's best poem 'Climb in Torridon Liathach, 1947.' She seems to have lacked a literary mentor during her writing career. If Macrow had had such a person in her life, might they perhaps have steered her away from the over-use of rhyming couplets? We'll never know.

Her decision after 1950, to write almost exclusively in the rhyming couplets used by the poets she most admired, Swinburne, R L Stevenson and Gerald Manley Hopkins seriously constricted her creativity. In seeking to emulate poets she loved Macrow dressed her poems up and sent them out into the world in tight, ill-fitting suits.

I never met Brenda G Macrow. My only contact with her came not long after I bought a copy of *Kintail Scrapbook* from the second hand bookshop in Edinburgh where my nephew had his first Saturday job. Several years passed before I had the idea of writing about Macrow. While glancing through the small ads at the back of *The Scots Magazine* I spotted one for *A Red, Red Rose*, an anthology of poems by one Brenda G Macrow. *Kintail Scrapbook* was published in 1946. I was amazed the author was still living as the second decade of the twenty-first century dawned. I posted a cheque for £5.50 to Mrs Brenda G J Prior at Myrtle Cottage, Chichester and duly received by post a few days later a signed copy of Macrow's last book, a slim volume of poems. On a slip of paper tucked between the pages a shaky hand had written: 'Many thanks for your cheque. I hope you enjoy the poems. Brenda G Macrow.'

Sue Collin is a retired English teacher and creative writing tutor with many years of experience, who also happens to be the author's mother. When I gave her Macrow's first book she commented that *Unto the Hills* was an: 'odd mixture of felicitous phrase and verse.' Whereas 'Climb in Torridon Liathach, 1947' captures the mood of the moment: 'Only the click of nails on rock—the quickened breath.' By contrast Macrow is at her weakest in poems like 'Autumn in Affric' with its 'laboured, artificial personification: 'Now softly spills the sun her golden tears.'' Or her use of inversion as in 'Fingal's Cave, Staffa': 'Sleeps here the saga… ' Her writing has echoes of RLS as in 'Lochnagar' with its opening line: 'Blows the moss-campion… ' and in the next verse 'Wails the wind eerily… ' and of the work of Gerald Manley Hopkins. It's a shame that Macrow was rather too heavily influenced by the artificial style of the Victorian poets she loved.

Rhyming couplets, as used extensively in Macrow's last anthology *A Red Red Rose* (Brenda Prior, 2007) can sound glib. Rhyming couplets are not good for expressing profound emotion. The structure of many of Macrow's later poems is: first, description in rhyming couplets followed by somewhat sanctimonious reflection. Compare this to the poem 'Magic Memory' which contains no reflection and is all the better as a result: 'I waited where the tides ran slow and silver ripples lapped the lonely shore.'

Macrow was prone to using archaic language in her poetry, often using words such as 'hue' and 'anew' and also over-using alliteration. Nor was she good with titles, particularily in her final anthology which contained a poem entitled 'Eternal Spring' and the even more grating 'Lovely Lochnagar.'

But despite all the above faults a passionate love of the hills and wild places shines through poems like 'Smoo Cave, Durness.' To a mountaineer Macrow evokes the emotions aroused when in the hills, as in these lines from 'Walking in the Wind': 'It was a day when the hill-wind cried like a lost child.' 'At the Shelter Stone' is, in the words of Sue Collin: 'an excellent evocation of the spirit of 1930's plebeian mountaineerinG' Macrow writes well when she can free herself of rigid rythmns and rhyming schemes. When Macrow keeps it simple, she writes very well indeed as in 'Lines Composed in the Sma' Glen': 'These be my solace in sin or sorrow: the mist on the meadow; the changeable shadow; The cloud in the chasm… ' Likewhise 'A Hillwalker's Dream' captures the rythmn of walking: 'To start in the early morning, When the mist is on the ben, And the sound of the curlew calling, Stirs echoes along the glen… '

So then, a poor choice in creative direction was one factor in bringing to an end the immensely productive and creative period that lasted from 1945 to the mid 1950s. We have already seen how Macrow's life changed for ever when she climbed her first Scottish mountain, Cairngorm, in 1941. Almost ten years later, in August 1950, a second life changing event was also to happen to Macrow in the Cairngorms. As a child Macrow described herself as having: 'a delicate constitution.' At the age of 31 while six months pregnant, she set out to cycle and walk from the Dell of Rothiemurchus to the summit of Braeriach, a round trip of some 34 kilometres. Writing to the journalist Colin Gibson in 1985, Macrow recalled how following this arduous hill-walk she suffered: 'serious health problems.' Recurrent attacks of thrombosis coupled with arthritis forced Macrow to give up mountaineering in the mid-1950s and led her to hang up her walking boots well before she turned 40.

The end of her mountaineering career had a knock on effect on her writing career. Shorn of day-to-day contact with the high hills and the wild places she loved, her creativity, inspired as it was by the great outdoors, began to dry up. Deprived of access to her beloved mountains her writing lost the freshness of experience. Much of her writing about Scotland served up after 1953 was a stale rehash, reheated memories of fondly remembered trips to the Highlands. Pieces like 'Land of Enchantment' which she wrote for *The Scottish Annual and Braemar Gathering Book* in 1954 concentrated exclusively on the history of Deeside. Athough she mentions a hillwalk to the Shelter Stone, by now it is clear she is writing from memory. Like much of Macrow's later work it lacked the mixture of personal experience, anecdote, folklore and history that had been the recipe for the success of her earlier books. To be fair, in *Kintail Scrapbook* Macrow included lots of history but back then the mix was leavened by descriptions of her climbing expeditions, something she was unable to do after about 1953.

The last of Macrow's Scottish books, *Speyside to Deeside,* was published in 1956. It is a smaller format, less lavishly produced hardback than the earlier *Unto the Hills.* The book contains very similar content to her articles for *The Scottish Annual and Braemar Gathering Book* . The lack of personal anecdotes and too many facts make *Speyside to Deeside* the weakest of Macrow's Scottish books.

In the 'Acknowledgements' in the opening pages of *Speyside to Deeside* , Macrow thanks the keeper of the National Library of Scotland and the Honorary Secretary of the Cairngorm Club. And I think of Macrow standing at the issuing desk in the National Library, Caleb George Cash's *Bibliography of Scottish Topography* looking haughtily down at her from the top shelf. Caleb himself departed these 30 years and me, another writer, coming to the library 75 years on, while sleet falls on the pavements of Edinburgh.

In common with many women of her generation, marriage and married life also seems to have negatively impacted on Macrow's career. In the early 1950s society had certain widely held expectations

THE WILD SWIMMER OF KINTAIL

as to the role of a wife and these included creating an ideal home and putting her husband and his career first. A married woman going off to spend six months in a cottage in a remote area of Scotland fell far outside the norms and expectations of the time. While Macrow had what was, by all accounts, a long and happy marriage to her second husband Dennis Prior, it does seem to have clipped her wings and negatively impacted on her writing about Scotland.

After health problems forced Macrow to give up mountaineering, she chose not to return to Torridon until 1985, by which time she was 69. Perhaps the sight of her beloved mountains whilst being unable to climb them was just too much for her.

So far then personal reasons: a poor choice in creative direction, health problems and marriage are some of the factors that caused Macrow's writing career to falter. But there were other factors too at work out in the wider world. Scotland was changing. Scottish National Party candidate Winnie Ewing's shock victory in the 1967 Hamilton by-election was the culmination of a long, slow change in the political weather.

Culturally too, Scotland was changing. By the early 1960s new poets, writers and entertainers were emerging with a different slant on Scotland's culture and history. Macrow's was a very romantic vision of Scotland. A Victorian vision of Scotland you could say, the proud Highlander toiling on his croft, the wild mountains, the cool breeze from the snowfields. Never forget that the Victorians were as close to Macrow's generation as The Beatles, Joe Orton, Marianne Faithful, Harold Wilson and Twiggy are to us today.

The new figures emerging onto Scotland's cultural scene included the poets Norman MacCaig and Edwin Morgan and the novelist Muriel Spark. The historian John Prebble was writing much more realistically about Scotland's history while entertainers like Billy Connolly made Macrow and Adam's romantic vision of Scotland, as exemplified in books like *Unto the Hills* look distinctly dated.

All these factors then must have contributed to Macrow's decision in the late 1950s to cease writing non-fiction about Scotland, switch genres and begin writing children's fiction. In the world of books, switching genres is something today's struggling writers (that's the 89 per cent of us who can't make anything near a living from writing alone) are frequently encouraged to do, in order to try and find commercial success. One reason Iain Banks was a best-selling author is because he wrote both Scottish literary fiction and sci-fi.

Macrow had read and enjoyed both J R R Tolkein's *The Lord of the Rings* and C S Lewis's *The Chronicles of Narnia*. Perhaps too, like many writers of her generation, Macrow was hoping to find fame and fortune by following the example of Enid Blyton. Blyton's phenemonal success in the 1950s and '60s (when she sold 26 million copies of *Noddy* alone) inspired many a writer to turn his or her pen to writing children's fiction.

I remember when my niece was little she was a big fan of the Famous Five books. When I got my first dog Cuilean as a pup, my niece said she looked just like Timmy when George found him on the moor. How many other aspiring Enids were there out there in the late 50s, I wonder? A legion of failed Enids, like when you read on publishers' websites today: 'No unsolicited manuscripts. No science fiction or fantasy.' Ah, Enid Blyton: *The Island of Adventure*, that was my favourite, especially the bit where the boys strip down to their underpants to go swimming. Such childhood homoeroticism, as a kid I read that page again and again.

In 1953 Enid Blyton sold six million copies of the Famous Five. Was this the plan for *The Amazing Mr Whisper*, Macrow's first children's book? 'Amazing,' now there's a good word. Derived from the Old English *āmasian*, according to Google, the use over time of the word 'amazing' in books peaked around 1950 and again in 2010.

THE WILD SWIMMER OF KINTAIL

Did Macrow sometimes dream of achieving Blyton-like sales while she peeled potatoes in the long afternoons in Chichester while the baby Lesley slept and she waited for Dennis to come home from work? A few lines of an unfinished poem scribbled on a notepad on the desk by the open window in the upstairs bedroom. The pages flutter in the breeze from the Downs.

But some things never change in the world of books. Just look at all those would-be, best-selling writers trying to follow in the footsteps of J K Rowling and Harry Potter today. It's like when you go into a charity shop – always a serious reality check for a writer – all those second-hand books. All that effort to write them and get them published and now they're for sale at 30p each. After all's said and done then, it's a chastening experience to be sat here. An obscure Scottish author writing about another little-known writer, all that time spent writing, all that work, all those words, mostly forgotten now.

The Watchplace

Here and there a wisp of forgotten gold to bring back rememembrance of strange beauty.
BGM, *Kintail Scrapbook*, 1948

The long, hot spell of weather is going to break tomorrow. I'm standing, rucksack on my back, on the jetty at the north end of the bridge by Dornie Hall. A Rabbie's Trail Blazers minibus pulled up in the car park a few minutes ago. Bleary-eyed tourists mill around the toilets, taking photos and pointing their iPads across the glassy smooth surface of the loch in the direction of Eilean Donan Castle. A couple Spanish twenty-somethings stand near the minibus chatting to a grey haired man in a crumpled kilt (the driver).

Macrow 1946: *It began well enough. We crossed the ferry from Dornie in sunshine and a light, salty wind blowing from the Isles. We did not forget to make an arrangement with the ferryman to take us back at about six o'clock. The ferryman lived at Letterfearn, about a mile from Totaig, and the customary procedure in getting a message to him was to telephone Letterfearn Post Office. They then passed on the message, and the ferryman proceeded to Totaig on his motor-cycle.*

On the rocky shore beside the jetty a young Dutch guy and his girlfriend are getting sea kayaks ready for a paddle. The blond, bearded Dutchman peels off his wet suit top to reveal lightly tanned skin, wispy golden chest hairs, a flat stomach and muscled arms.

Macrow: *...some fellow-cyclists passed me... puffing and sweating up the hill while I stood still and surveyed the landscape. One of the*

THE WILD SWIMMER OF KINTAIL

young men, naked to the waist, was a rich golden colour, including his hair, as if he just stepped out of the cast of Ben Hur.

The sunlight glistens on bubbles of bronze coloured kelp floating on the surface of the loch, the water so clear I can see the stones on the sea bed. Across the blue waters of Loch Duich beyond Eilean Donan blue hills, the Five Sisters at the head of the loch stand out against the azure sky. A fast white motorboat rounds the rocky shore of Eilean Donan slicing a frothy white wake across the blue surface of the loch. I think this must be my boat.

I'd spoken to Lachie on my phone a couple of nights before. He runs Loch Duich cruises from his house named Mullardoch in Inverinate. Mainly it's fishing and wildlife watching he does.

'Recreate the old ferry run from Dornie to Totaig? That's an unusual one,' Lachie had said.

Now the boat's close enough for me to see Lachie standing at the wheel peering anxiously at the clear waters of Loch Duich washing over the old yellow stone blocks white with barnacles of the Dornie Hall jetty.

Now Lachie's standing at the bow of his boat with a boat hook.

'Kellan?'

He pushes the gleaming fibreglass hull of the boat away from the stone jetty.

'There's a bloody big tyre down there.'

He's got the boat up against the jetty.

'Could you just hop on now please?'

I lift the Labradoodle over the side of the boat, paws scrabble on shiny white fibreglass. Then I climb on board and plonk my bottom on a bench in the stern. Lachie is nudging the boat away from the jetty with bursts of the propeller. There's a grinding sound from the back of the boat.

'The council should do something to clear these old jetties. The seaweed has stones in it, they catch in the propeller,' he complains.

A couple more pushes with the boat hook and we're away. Looking around at the beige interior fittings of the cabin and the impressive sonar and GPS beside the wheel, it occurs to me this boat must have cost a lot, like a new car. Already the jetty and the sea kayakers are receding into the boat's foaming white wake.

During the short crossing I grasp the Labradoodle's collar and look over the gleaming chrome handrails and watch the salt seawater of Loch Duich swirl under Dornie Bridge. Lachie tells me how his sisters lived in Leachachan when they were kids and used to cross on the ferry from Totaig to Dornie every day in the 1950s. A bus would be waiting at Dornie to take them to school in Plockton.

The Five Sisters look like the Caribbean, like somewhere Captain Cook might have gone ashore. They remind me of the mountains of Paros seen across the Aegean Sea from the Greek island of Naxos.

Macrow: *We had the finest view of the Five Sisters... in the deep blue gulleys between them, a few frail ribbons of mist yet lingered, like the wraiths of old warriors...*

All too soon the boat slows as we approach the white ferry house at Totaig across aquamarine sea. The water so clear I can see fronds of seaweed waving in the current on the seabed. A heron stands as if in silent vigil among the rocks on the shoreline. Lachie edges the boat into the jetty and I hop ashore closely followed by the Labradoodle. Lachie's anxious about seaweed in the propeller again and quickly pushes away from the slipway and turns the boat back in the direction of Inverinate.

The ferry house at the top of the slipway at Totaig is empty. An old fridge minus door lies in the grass. A ladder is propped against the porch. Robert M Adam's photo in Macrow's book shows a dilapidated corrugated iron shed attached to the Ferry house. Lachie told me this was a pub and we concurred it was very civilised to be able to have a drink while waiting for the ferry.

The chug of the boat's engine soon fades. I can see a line of coaches across the loch at Eilean Donan Castle. Weeds poke up in the gaps between the greasy grey stones on the slipway at Totaig as the sound of bagpipes from the castle drifts across the loch.

I nearly trod on him. Lying still, camouflaged among last autumn's orangey-brown oak and birch leaves at the edge of the track. An olive and black, wart-speckled toad, his wet skin glistens. On the top of his head his eyes bulge. He's motionless. I walk on.

The track runs along beside a low sea wall. The tide is out revealing rocky skerries blanketed in kelp and grey sands pockmarked with wormcasts. On the far shore of the loch, framed by bright splashes of yellow whin, stand the buildings at Ardelve. I can see the low rise of Fireach Ard and the familiar outline of the hillside behind Shepherd's Cottage.

In a cove the rusty, red hull of a fishing boat lies beached among the rock pools and sea pinks. The path climbs up through scattered birch trees and crags on the steep, grassy headland. Among the brown stalks of dead bracken, the silver birches and green ferns stands a large mound of white lichen and moss-covered stones. It takes me a few moments to realise, it's the broch. Like all brochs there's only one small doorway marked by a triangular lintel stone. I crouch down to walk through the low gateway into Caisteal Grugaig. The walls are thick but they are hollow and on my left, in the dark passage, another narrow doorway leads to the remains of a flight of stone steps.

I scramble up on to the walls of the broch and look across to Dornie Bridge. I realise, like Eilean Donan castle on the far shore of the loch, Caisteal Grugaig is strategically located, controlling access to Glen Shiel at the meeting place of Loch Alsh, Loch Duich and Loch Long. The Gaels named the hill behind the broch Faire-an-Dun which means The Watchplace.

Sitting at the PC, in front of the screen, writing. I reach across to the filing cabinet. The steel drawer slides open and I pull out a small blue baG I unzip it and strap the grey nylon cuff of the blood pressure monitor to my arm. I gaze at the computer screen and its font of Courier New, reminiscent of and chosen because, it is like the typewriter fonts Macrow used in 1946. Or I wonder, did she write in longhand, walking briskly across a sun-drenched courtyard off the Royal Mile with a thick, heavy, handwritten manuscript in her shoulder bag that summer in Edinburgh 75 years ago?

I touch the button on the front of the blue and white plastic box. The screen fills with number 8s like a pocket calculator. Five seconds elapse then, the whine of an electronic motor, vibrations from the white plastic box and the cuff starts to inflate and tightens hard above my elbow. The numbers on the screen begin to fall. Ten seconds. Then with a hiss the cuff relaxes and the blood pressure reading appears on the screen with a warning heart symbol. Am I living now with the health problems associated with getting older? Or did HIV cause unseen damage in the decade or so in the late eighties and early nineties when the virus raged unchecked in my feverish veins, free to invade any organ of my body unconquered as yet by anti-retro viral drugs with names like the Knights of the Round Table: Saquinavir, Epivir and Abacavir?

THE WILD SWIMMER OF KINTAIL

Back in Kintail in the second decade of the twenty-first century, I'm standing on the grassy hillside looking out across the quiet waters of Loch Duich in the still air of a Highland morning. To the west, across the low grassy Glas Eilean, lie the Cuillins and Skye. The sweeping arch of the Skye Bridge rises on stilts of concrete then vaults across the narrows and the island where Gavin Maxwell once sat on a boulder on the shore and watched the otters in the bright water.

Macrow: *The little lighthouse, like an ivory tower, on Eilean Ban, and the ferry to Kyleakin, crawling like a lazy black-beetle across the frosted glass of the sea.*

As I begin my descent to Ardintoul through an area of clear felling, the bay has a mournful look to it, even in warm sunshine. There are abandoned, overgrown fields bordered by lines of mature trees. Two fish farms, each with a dozen circular tanks, float in the sea on either side of the shingle spit that is Ardintoul Point. The burned-out ruin of a large farmhouse adds a further melancholy note to the scene. Ardintoul appears completely deserted and I start to imagine drug smugglers and yardies with guns.

1946: *It was beginning to rain as Jeannie and I began our scramble down down to Ardintoul. Nothing, however, could have damped my enthusiasm for this delightful little cluster of houses, hugging a shell-strewn shore, backed by the heathery slopes of the hills.*

At Ardintoul Macrow saw red roofs and bright green trees, and golden whin. Where Macrow found a little settlement full of colour and life, Ardintoul today has an air of abandonment. It reminds me of the deserted villages in the mountains on the Greek island of Naxos, abandoned when the wells ran dry or the local emery mines closed down. All this I think about as I begin my descent through the rotting stumps of felled conifers.

When Macrow came to Kintail, salmon was one of Scotland's luxury items, like lobster and crab, prawns and langoustine, Bruichladdich and Laphroaig. Caught by skilled anglers with line and reel and net, back in 1946 salmon was a luxury food you might serve at your wedding or order in the restaurant of a posh Edinburgh hotel high above Princes Street looking across the tram wires to the castle on its rock.

I follow the track down to the burnt-out farmhouse. It is sheltered by a windbreak of tall pines. The walls of the house still stand. The roof is just a few charred rafters at one gable end. It's like looking into a blackened dolls' house. The floors have gone but a corner of an upstairs bedroom remains intact. Scorched furniture teeters on the edge of charred floorboards. Melted plastic drips from the ruins of the attic. The heat of the blaze has distorted the surviving glass in a charred upper sash window. A corrugated-iron generator shed stands next to the house and the fire must have spread to here too. Blackened petrol cans lie buried in ash among a tangle of charred beams and sheets of rusty-orange corrugated iron. Spray painted onto the boarded up doorway are the words: 'Dangerous Building Keep Oot' [sic].

A new-looking polytunnel stands behind the house, untouched by the flames. A green wheelie bin and window boxes in a row on the ground, a vegetable plot with small currant bushes, still clear of weeds. Rhubarb sprouts in a corner. Later I ask the red-faced guy, who collects the money at Dornie campsite, what happened and he tells me the building was in the process of being renovated. The owners left home thinking a coalfire in one of the fireplaces would just go out. But somehow it spread and consumed the whole house. Seventeen firefighters attempted to save the building. And they had no insurance, he says.

I wander down the track from the burnt out house to the shore. A gate bars access to the jetty: 'No Unauthorised Persons Beyond This Point.' Behind it is a ramshackle collection of fish farm detritus, three-foot-high coils of rope, floats, concrete blocks, a skip and a fibreglass rowing boat on a trailer. Much more sinister though is the wooden hide. About twelve feet off the ground, built around the trunk of a sturdy Scots pine on the edge of the windbreak that shelters Ardintoul House and complete with camouflage webbinG I stand there with the Labradoodle. I'm puzzled. It looks like the treehouse the kids who live in Mill Cottage in Roy Bridge built in the woods by the River Spean. This is a watchplace too. But what are they watching for here? Then the cold truth dawns on me. This is no childish treehouse. This is a hide. They shoot seals from here.

The sun beats down on the car park outside Morrisons in Piershill. It's half-five on a weekday afternoon. The shop is busy. Tired-looking men in suits and mums pushing buggies jostle between young Polish couples holding hands. After the July sun blazing down on the car park outside, there's a welcome blast of cold air from the cool cabinets as I turn the corner from the pizza and ready meals aisle. On the lower shelf of the chiller cabinet, under the tubs of hollandaise and parsley sauce, resting on plastic trays wrapped in clingfilm. Two pink fillets of salmon from Rhuabh Sillaig, priced at £2.20.

Then, suddenly I'm back on the shingle shore at Ardintoul Bay. I'm standing beside the burnt out farmhouse, looking out across the oily foam floating on the surface of the sea, to the cages in the water and the marksman's hide up in the tree by the shore with its clear line of fire to the fish cages in the loch. Standing in the bright, neon-lit supermarket aisle, the neat parcels of salmon flesh seem to seep blood through their plastic packaging. For who could shoot a seal?

Macrow 1946: *It was still raining hard... I went up to the attic... And here, for a while, I lost all count of time. Wandering about in the semi-darkness, among cans of sheep-dip, tar and marking-irons, I blundered into a pile of steel traps... I picked one up ...and tested the spring. I could hardly force it apart...* [It] *could hardly fail to break the captive's leg... And if no-one came by for a day or two . . .*

I sat there miserable and confused, holding the gin-trap in my hands... Admitting that 'vermin' are a 'pest' and must be destroyed, I could not help wondering what they had done to deserve an end like this. Even the fox cannot help his nature...

I leave the scorched shell of Ardintoul House behind. A little further along the track, behind a six-foot-high fence supported by concrete posts and topped with barbed wire, there's a rectangular, grass-covered mound sprouting yellow, gorse bushes and a radio mast. A secret bunker, I wonder, some remnant of the Cold War? My mind races, I see Harold Wilson arriving in a black Jaguar to escape an impending nuclear attack on London.

1946: *Soon we were walking across the machair, on a carpet of short turf dotted with sun-bleached shells, while gulls and oyster-catchers screamed on the fringe of the ebbing tide. Along the pebbly shore, nets were spread over the sea-wall to dry*

The oyster catchers are still here, pecking among the green weed on the shoreline. But the fishing nets spread to dry on the wall and the painted wooden boats pulled up on the beach are gone. The machair too is gone. There's just a strip of long grass and weeds by the shore now. The Forestry Commission must have planted conifers across the machair, right down to the edge of the shingle. The shoreline here covered by forest for 50 years then clearfelled. Leaving tree stumps, dried rushes, bleached branches of pine, abandoned rolls of wire fence and dead bracken in its wake. I walk on across the old fields but I'm not clear of the ruins of Ardintoul yet. I come to a substantial, stone built, slate-roofed and utterly derelict farmyard and stables block.

Macrow: *The general impression of this little settlement was one of colour, life and industry. Even the geese, emerging in an orderly squad from a farmyard, were full of vigour, and quite prepared to chase us down the road...*

Then the penny drops. This is the cobbled farmyard, now choked with hawthorn, nettles and brambles, where the geese ran out and squawked at Jeannie.

Some time in the early 1980s: my mum and my stepdad were having a row. The argument was taking place over the three landings of the sunny tenement on the corner of Spottiswoode Road and Arden Street. Me, my little sister, we were all helping unload the family car after a summer holiday. Can't remember where we'd been. Ireland, the west Coast of Scotland perhaps, maybe it was just a weekend away. Anyway, it doesn't really matter.

There was loads of stuff: windshields (remember them?), boxes of Alpen, blackened bananas, rusty tins, orange cagoules, canvas rucksacks and fishing rods. There was a sort of relay system operatinG

My sister and I were carrying the stuff from the first floor landing to the top flat. My mother and stepfather were carrying the stuff from the car to the first floor. Ostensibly this was so my stepfather could 'keep an eye on the car.' But really it was because, hooked on 20 'Embassy Extra Mild' and ten 'More Cigarillos' a day, he just didn't have the breath to get up three flights of stairs more than once.

My mother and stepfather had fallen out because he'd left a white chamber pot outside the Miss MacDonalds' front door on the first floor. The chamber pot my mother used so she didn't have to pee outside the tent in the wet grass in the dark. But she didn't want the neighbours to see it. Furious with him, she snatched it up and concealed the potty under a heap of damp, orange cagoules.

'But everyone has to go to the toilet,' he protested.

From the derelict farmyard, the track leads across a grassy field down to the shore. I walk through a gap in a drystone wall along the edge of the shingle beach. The wall where the fishing nets were hung to dry when Macrow passed by.

I tramp across pebbles and crispy, black seaweed. A heron stands one-legged at the edge of the water, staring across at Beinn na Caillich on Skye. A rib buzzes between the fish cages and a black, submarine-like hulk out on the loch. It's very hot. I think about swimming. But the pebbles discourage me and the water has a foamy residue where the saltwater laps the grey and white shingle. I'm not worried about the men on the boat seeing me naked. But I think about my big, white bum being a target for the one in the treehouse with the rifle. I walk on.

A flock of feral sheep huddle together at the edge of the shingle. The Labradoodle strains at the leash. A line of pylons marches down

THE WILD SWIMMER OF KINTAIL

the hillside and across the narrows of Kyle Rhea to Skye. I can see the flat top of Macleod's Tables on the horizon.

At last we leave the beach behind and follow the path, up through ferns and clumps of soft rush, up into the birch trees. At every mossy stream crossing an otter spraint lies on the path. Over the young bracken, through gaps in the trees, I can see the swirling tidal race surging through the narrows between the Glenelg peninsula and the light house at Kylerhea.

I walk under a tall pylon like a giant frozen on the hillside. The footpath becomes a track. I glimpse the stone slipway at Kylerhea. The sea is churning and aquamarine. A wooden deer gate, two five bar gates and finally I've arrived at the car park beside the Glenelg to Skye ferry. I sit down gratefully on a park bench and watch the *Glenachulish* take advantage of the current to execute a perfect ferry glide across the narrows.

I need a dump. For the last couple of miles or so, thought the urge had gone away for a bit, but now it's back. Some people hate having to go in the great outdoors but I quite enjoy an alfresco shit. No point in a buttock clenching walk all the way back to Dornie so I take off my rucksack, drop it on the path and clip the dog's lead to it. Then picking up a flat, pointed stone, I walk fifty yards from the path. In a little hollow among the bracken I scrape out a shallow hole with the pointed stone. Shorts and pants round my ankles I squat over the hole. My sphincter relaxes and opens. Perfect aim, tubes of excrement neatly coiled like a chocolate Mr Whippy ice cream. I stand up and wipe my bum. Then use a twig to poke the crumpled sheets of white toilet paper into the brown keech before burying it all with earth and grass so no trace remains. As I pull my pants up and walk down to the burn to wash my hands, tied to the rucksack the Labradoodle watches anxiously.

Like the man said, everyone has to go to the toilet.

The Right Way up a Mountain

The right way up a mountain is straight up.
Dougal Haston

Rucksack over my shoulder I'm making my way along the aisle of the yellow citylink coach, holding onto the seat backs as the bus bounces along the A87.

'Can you let me off at the Kintail Lodge Hotel please?' I ask the driver. I'm holding the Labradoodle by the collar as the bus careers around the last big bend in the road after Shiel Bridge. The bus slows then comes to a halt in a hiss of airbrakes and I step down onto the grass verge to a tang of seaweed.

> 1946: *The Kintail Lodge is a converted shooting-lodge, recently opened by the National Trust as a hotel... When Jeannie and I arrived on the evening 'bus... Two children played gaily on the lawn, chasing a golden retriever puppy...*

The bus pulls away as I push open a white painted wooden gate in a drystone wall and walk up a gravel drive between neatly mown lawns and rose bushes and yellow bedding plants. Red fuschia, rhodendron and stacked garden chairs and beyond the fence little crags climb the grassy hillside. All just like Macrow described back in 1946.

I climb a carpeted staircase to room 16. I turn the key in the lock and my eyes take in a pine wardrobe, a dressing table and a tartan bedspread. Somewhere under the wallpaper of my hotel room is Macrow's dainty green bedroom. Did Macrow write here at the Kintail Lodge Hotel, I wonder? I push aside the curtain and open the metal framed window. My room's at the rear of the hotel overlooking a wooden hut and the two static caravans which sit, curtains drawn, at the back of every Highland hotel and provide the accommodation for seasonal workers from Poland, Rumania and the Czech Republic. I wonder if there's a handsome barman but there never is.

Macrow: *We were shown to a comfortable room at the top of the house, and given sea trout and salad for dinner.*

That first night in the bar of the Kintail Lodge Hotel I order pan fried trout and salad in homage to 1946 but with the addition of chips.

Macrow: *Then I went back to my dainty green-and-primrose bedroom and set about oiling my boots.*

Sitting alone at the bar I get into conversation with a Glaswegian hillwalker who is downing pints of cider and admiring the Labradoodle. Turns out he's in Kintail for a last Munro party the next day. I can't recall now what hill he said they'd chosen for the last Munro. Maybe it was A' Ghlas-bheinn, disnae matter like. I bought him a pint and we got to talking some more.

'Have you done your Skye Munros then?' I asked.

It's the question Munroists always ask. The Skye Munros are the crux of the climb, the difficult move that spells the difference between success and failure for the aspiring compleat Munroist.

'Did you use a guide?'

That's the next question you always ask. (The subtext being you're not some shit hot rock climber who did the In Pin on your own are you?)

'Nah, I did them with Glenmore Lodge.'

Glenmore Lodge, located at the foot of the Cairngorms, is the Scottish national outdoor training centre and their instructors set the

Brenda G Macrow and Jeannie, the Skye terrier.

Kellan MacInnes and the Labradoodle.

Brenda G Macrow (and friends) on the hill and wild swimming.

The outflow of Loch Mullardoch photographed by Robert Moyes Adam in 1930. Photos of Glen Cannich taken before the Second World War show scenes of great beauty. Today the vast, concrete Mullardoch hydro-electric dam stands at this spot .

ABOVE: Blue Remembered Hills. Looking across the mountains of the north-west Highlands to Kintail. BELOW: Loch Dubhach.

ABOVE: Loch nan Eun. BELOW: Loch Coire nan Dearcag (located at a height of 2,400 feet) nestles below the summit of Sgurr nan Ceathramhnan.

ABOVE: Loch an t-Sabhail. BELOW: Loch a Chlèirich, high on the mountain A'Ghlas bheinn.

ABOVE: Iron Lodge and upper Glen Elchaig. BELOW: Glen Affric: hydro-electric development here was carried out more sensitively than at nearby Loch Mullardoch.

TOP: The Five Sisters of Kintail. BOTTOM: The lodge under the loch: Benula Lodge where Macrow stayed the night in 1946 was later submerged by the Loch Mullardoch hydro-electric scheme but, during a prolonged dry spell in the summer of 2021, the gates of Benula Lodge reappeared.

Dornie in 1946 and Dornie now.

gold standard for mountaineering in Scotland.

'They warned us against using the guides on Skye.'

The Glaswegian hillwalker takes another gulp of cider.

'The Glenmore Lodge guys reckon they're a bunch of cowboys.'

Macrow: *Outside, the dying sun hung like a huge red lantern over the black-and-gold expanse of the loch… In the dusk, we walked along the pebbly beach… shell-hunting until it was too dark to see.*

In Edinburgh I turn the key in the lock, it clicks and the wood-panelled cupboard door opens. In my flat I'm blessed with three walk-in Victorian cupboards. Or is that cursed because it results in a tendency to horde stuff? If I had no cupboards I'd have to be ruthless and chuck stuff oot. Last autumn, when I got back into my flat after the Airbnb summer, I threw out 14 black bin bags of 'stuff' while thinking I've lived all summer long out a travel bag and a rucksack and you know what? I don't need all this crap.

I'm in the cupboard looking for another white towel. One of the new ones, I got in the John Lewis clearance, not the old 'white' ones from Jenners which, to be honest, when seen in bright sunlight are more grey than white. Or maybe I'm getting a couple of toilet rolls out the cupboard. I'm in my flat in Edinburgh and it's the height of the Airbnb madness. Corentin and the French boys left at 10am this morning leaving behind them a faint aroma of trainers and male deodrant. Enza from Germany and her sister ('Ve vood like to make an excursion to ze Highlands, can you recommend a company?') are due to arrive at 4pm this afternoon. I'm down at the flat to change the beds and clean the bathroom and mop the kitchen floor, an Airbnb changeover. I have three hours to get the flat back up to five star review level. Then I pedal across town, grab something to eat then I'm off to drive the van all evening. Or, as I like to put it: 'I'm off to feed the starving hordes of Morningside.'

Or maybe I'm getting some miniature guest soaps or shampoos out the cupboard. And that's when I find the jamjar of shells, all white and dry, not wet and sandy like they were when I picked them up on the shore of Loch Duich at the end of the summer. Macrow's shells, I was walking in her footsteps remember, so before darkness fell on the loch, I too clicked open the gate at the end of the garden and with the dog at my heel, stepped onto the shingle beach. The sea pinks trembled in the breeze, the sky yellow through orange behind the mountains at the head of the loch as I walked the shoreline collecting shells and breathing in the seaweed tang of the salt water. It didn't seem long since 1946. Seventy-five years gone by since Macrow and Jeannie crunched over the shingle and watched the fishing boats at anchor. Macrow's shells from Kintail: they sit on my desk in a row as I write this, the razor clam, the oyster shell and the cockles. I pick one up, press it to my ear and hear again the waves lapping the shore of Loch Duich.

Pretty Soon Colin Was Going To Be Dead

Macrow 1946: Loch Duich gleamed orange in the sunlight… the wet rocks of Sgurr na Moraich shone like sheets of mica let [sic] *into the hillside.*

I've found a typo! An Oliver & Boyd 1940s typo. Macrow *must* mean 'set' into the hillside not 'let'. A 1946 typo when typos were rare things, but how times change. Twenty-first century reviewers lament the poor standard of editing and proofreading in books published today. But then there are so many more books now than back in Macrow's day. I read somewhere that there were more books published in 2018 than in the whole of the eighteenth, nineteenth and the first half of the twentieth centuries!

Macrow: We were away from the hotel by ten o'clock, tramping down the road towards Morvich in a quite unexpected shower of fine rain.

Puddles shine on tarmac and over on the far shore of Loch Duich, the cloud's right down on Mam Ratagan. Past the boats on their moorings, rucksack on my back, walking poles clacking, 75 years later it's me tramping down the road towards Morvich. Blue forget-me-knots and devils bit scabious, the herald of autumn, flower in the long grass at the edge of the tarmac. But the smirr of rain's not unexpected.

1946: Before us, the great, uneven ridge of Beinn Fhada blocked the eastern sky, looming ever closer like a dark fortress…

A car, a mobile home and a lorry roar past. I'm walking the verge of the A87, Macrow's road buried beneath the asphalt, white lines, crash barriers and chevrons of the trunk route to Skye. But only for a couple of hundred metres until I turn right at a sign post to Morvich and Innis a'Chro, Innis a'Chro, a name to roll around your mouth. After World War Two, Macrow was told by the locals the name Innis a'Chro comes from the topography of the land at the head of Loch Duich. A flat valley surrounded by high hills, like a cattle pen or *Cro* and so they called it Cro Chin-t-saile, the cattle pen of Kintail.

The stone but 'n' ben and the byre beside the road and this tree, they were all here then. Macrow must have walked beneath the branches of this tree on that morning in 1946 at the dawn of the new world. This year, 1946, Berlin lies in ruins. This year 1946, the newly elected Labour government, clad in belted mackintoshes, thick black-rimmed spectacles and hair slicked down with Brill cream, set out to slay the five monsters of Want, Disease, Squalor, Ignorance and Idleness. Aneurin Bevin worked tirelessly through the night to implement the new National Health Service from his office high above Whitehall in London, the city Macrow left on that evening of blue twilight and gentle rain.

Macrow: *...I believe in the New World we are trying to build together. The sorrows, the inequalities, the barbarities of the old have had their day... '*

Maybe the white washed buildings of the Kintail Ranger Visitor Centre were a farm in Macrow's long ago time. There's a car park here today and the Labradoodle greets my pal L ecstatically, jumping up at her like the puppy she still is at heart. L has driven up from Edinburgh again to do some more of the 'book walks' with me and tick off some remote Munros at the same time. The Labradoodle sniffs the sunny July morning air as we pass Morvich Caravan Club campsite, screened by a tall hedge of Leylandii, adding a touch of suburbia to Kintail. Now I've never stayed there, preferring the more basic site at Dornie. There's just the caravan site at Morvich and a few houses. No hotel you see and when choosing a campsite I usually adhere to my old drinking buddies' D&G's golden rule of campinG That's camping in a tent rather than being being flamboyant and effeminate btw. And what is D&G's golden rule of camping I hear you ask? For the record, it states: 'A Campsite Must *Always* Be Located Within Staggering Distance of a Pub!'

Macrow: *The air was hot and sultry, the field-flowers drooping or dead save for vetch, cow-parsley, buttercups and a few starry-eyed daisies. But already the ling was budding...*

Beyond the birch trees A' Ghlas-bheinn, its steep, grassy flanks riven by deep gullies, rests like a giant's green fist at the end of Strath Croe. We're headed for the sheet of grey-green water that fills a hollow in the flank of A' Ghlas-bheinn and is called Loch a'Chleirich, the loch of the priest.

The road is tarmac now, dust and gravel in 1946. Beyond low bushes of yellow whin the Five Sisters of Kintail shimmer in the June sunshine. Birch and oak trees grasp the white shingle banks of the River Croe. Bluebells shine in the long grass at the edge of the road and the hawthorn in flower.

The track leads through a field. There are cows. Now when I was a child cattle held no fears for me. The cows came down onto the shingle beach at Ardmucknish Bay and waded into the sea. And when the cattle on the machair lay down, my mother said it was going to rain. When we stayed in the old caravan and the sleeping bags leaked feathers and there were midges outside and our clothes smelt of woodsmoke and the sky turned orange–red behind the mountains of Morvern I'd one day climb, cattle held no fear for me. But that was before I got a dog. People tell you cattle can be aggressive around dogs. Just like they tell you farmers shoot dogs for chasing sheep. So now I worry and instead of marching along the path straight through the field of cows, the Labradoodle and I take a long circuitous route around the perimeter of the field. The dog gazes up at me and I think I see a quizzical, mildly exasperated look on her hairy face.

Macrow 1946: *Along the side of the tree-fringed Shiel River, we wandered through a herd of young bulls which looked at us in such a manner as to side-track us for some time from the marked path.*

Dripping with sweat from a long and arduous circumnavigation of the perimeter of the field, in order to give the dreaded cows a wide berth, the Labradoodle and I finally rejoin L at the gate at the far end of the field. L gives me a long-suffering look. She's used to my machinations around fields of live stock on hill walks. But I can't help feeling the look in her eyes says: 'Man Up!' A real climber and his dog would have marched straight through the middle of that field of cows. Still she knows what I'm like and loves me dearly, no doubt, to put up with me. Once safely through the cows I almost immediately started to stress about crossing the field again at the end of the day. I'm a born worrier me. Suppose the cattle have moved? Suppose when we come back they're clustered around one of the gates and we can't get back to the car…

Oh shut up, for fuck's sake!

It's a beautiful summer's morning in the Highlands. Give yourself a slap on the geggie. You deserve one pal!

Amen, sayeth the Labradoodle.

Ahead, streams cut deep gullies and clefts down the flanks of A' Ghlas-bheinn. Back in 1946, it was by climbing up beside one of these gullies that the indefatigable Macrow planned to reach Loch a' Chleirich. The aforementioned loch also being L, the Labradoodle and my objective for today too plus L is kind off ticking off Munros while pretending she's not and refusing to say how many she's done. She's the opposite to me. I've got them all counted down to the last Corbett. Ticked off in the book, carefully checked section by section, scored off in spidery, blue biro five-bar-gates. As we were taught to do in arithmetic in primary three in the stone-built Victorian primary school that still stands on the corner of Dalhousie Terrace and Morningside Road.

One night oot in the van, rattling down Morningside Drive, James is sitting in the passenger seat on his i-phone, texting his girlfriend in France for like the 500th time that day. Makes me remember my ex and I were like that once and now it's all lawyers and money and hatred.

James is 29, dark haired, beard: 'Cos she likes a bit of stubble mate' and I guess I do fancy him a bit and sometimes just sometimes find myself wishing he was gay. James is always telling me about *his* sex life. Sometimes there's like just too much detail bud, I say a smile playing on the edges of my lips. Like when he tells me, 'She gets so wet mate, it takes me ages to come.' And he seems quite interested in *my* sex life too. But I digress, we're mates, no really, bit of an unlikely friendship, I'll give you that. But it works and on Friday nights we skive off early and go for a pint and a game of pool in the pub across the road from the supermarket.

But back to the night oot in the van: we're rattling down Morningside Drive when I make the mistake of saying:

'I used to walk to school along this street, you know.' James looks up from whoever he's messaging on his i-phone now and grins.

THE WILD SWIMMER OF KINTAIL

There's a cheeky look in his blue eyes as he says:
 'Wis it all like horses and carts back then mate?'
 'Fuck off,' I reply and he starts laughinG

Back in Kintail we're heading for A' Ghlas-bheinn so L can tick off another of the Munros she's not counting and I can follow in Macrow's footsteps and visit another of the hill lochs of the parish of Kintail. Except, ah, true confessions time, the naked writer and all that, I have to confess I'm not following exactly in Macrow's footsteps. Like I said, at times over this summer in Kintail I've has the distinct impression I've been following in the footsteps of a mad woman with Amazonian tendencies to boot, the 15 mile 'walk' from Totaig to Glenelg being a case in point.

Back in 1946 Macrow had picked a bit of a crazy route up to Loch a'Chleirich. I'm sure she'd be the first to agree that this was not the best route she could've picked. It does have a certain logic to it when you look at the map though. Following the stream that flows down from Loch a'Chleirich to its source would make for easy navigation and reduce the risk of getting lost if you were not too confident with map and compass which Macrow probably wasn't. There's not much about navigation in *Kintail Scrapbook*, leading me to think that her navigation was a flying by the seat of her pants kind of affair. Like I say though there's a certain logic to her choice of route following the stream straight up the hillside to Loch a' Chleirich but, oh my dear, the contour lines! It seems as though, sitting in the garden of Shepherd's Cottage, studying the Bartholemew's map with its brown hachures and green forests, Macrow appears to have failed to appreciate the implications of lots and lots of contour lines *very* close together. I'll leave the lady to explain in her own words: reading between the lines the problems seem to have begun even before Macrow and her bedraggled Skye terrier Jeannie reached the foot of A' Ghlas-bheinn:

1946: *And now we were plunging through long wet grass, bracken and young pine... I was sticky, breathless and irritable. Flies buzzed incessantly over the swamp, and midges contributed their unwelcome attentions to my perspiring face.*

Things got worse when Macrow and the long suffering Jeannie eventually reached the foot of the mountain.

1946: *Heavens, but that hillside was steep—and wet! The burn frothed down through a fierce gorge, and ...I hope no-one will be 'fooled' by the shortness of the distance to this loch as shown on the map...*

Ah, poor Macrow. We've all been there hen. We feel for you swatting the midges away as the raindrops ran down the back of your neck. 'The epic is always unplanned' as Ralph Storer wrote in his book *The Joy of Hillwalking* before going on to describe a hillwalk in the Mamores that ended up with the group having to abseil down a waterfall.

'Well that looks pretty straightforward,' is a phrase I've learned never to utter. Don't speak those words! The mountain gods are listening and if they're in an ill temper they'll make a burn rise in spate or a dense forest spring up blocking the way just to spite us lesser mortals.

So, learning from bitter experience, me, L and the Labradoodle have opted for the tried and tested route followed by many a would-be Munro bagger up A' Ghlas-bheinn with a minor deviation to vist Loch a' Chleirich. So I hold my hand up and say sorry to all the purists and perfectionists reading this. I confess that hot summer's day I wasn't following print for print in Macrow's footsteps.

The giant fingers of the grey mountain reach out to us. Little red painted signs at junctions and deer gates on stony forest roads steer us on our way. Purple flowers of common butterwort shiver at the edge of the track among the golden stars of yellow tormentil. At the highest point of the path the giant's finger nail rests on the stony track and it is here we strike up the ridge of the grey mountain following a line of old iron fenceposts.

I'm sweating and pull the black headband from the side pocket of my rucksack to stop the perspiration dripping into my eyes. Higher up the angle of the ridge eases, the grass is less tussocky and red-faced I stop to gaze down on the distant blue waters of the sea loch. Below us on the far side of the steep defile of the Allt an Leoid Ghaingamhaich (how's that for a Gaelic tongue twister?) the path to the Falls of Glomach cuts a thin white line along the green and brown hillside.

Macrow: *Behind us, mighty Beinn Fhada shut out the sky, and the white house of Dorusduain lay in a deep, dark hollow.*

From up here the clearing stands out. A handful of tall trees and a patch of green among the dark sea of conifers that washes the foot of A' Ghlas-bheinn are all that remains of the white house of Dorusduain.

The ridge climbs up over slabs and rivers of scree and boulders. From behind a rock a pair of ears and a head poke up. The Labradoodle's had her nose pressed to the ground rather more intently than usual for the last few hundred metres or so. I clip her onto the lead. Precautionary measures I explain to L as the Labradoodle looks up at me, her big brown eyes wells of innocence. I wouldn't touch them you know, says the look on her face. The breeze catches her beard which has gone quite grey over the last couple of years and I reflect she now looks a bit like Gandalf.

Macrow: *Beyond Dorusduain… I saw, on a nearby mountain-side a herd of the rumoured wild goats of Kintail, led by an enormous grey and black Billy with a flowing coat and great horns curving over on to his shoulders.*

A dragonfly whirrs past in the warm summer air. We climb another little rise and suddenly there in a hollow 30 feet below lies the loch of the priest. I scramble down a grassy slope between boulders splashed with orange lichen and the spikey leaves of alpine ladies mantle and wash my face in the cold peaty water.

1946: *Rain was again blurring the surrounding landscape, so we turned northward and, at last, found our loch, a long, bare pool set between grey crags.*

There is alpine ladies mantle, club moss and cowberries among the rocks as we climb up from Loch a' Cleirich making for the summit ridge of A' Ghlas-bheinn where a faint path, a mere scratch on the ridge will lead us north to the rickle of stones marking the summit. I've got my tick, now it's time for L to get hers.

Macrow: *In just under an hour, we were back at the forest fence, and I was drinking out of my mackintosh hat beside the swift stream…I looked at Jeannie, and snapped my fingers—and she wagged the ever-ready tail [and] we set off gaily along the forest trail towards the Kintail Lodge.*

THE WILD SWIMMER OF KINTAIL

For most of our two decades together my ex and I had an open relationship. Open relationships are common among gay men, one special, long-term partner plus other casual partners, just for sex. It tends to be that or serial monogamy. Sometimes open relationships work, sometimes they don't. When I was in my twenties and thirties it seemed unimaginable, that just because I was with someone, I'd never have sex with anyone else, ever again.

Only thing was it always seemed to me that the relationship was more open on my ex's side than it was for me. I can't remember the last time we had sex but I do remember the last threesome we had. It was with a guy called Colin who lived in a towerblock in Leith. I remember it because pretty soon Colin was going to be dead.

It's funny all the stuff you think about when you're out in the hills. Thoughts drift in and out of your head like the mist coming and going on the Five Sisters. I don't know why, it had been a while since I'd heard the news, but for some reason, in my mind's meanderings, climbing down the steep hillside towards the white houses at Morvich, it was Colin's story that suddenly came into my head.

Colin went to the big white high school that stands on concrete stilts in the shadow of the Mamores overlooking the Highland village once destined to be called Aluminiumville. It was 1975 and he was in primary six and it was the last period in the afternoon. At the back of the classroom Colin gazed across at Lachlan Strathearn. The teacher was handing out the reading books, the Norman Conquest, the Spanish Armada and the Battle of Britain. Over the white cliffs, inky black spitfires in dogfights with Messerschmitts, flew off the edge of the page. The textbook took a very Anglo-centric perspective on Britain. Of course this class of ten year olds didn't know that, though their parents' generation was beginning to wake up to the idea of an independent Scotland. This was 1975 after all and a record breaking eleven SNP MPs had just been elected to the Westminster parliament five-hundred-miles to the south. In previous lessons in earlier weeks the children had learned about the Wars of the Roses and Henry VIII but the textbook, published by Blackie and Sons of Glasgow, made no mention of the Robert the Bruce or Mary Queen of Scots.

'Pick up your books please,' said the teacher.

She liked to think she was in the business of putting old heads on young shoulders. No-one suspected that day, in the school among the dripping birch trees what the future held.

'Now turn to chapter twelve,' said the teacher, 'Tomorrow's World. How old will you be in the year 2000?'

Colin was an OK sort of kid, 1975 and it was the last period of the day for the primary sixes. The lesson was Tomorrow's World. But who was to know? Who could know what the future held for these 30 ten year olds? For who can bear to look into the future? It was best they couldn't look into the future because for some of the kids the future would be no child's storybook.

Colin sat at the back. A good thing he had no palantir of Orthanc to see into his short future. Couldn't foresee his fate was the saddest. Working-class, gay-boy from a small Highland community, it was never going to be an easy call in life. At 20 he will move to Edinburgh. Of course he will. Or it could've been Glasgow. But he'll leave the dripping birches and the Grey Mare's Tail waterfall behind.

His mother will take their old shaggy brown sheep dog on the train down to Edinburgh and they'll go for a drink with his friends in the Bow Bar. He'll notice his mum's clothes are covered in dog hairs because she's always cuddling the dog. His new gay Edinburgh friends will look down their noses at his Mum and the dog.

'I hope that's not Colin's mother,' a fat bitchy old queen will say as she pushes open the brass handled, glass half-doors of the pub. But then she loved that old dog. A gay-boy, from a village in the Highlands that narrowly avoided being renamed Aluminiumville, it was never going to be an easy call. Unemployment, the benefits trap, depression, loneliness and Scottish men use alcohol when stressors apply.

In 1975 it was the last period of the day for the primary sixes. The lesson was 'Tomorrow's World.' The teacher was in the business of putting old heads on young shoulders. No-one suspected that day in the school among the dripping birch trees what the future held. That far from Aluminiumville, on the ground floor of a towerblock in Leith, Colin will be found dead at the age of 44, his legs sticking out the lift doors, naked from the waist down with a plastic carrier bag over his head, a victim of homophobic violence.

The Man in the Waterfall

'Have none of you guessed where we are?' said Peter... 'We are in the ruins of Cair Paravel.'
C S Lewis, Prince Caspian, 1951.

Macrow: *The name, 'Iron Lodge', had long fascinated me on the map... Lying well beyond Loch na Leitreach, at the very end of the green glen...*

'No there's no question of it,' said the cheery sounding voice at the end of the phone, '—no question of it at all.'

1946: *I scrambled out of the car, collected Jeannie and the baggage, and tramped over a wooden bridge. The road ended here, only a rough track running on and over the hills to Pait. Behind the white house, a waterfall leapt down the green hillside, and a few silver birches tossed their leaves in the sunlight. The hum of the vanishing car died along the lonely green glen.*

'Health and safety reasons... ' continued the cheery-sounding voice, and I had a brief vision in my mind of the telephone wire leading out the bathroom window in the flat and the exchanges relaying the call across a line of telephone posts beside the A9 to the estate office among the birch trees on the shores of Loch Duich. The cheerful sounding voice at the other end of the phone belonged to Janet. Janet's husband, it turned out, was the estate's gamekeeper, the couple were both employees of the slightly sinister sounding Smech Estates. I couldn't help thinking it sounded a bit like a cover organisation for arch-villain Blofeld in a Bond movie.

'No there's no question of it,' said Janet again after I'd explained I was writing a book retracing the journey of a female poet who spent six months in Kintail in the summer of 1946.

'It's for health and safety reasons. I can't rent out Iron Lodge for a week in July because the building… '

And here Janet paused for effect, ' …is uninhabitable!'

I had kind of guessed that I said, explaining that on a previous hillwalk a few summers back I'd looked through the windows of Iron Lodge and seen plaster had fallen from the ceiling, though the building had clearly been renovated fairly recently.

'Oh yes,' continued Janet, the Sheikh, as she called her employer (rather in the manner the foot soldiers of Al Qaeda once referred to Osama Bin Laden) spent money doing it up when he bought the estate back in the eighties. That AGA I glimpsed through the window is a great machine and a fitted kitchen to die for but with the winters we get up here you know and the house kept getting broken into so at one point they had to board up the windows.

'I'm used to staying in remote bothies,' I persist, 'would the estate give us a key and let us doss in Iron Lodge?'

'Oh no that would be breaching health and safety… '

'No we can't rent you the house at Carnach either.'

Hmmmm. Macrow had considerable difficulty finding accommodation for herself and Jeannie in Kintail in 1946 at the height of the post-war housing crisis. I'm beginning to know how she felt.

'Fair enough,' I said, 'we'll just have to camp outside then.'

Janet was helpful in other ways though, offering to hunt out old photos of Iron Lodge and better still she offered to put me touch with an old gentleman called Ian Mackay who knows something of the family who lived at Iron Lodge in 1946. Now in his eighties he once lived at Pait.

'By Loch Monar? ' I asked, the penny dropping, realising this must be the Iain Mackay who features in Iain R Thomson's classic account of life in a remote Highland glen, *Isolation Shepherd*. A man who lived only a few miles away from Iron Lodge in the 1950s and knew the glen and these hills before the Hydro came. A man who is a living piece of Highland history I reflected as Janet spelt out her e-mail address.

Three months later:

'Are you going to be OK cycling with that?'

L is struggling to haul an enormous rucksack onto her back. When she eventually gets it on it's so big it pushes her head forward so she's walking like Charles Laughton in the Hunchback of Notre Dame.

'What on earth have you got in there? Are you really sure we need two wineboxes?'

'Well it's not like we can just pop out to the shops if we run out of something... '

We're standing beside L's VW Golf in the car park at Killilan where the public road ends at the head of Loch Long. *Private: No Vehicle Access* declares the sign on the stone gate posts. For once we're stealing a march on Macrow in the fitness stakes.

1946: *I had planned to tramp up the whole length of Glen Elchaig and spend a week at the ' Iron Lodge,' discovering the more remote hill-lochs of Kintail but my good neighbour, Mr Ingram, had business in that direction on the day in question, and drove me up in his car.*

'It's a two hour plus cycle on a pretty rough track and most of it's uphill,' I say, pulling on black cycle shorts.

'Can't you get changed behind the car?' she complains, 'I can see

THE WILD SWIMMER OF KINTAIL

your bum.'

I stick my tongue out at her.

'Och, you've seen it all before.'

We roll off down the first mile of road – smooth well-maintained tarmac between moss covered drystone walls and old birch trees – quite the thing, me with my cycle panniers and mountain bike. And L still doing her Charles Laughton impersonation with the giant rucksack jampacked with glamping essentials.

The tarmac ends abruptly and we bump along a stony unsurfaced road, with me fearing for L's spokes. Mind you she's a lot lighter than my 13 stone and I'm carrying loads of crap too (sorry, essential items for camping in a remote location 15 miles from the nearest shop).

For all the slagging he gets I think RyanAir boss Micheal O' Leary did the world a favour with his strict eight kilos of handluggage or you get a £50 surcharge rule. Think how many people he saved from dragging heavy suitcases across airport concourses. They do have shops in foreign parts, you know. You can just buy a pair of those flip flops that tipped you over from 7.9 kilos to 8.1 kilos. Unfortunately, though, we're not flying Ryan Air to Iron Lodge and a certain amount of anxiety about camping in the wilds means our bikes are creaking under the weight of loads of crap. I guess part of the problem here is materialism. Back in 1946, Macrow didn't have half the stuff we encumber ourselves with today. She was happy at Iron Lodge with just her old overcoat and disintegrating walking boots and Jeannie and the collie dogs and Bonkie and Snookie the cats, and not a lot else.

We stop to fix a rear reflector that's pinged off L's bike and drink a long drink of cold water while gazing down Glen Elchaig at the black witch's hat of Carnan Cruineachd standing guard over the Falls of Glomach. A herd of shaggy Highland cattle stare curiously at us through long matted fringes.

Macrow: Looking back along the glen, we saw Loch na Leitreach lying at the foot of fierce Carnan Cruineachd, and the yellow road running away back towards Killilan.

We set off again, me ringing the bell on my bike to clear sheep from the track and suddenly feeling very 1940s. There's something a bit camp about a bicycle bell. There's something of the legendary Edinburgh school teacher Jean Brodie about a bicycle bell. High up the steep-sided glen a large herd of deer graze on the hillside. The track's heavy going now and we've been pushing the bikes for the past five minutes. L is looking a bit pink and drips of sweat are running down my back.

After what seems an age we reach Loch na Leitreach at the far end of which stands the lonely white house at Carnach, once the nearest neighbours to Iron Lodge. A gentle downhill bump bump bump rattle rattle rattle, more sheep, a last push uphill and then, there below us lies Iron Lodge.

1946: Mrs. Munro met me at the gate, seeming really delighted with the few red roses I had brought her from my wild garden. She was young, slim and fair-haired, and Jeannie and I felt at once at home.

But at the end of the second decade of the twenty-first century, there is no-one to welcome us to Iron Lodge. Only the deer grazing high on the hillside and the starlings nesting in the broken drainpipe at the back of the house, only the wind in the grass, only the lonely hills that stand silently all around.

In our whole three days at Iron Lodge we will not speak to another living soul. This is a glen deserted. The house sits on the far side of

THE WILD SWIMMER OF KINTAIL

a gorge spanned by a concrete bridge with gates and a rusty, illegible sign. The house lies between two streams and what makes Iron Lodge unique among the lonely houses of Scotland, what makes it one of the special places in the world is the white waterfall that cascades down the hillside behind the house.

But the house is sad and neglected. At the back, large sheets of harling have fallen off exposing bare brickwork. The house has such a beautiful situation but is so neglected. No-one cares for Iron Lodge now, least of all the Sheikh in his faraway land. A few more winters and the roof will be gone.

The house stands in a meadow. Yellow buttercups, tormentil, common butterwort and white tufts of bog cotton shiver in the breeze. A pink orchid stands proudly erect among the long grass and rushes. Across the meadow, behind the house is the waterfall and it is this waterfall and the deep pool below it that give Iron Lodge its magic.

Our bikes rest side by side against the red, fuel oil tank that stands rusting at the gable end of the house. Iron Lodge and the house at Carnach are painted in the same estate colours (maroon and white) as the still-maintained buildings we cycled past, further down the glen, at Killilan. I plan to pitch my one-man, green tent, a veteran of many a wild camping trip in the long grass, well away from the house. I don't want slates raining down on me in the night if the wind gets up and besides the whole place has a Scooby Doo spookiness to it. If the creepy caretaker guy turns up L will have to deal with it. She's the brave one after all. I'm just a big Jessie me.

My sister asked, 'Are you going to do that thing where you stick different coloured stickers on bits of furniture and DVDs?' We didn't, though I did compile an inventory, complete with comments on the condition, origin and estimated value of the contents of the flat me and my ex had shared for more than ten years. Stuff accumulated over nearly two decades of being married to someone who worked in a department store. Some of the entries in the inventory were a little tongue in cheek. It was the writer in me coming out I guess. In the darkest days of the fight against AIDS we learned to use humour as a weapon and it's one I rely on still in difficult times. What follows is a selection of entries from the divorce list, just to give a wee flavour of it. I suppose it's like a gift list gone over to the dark side. Anyway here it is:

The Divorce List
1. One sofa *Comments:* needs cleaned P*
5. Wicker dogbasket and occupant (asleep)
12. Twenty-year-old Raleigh mountain bike. *Comments:* brakes don't work.
17. Blanket chest *Comments:* dog likes to sit on this, bucket rake, needs re-upholstered
39. NintendoWii… pls take this item. I don't want it.
6. Art-deco cocktail cabinet… antique… third party gift.
23. 1 x dogbed… occupant snoozing, condition: smelly P*
24. Coal scuttle… rusty… hole in bottom…
47. 3 x houseplants… unhealthy… wedding present?
51. Toaster… fire hazard…15+ years old…

I don't think my ex saw the funny side of it.
Suppose there was the £300,000 Edinburgh flat too but we won't go there this trip.

*P = purchased during civil partnership

'Hmmm, not greatest camping place is it? Is it any drier over there? This bits awfy boggy… '

'I'm going to put my tent here,' says L.

'It's a bit close to mine'

L raises an eyebrow.

So?'

'Well it's just you'll hear me snoring and grinding my teeth and shouting out in my sleep,' I reply. Truthfully – must be my guilty conscience about murdering my ex and burying him under the patio like happened to Trevor Jordache in the 1980s Channel 4 soap Brookside – only kidding hah!

'I'm a sound sleeper,' she says.

'And farting… '

She shrugs.

'You might hear me having a wank.'

This is true too. You get horny after a day hillwalking. It's something to do with your bits shoogling about all day plus the fresh air and exercise and blood flow and all that.

'Oh, for fuck's sake,' she says and drags her tent out of hearing distance.

This Tree

This solitary old birch tree stands in the yard in front of Iron Lodge. This tree must have stood looking down the glen for all these long years. This tree must have seen Macrow come and go and leave Iron Lodge for the last time, never to return. This tree must have seen the ghillies bring a stag down from the hill. This tree must have seen the rain sweeping across the glen. This old tree must have seen the storms roll in from the sea. This tree must have seen the ice melt. This tree must have seen the bracken turn. This old tree must have seen the stalker tether his pony on his way home from the hill. This tree must have seen the winter snows and the brown swirling leaves of autumn, the first snowdrops of spring and the wildflower meadows of summer. This tree must have seen the last family leave the glen. This tree must have seen the van, packed up with their belongings, rattle off down the hill towards Carnach. This old tree must have heard the noise of the engine fade. This old tree must have felt the silence fall all around. This tree must have listened to the voice of the waterfall all its life. This tree must have seen Jeannie skipping around the yard. This tree must have seen Macrow open the door of Mr Ingram's car. This tree must have seen the yellow light of Mr Munro with his lantern come back from checking the sheep. This tree must have heard the banter of the workies hired by the Sheikh to fix up the Iron Lodge. This tree must have seen the house fall quickly back into disrepair. This tree must have seen the seasons come and the seasons go. This tree must have seen the swallows arrive and watched them leave. This tree must have seen us wheel our bikes down the stony track and across the bridge to Iron Lodge. This tree will watch us leave. This tree will hear the silence fall.

THE WILD SWIMMER OF KINTAIL

We scramble down between foxgloves, thistles and rushes to where the roots of the silver birches grasp the steep bank of the stream to wash the dishes. We slither across round boulders a few metres upstream to fetch drinking water. When the sun comes out I cross the meadow behind the house and strip off and wash myself in the clear pool beneath the white waterfall. While I'm standing there naked under the torrent of water I have sense of folk bathing in this pool in years gone by, long before the man in the waterfall came.

Before it gets dark I walk around the perimeter fence that encloses the house and the meadow. I close two rickety old gates just in case the herd of Highland cattle that roam freely along Glen Elchaig get in and trample our tents and gear while we're up the hills. It would be a bit *Dads Army* if we got back to find the tents flattened and the supplies trashed by muddy hooves and OK I'd probably be pretty Captain Mainwaring about it, going apoplectic and purple in the face. Or worse still: trampled by a hoof on the head while asleep in my tent because, like I said before, I'm a born worrier. Anyway I shut the gates and the cattle stayed on the far side of the glen the whole time we were there.

There's a photo of me. A diffident look on my face standing hands in pockets on the front step of Iron Lodge where Macrow must have stood as Mrs Munro came out, wiping her hands on her pinny, to greet her that first, bright morning in 1946.

Across the meadow behind the house, the white waterfall cascades from a leafy gorge, down into a dark peaty pool. Beyond the waterfall a path climbs the brae behind the house. This is the hill track that once led to Benula Lodge. This is the hill road that mounted swiftly up the brown brae that sunny morning long ago. Its eastern end now drowned beneath the shallow, grey waters of Loch Mullardoch. This is the hill track Macrow stumbled down, hardly able to walk on her way back from climbing Sgurr na Lapaich. This is the meadow

Jeannie ran joyfully across and wriggled under the fence to greet Macrow, back from the high hills at last.

'Shall we have a look inside?' says L.

Like I said, she's the brave one.

'It's all locked up and Janet at the estate office said we couldn't go in.'

I've always been the cautious one.

I place my hand on the cold, metal door handle of Iron Lodge. The handle turns and the door swings open with a creak. Despite all Janet's protestations the Iron Lodge is unlocked. I push the door wide open and enter the house. From down the years I can feel Macrow at my shoulder. The door swings opens to reveal a small porch and two rusty electric mains switches. A door on the left is ajar and what looks like a small scullery with a 1980s type sink unit. The floorboards have been torn up and the joists are exposed. Beige vinyl, of a pattern that was popular around the time the Pet Shop Boys were singing about Suburbia, is torn up in a heap in the corner.

Another door leads into the kitchen where the splendid, double-ovened Aga I glimpsed through the window, on my way back from climbing one of the An Socachs, sits quietly rusting. The house is cold and damp. I breathe in the fousty smell of wet plaster and soot. There is an electric hob with two rusty rings built into the laminate worktop. A pane of glass is missing from one of the kitchen windows and a piece of hardboard has been jammed behind the handle to keep out the rain. The piece of hardboard flaps in the breeze as the wind rattles the windows of Iron Lodge.

In a panelled alcove there's a bench and a ringmarked wooden table. And it's here we'll sit in the evening as dusk falls over the hills. I'll pour a dram from my plastic waterbottle of Glenlivet and we'll sit here in the freezing kitchen of the house. Me with my woolly hat on, as the rain batters at the windows and the wind rattles the glass in the rotting window frames. My headtorch casting shadows on the walls. While outside on the steep, grassy hillside behind the house, the deer see the faintlight that gleams once more in the window of the kitchen of Iron Lodge.

It was in this kitchen that Macrow sat and chatted with Mrs Munro in the long evenings by the fire. As I sit there in my Rab down jacket, all Macrow's tales of the firelight and the stove and the warmth and cosiness of the Iron Lodge of 1946 run through my head, because the Iron Lodge of today is a cold, chilly, haunted kind of place.

Through the kitchen is the hall, still carpeted (red of course) and a flight of stairs leading to the upper floor of the house. A door stands ajar. An empty room, in the corner of the ceiling the lathe is exposed and fragments of plaster dangle in the air. More triangles of white plaster are scattered across the corner of the room by the fireplace. It looks like in some long ago winter, a pipe froze. Then as the ice melted and out in the yard, beneath the old birch tree the first white snow drops shivered in the breeze from Sgurr nan Ceathramhnan, the pipe burst and water cascaded down from the bathroom upstairs. Until the tank in the attic was empty.

This poor old house is so neglected. The Sheikh probably doesn't come to Scotland more than once a year. As I look around at the dereliction of Iron Lodge, it makes me think of the beggars under blankets in Sauchiehall Street and the man who sleeps in an orange survival bag on a bench in Regent Road Gardens and the Sheikh walking the marbled corridors of his palace far faraway.

'Uninhabitable!'

I can hear Janet's voice on the phone from the estate office on the shores of Loch Duich. She was right about that anyway. Uninhabitable is a pretty accurate assessment of the present-day condition of Iron Lodge.

But not so uninhabitable we can't come inside of an evening and sit round the table just like Macrow did seven decades ago. Look out the windows of the kitchen of Iron Lodge. See the deer grazing on the steep, grassy hillside outside pause and lift their heads, sensing the presence of people in the derelict building beside the waterfall.

L hangs her soggy paramo jacket from a brass light fitting on the wall of the empty room with the fallen ceiling. There are ashes in the fireplace and a section of chipboard torn from one of the Banarama-era fitted kitchen units. Someone's had a fire in here. We try not to think about who. Then I see Macrow walk across to the window and rub the condensation off the glass with the sleeve of her cardigan, then gaze out at the rain sweeping across Glen Elchaig. And Mrs Munro sitting in the armchair by the fire with her knitting, the Iron Lodge is all ghosts now.

Now I'm really wishing I'd brought the Labradoodle with me but she's not very good at riding a bike yet, still needs stabilisers I tell folk. But this too is true to following in Macrow's footsteps, because she sometimes left Jeannie at home before setting off on her longest stravaiges. At least if we had the dog with us her barking would give us warning of the return of the itinerant, wandering tramp who lit the fire in the front room of Iron Lodge and left the empty vodka bottles and ashtray full of roaches in the kitchen. I hope it's not the scary looking guy in the leather coat carrying a plastic shopping bag that the Doodle and I once spent a long wait on the platform of Corrour station with.

'I'm really glad we brought the tents,' I say, 'I wouldnae fancy sleeping in here.'

'Uninhabitable is the word that springs to mind,' replies L looking around at the ruins of Iron Lodge.

Then she drags two of the wooden chairs from the kitchen outside and we sit on the grass in the sunshine by the tents and watch the starling feeding its nest of young at the top of the broken drainpipe.

THE WILD SWIMMER OF KINTAIL

Before it gets dark we climb the creaky staircase that leads to the upper floor of Iron Lodge. That creepy caretaker's going to appear at any minute for sure. The flood damage is worse in the bathroom with its early George Michael rose-coloured bathroom basin. In one of the bedrooms a dressing table's been left behind, one drawer pulled out and lying on the carpet. I look in the mirror at the stubbly, unshaven face with black rings under the eyes that gazes back at me and think of Mickey Bell.

Later that night I twist the cap off my waterbottle. I pour a dram into a plastic cup and take a sip of Glenlivet and as the shadows lengthen outside the years start to fall away, spinning back in time to 1946. Macrow sits by the fire, Jeannie chases the two cats Bonkie and Snookie. They're all the ghosts of Iron Lodge now. All ghosts. All gone. But I sense that in some parallel universe the animals at Iron Lodge are still there playing together while the cat casts a cold yellow eye from its perch on the window sill.

Outside a blatter of rain of rain rattles the window and the square of hardboard over the broken pane of glass flaps in the wind. Shadows creep down the steep slopes of Sgurr na h-Eige where the track to Loch Mullardoch climbs the hillside behind the Iron Lodge. It will be dark soon. I twist the cap off the waterbottle again and pour another two fingers of Glen Livet into a plastic cup and slide it across the table to L.

'Do you want to hear a ghost story?'

Her eyes look expectantly up at me.

Well, it all started at the book launch of *The Making of Mickey Bell*. I'd invited several old school friends and word got round as it does and on the night another friend of a friend from school, Al Smith shall we call him, turned up. The book launch was in September and still the Edinburgh summer lingered onto into an autumn of blue skies. We had a great night and a piano accordion player and I said how pleased I was so many folk had turned out to give *Mickey* a good send off out into the world.

A few weeks after the book launch party, it was into October by now, Al Smith shall we call him, got in touch. He'd very much enjoyed my first novel, he said and could we meet up for a pint and a chat about *The Making of Mickey Bell* and oh yes he'd like me to sign a copy.

A cold night in early November, we were sat nursing pint glasses at a table by the fire in the Barony Bar in Broughton Street. The tall windows looked out on to Broughton Place and the Georgian houses of the New Town. The hands on the clock on the wooden panelling above the fireplace said ten to seven and the flames flickered and were reflected in the pub mirrors hanging above the yellow-white Victorian tiles and green dado rail.

Al was telling me one of the reasons he enjoyed *Mickey Bell* so much was because some the book is set in Assynt in the far north-west of Scotland.

'Aye, it's grand area. I once spent three weeks house-sitting and looking after the post office in Stoer,' I told him.

It turned out Al spent a lot of time at nearby Drumbeg in the late 1990s.

'That bit in the book, when Mickey gets queerbashed outside the Wheelhouse Bar in Lochinver. It never happened you know,' I explained, 'It was just an amalgam of when I was in the Drumbeg Hotel one night with two gay mates and we overheard a couple of the local rough boys saying 'Look at those poofs – let's give them a doing,' and the time Donald Quested kicked me in the face beside the railings by the tennis courts at the foot of Ettrick Road, after a teenage party. He was wearing black Doc Marten shoes, I remember, my nose has never been the same since.'

Donald Quested was one of the bad boys at secondary school.

THE WILD SWIMMER OF KINTAIL

'He was a wanker,' said Al.

The firelight flickered in the the Victorian tiles and the conversation and the evening moved on.

A Friday night a week or two before Christmas. I was oot in the van. I'd just done a delivery to the Old Coach House deep in the countryside near Romanno Bridge. I was stopped in the dark, narrow, tree-lined lane leading up to the house from the main road, checking the paperwork for my next delivery when I heard the van assessor's voice in my head:

'You're losing points on engine idling time. Always switch the engine off when you're stopped for more than two minutes.'

I turned the key in the ignition and the Mercedes diesel engine died. Silence fell. Just the creak of the branches of the tall, old, pines out there in the dark.

Bzzzz! My phone went off. A text. From Al Smith:

'You'll take no pleasure in hearing this I know but... '

I read the words on the screen in the dark.

'Donald Quested's Dead!'

'Fuck me! What happened to him?' I texted back.

'Dunno,' came the reply (by now I was somewhere on the road near Leadburn) 'It was sudden like, a few weeks back. My sister saw the obituary. She looks at that kind of shit.'

Now Friday night's a busy night at work. There's always pressure to get back for the Labradoodle lying in her basket by the Rayburn, home alone. So pretty soon I'd forgotten all about Donald Quested and the texts.

My last drop that night was in Midmar Gardens, to an old lady living alone in one of the vast houses that border Blackford Hill. It was a damp, murky night and a light drizzle of rain was falling as the old woman locked and bolted her front door and I loaded the last of the empty green crates into the back of the van. Nine o' clock on a

Friday night, the street was deserted.

'Which way is it to the Inch, mate?' said a voice.

Suddenly from out of nowhere there was a young guy in a shellsuit standing behind me. Where the fuck did he come from?

'It's miles away… you'll need to get a bus mate,' I said pointing in the direction of Morningside Road.

'Are you going that way? Can you no' take me?' the youth asked. He had a murderous prettiness about him that was disconcertingly familiar but I couldn't place where I'd seen him before. But I thought it was long ago. It must have been long ago.

'Sorry, mate I'm not allowed to take passengers in the van,' I said pulling down the roller shutter door at the rear of the van with a bang.

And when I turned round he was gone, disappeared back into the night.

It wasn't until I was back home, sitting next to the Rayburn with the Labradoodle curled up at my feet that I suddenly shivered, as the realisation dawned, I must have seen a ghost, because the young guy with the murderous prettiness about him who'd appeared out of the night at the back of the van in Midmar Gardens, he was the absolute double of Donald Quested.

The Motorcycle Summer

O wad some Pow'r the giftie gie us
To see oursels as ithers see us!
                                   Robert Burns, 1786.

Macrow 1946: *I decided, on impulse, to try the long, circular tramp over to Loch Cruoshie and back by Coire nan Each. We set off without further delay, as the day was already well-advanced.*

The gate clangs shut behind us as we leave Iron Lodge in the bright sunshine of a July morning and set out along the track north. L and me, heading for Loch Mhoicean, Loch Cruoshie and Loch na Maoile Bhuidhe, three hill lochs situated in a vast tract of wild and remote country between Loch Mullardoch and Loch Monar. Ever the optimist I also plan to bag the Corbett Beinn Dronaig which rises to the north of Loch Cruoshie. We've allowed a long summer's day for three hill lochs and a Corbett. What could possibly go wrong?

Like I said what could possibly go wrong? After all Macrow had done this walk on her first afternoon at Iron Lodge, setting out when: 'the day was already well-advanced.' Ah, how I love the 1940s use of hyphens. I don't think my editor would bother hyphenating well-advanced today. But we shall see.

As I say, Macrow had done this walk in an afternoon. A wee look at the map while sat at the table in the chilly kitchen of Iron Lodge the night before had given me some cause for concern though. Firstly and unsurprisingly, this was a Brenda walk after all and I knew what to expect by now. It looked like a long way. A very long way. Macrow's 'long tramp' also involved crossing both the Allt a'Chreachail Mhóir and the Allt Lòin-fhiodha. The latter, if the Ordnance Survey were to be believed, looked like a fairly wide river. I was anxious, with the weather turning unsettled, there was the possibility in the event of sudden heavy rain we could end up trapped between the two rivers, unable to get back to Iron Lodge. Like I said I'm a born worrier.

Still, the sun was shining as we tramped up the dirt track road that leads from Iron Lodge to Pait at the head of Loch Monar. It was south across the loch that Iain R Thomson looked over to the lights of Pait in *Isolation Shepherd*. Somewhere I've always wanted to go but have never been. Yet.

I wrote this in December with the Rayburn lit and the lights of the Christmas tree twinkling in the bay window as dusk fell on Edinburgh. I looked at the photos I took in the summer and it all looks so green and bright. Sometimes in Scotland as the shortest day, the winter solstice draws near, it's hard to believe summer will ever come again and I wondered if the Iron Lodge lies blanketed in snow.

The rough track skirts the lower slopes of Aonach Buidhe on its way up to lonely Loch Mhoicean. This is wild and remote country.

1946: Our path was now running close to the Allt na Doire Gairbhe, which flowed through a miniature gorge flanked with alder trees and ferns.

There's rhododendron growing in the gorge too, though Macrow doesn't mention it. We've gained some height now. We pause and look back and there is Macrow's view, just as she describes it on page 119 of *Kintail Scrapbook*.

1946: There, in the distance, lay the blue expanse of Loch na Leitreach, with the black peak of Carnan Cruineachd beyond...

The track has dwindled to a footpath, a ribbon of white across the grassy flank of Aonach Buidhe and here is our first hill loch of

THE WILD SWIMMER OF KINTAIL

the day, Loch Mhoicean. Hoof prints mingle with our bootprints in the sandy soil on the path by the lochside. The sun's out though the breeze is cool. Loch Mhoicean has a little sandy bay at one end and from the wild swimmer's point of view, looks to be one of the more inviting of Macrow's hill lochs. More inviting than the murky peaty waters of Loch an t-Sabhail anyway, where I heard the strange bellowing noise coming from the nearby peat hags.

A kilometre or so north of Loch Mhoicean the path reaches the head of the pass at a cairn and the green bowl of Coire Each lies below. The stony track ends here. An old, grassy stalkers' path leads downhill following each twist and bend of the Allt Coire nan Each. Through long-abandoned but still green fields, their boundaries marked by mossy, overgrown dykes and down past the ruins of the cottage where the Mackay family once lived. Yellow tormentil and white flags of bog cotton in the long grass which must once have provided lush, rich grazing. The land around here utterly abandoned in the 60 years since the hydro came.

Further down Coire Each the path draws close to the stream. OMG! Macrow didn't half tramp a long way. It's nearly one o' clock and we're less than halfway around the 19 kilometre circle. The morning sunshine is gone and cloud is rolling in from the Atlantic. Little wisps of mist are brushing the top of Lurg Mor and now Beinn Dronaig too. I'm faced with the dawning realisation that, added to a Macrow stravaig, there's nae chance of climbing Beinn Dronaig and getting back to Iron Lodge before nightfall. Nae chance at all. And I'm still worried about crossing the bloomin' Allt Lòin-fhiodha. Like I said, I'm walking in the footsteps of a mad woman.

The rustling, fluttering noise from behind the dressing table in the front bedroom, had been there all morning at the back of my mind, scrabbling away. In fact I'd been aware of the noise since I got back to the Victorian tenement flat, 48 hours earlier. I thought it was the mice at first. It wasn't until I saw a flutter of movement behind the ventilator grill in the skirting board behind the dressing table that I finally realised there must be a bird trapped behind the boarded up fireplace. Flown down from the sunlight on the roof, down and down

I fetched a screwdriver. The trapped bird fell silent as I removed the screws that attached the ventilator grill to the skirting board. Then I shut all the doors in the hall (because this happened once before ages ago) and opened the front door. While I was out of the room I heard the ventilator grill clatter on to the floor as the bird escaped, fluttering sootily around the bedroom.

I took shelter behind the glass door in the sitting room with the dog, while the starling, for a young starling it turned out to be, scrabbled at the Venetian blinds in the bedroom, seeking to reach the daylight behind the glass.

Then the bird flew out into the hall and after perching briefly on the wooden picture rail a foot or so below the ceiling, it sensed the sunlight and fresh air from the street and flew straight out the front door. I opened the sitting room door and still clutching the screwdriver in my hand, ran out the front door and down the steps that lead to the garden gate and looked up towards the roof of the tenement. Then I saw the trapped bird and its companion flying across the road to the rooftops on the other side of the street, tweeting joyous, alarm calls of relief.

'Kellan MacInnes!'

He was standing by his trolley in jeans and blue polo shirt.

'Kellan MacInnes,' he said again.

I couldn't have seen him for nigh on 20 years but my mind spooled back to the summer we rode round the Highlands on his motorbike.

THE WILD SWIMMER OF KINTAIL

To that hot day when I still wish we'd jumped off the end of the pier naked.

He still had that boyish charm and enthusiasm I liked. And I wondered? Did releasing the bird from its dark and sooty prison behind the boarded up fireplace somehow revive this long forgotten, old friendship and release it, out into the sunshine again? I looked at the lines on his face. I saw him glance at me a couple of times searchingly, as if he could see the virus under my skin. Shopping in Morrisons, so he couldn't be rich, he never became an architect in the end he told me. He built his own house though. He waved as he drove off in a 53 plate car. Though he must be late forties now and told me he had two kids of six and nine, like the bird flying free into the blue sky, we two boys were free in the sunshine of the motorcycle summer.

The path continues on and on down Coire Each then begins to fade as it climbs the shoulder of An Cruachan. So we follow vehicle tracks that continue by the side of the stream. The paths marked on the map in this part of the world are very faint and very, very old. Once again we're well into the Ordnance Survey's equivalent of 'Here Be Mermaids.'

Cursing Brenda under my breath, I press on. L is flagging and a long way behind. The much worried about Allt Lòin-fhiodha is low and turns out to be a bit of a pussy as my mate James the van driver would say. We get across without even getting our feet wet. But it would be un-crossable in wet weather – completely – don't even think about trying to do this walk in bad weather. But you see dear reader, unlike Macrow I'm going to be sending you round the circle anti-clockwise, so you will come to the potentially un-crossable river first.

Once across the river though, it proves near impossible to find the path on the other side and soon we're wading through boggy moorland and cursing Macrow with every squelchy step we take. The ground around the Allt Lòin-fhiodha is a notorious bog, I later discover when reading up on the walk. General Monck is reputed to have lost 100 baggage horses here in 1654 and you can see how it might've happened! Eventually I spot the path skirting the edge of the hillside on drier ground around the 270 metre contour line and then, at last, Loch Cruoshie hoves into view.

> Macrow: *There are no trees around Loch Cruoshie… It has several tiny islands and a hint of golden sand; and we found some old cottages and ruins along the shore. The wind freshened as we took our tea, and puffy, sunlit clouds rolled in soft billows across the sky.*

We hasten towards the cheery sight of the white-painted, gable end of a well-maintained cottage at the west end of the loch as the cloud spills down over Beinn Dronaig and we feel the first drops of rain carried on the wind.

A line of rusty iron fence posts marches along the edge of the loch, on the boundary of the Parish of Kintail and there is Macrow's hint of golden sand by the loch. The ruined cottages where Macrow took her tea are now surrounded by a deer fence, there are well-established silver birch, Scots pine, and rowan, planted as a windbreak. But it's not the trees that really interest me, it's the deer fence itself. While the wire mesh looks newish the rusty, iron posts supporting it are unusual, most deer fences you come across on the hills are supported by wooden posts. Oh crikey he's going on about fenceposts now, I hear you say. Let's go play a video game. But bear with me for a few more sentences because I'm wondering if the rusty, iron fenceposts were once part of William Winnans deer fence. Winnans was an

THE WILD SWIMMER OF KINTAIL

eccentric American railroad tycoon who paid a lot of money to rent the Killilan estate in the 1880s. He had apparently limitless funds and was so incensed by the way deer from his estate wandered far and wide he constructed a fence that stretched from Killilan to Loch Monar. Iain R Thomson who was the shepherd at nearby Strathmore recalls that Winnans fence was still standing in the 1950s.

But could these iron fence posts have lasted from the 1880s to the 2020s? When the Ballachulish branch line, a long lost spur of the West Highland line was constructed in the early 1900s, the Caledonian Railway Company provided many miles of livestock fences. The original iron railings on bridges and at stations can still be seen to this day. So I guess it's possible some of the railroad tycoon's fence could have lasted into the second decade of the twenty-first century.

And billionaire Americans still own large chunks of Scotland today. Think only of Donald Trump, accompanied by his piper on the sand dunes on the Menie Estate he owns in Aberdeenshire. In many ways the history of the Killilan Estate over the last 150 years encapsulates all that is wrong with the pattern of land ownership in Scotland. Purchased by Colonel Wills of the tobacco dynasty in the mid-nineteenth century the estate was then leased to William Winnans, an American railroad tycoon and is today owned by Smech Properties Ltd, a company registered in the tax haven of Guernsey and owned by Sheikh Mohammed bin Rashid al Maktoum, the King of Dubai and Prime Minister of the United Arab Emirates. The Sheikh is one of the richest men in the world and he likes to bring his extended family to the Scottish Highlands to enjoy the cool summers.

The well-maintained, white-painted cottage the gable end of which was such a friendly, welcoming sight from the east end of Loch Cruoshie turns out to be a bothy, Maol-buidhe, maintained by the Mountain Bothies Asssociation, where we seek shelter from the rain to eat our sandwiches. There were only ruins here in 1946.

Inside, the bothy has recently been done up. The upstairs attic bedroom looks cosy and is reached by a steep wooden staircase. The front room is newly panelled and there is a fireplace and logs, a blackened frying pan and two teapots that look like they might have survived Chernobyl.

Maol-bhuidhe is one of the remotest habitable buildings in Scotland. Perhaps it was once a summer shielinG It is not marked on General Roy's eighteenth-century map of the Highlands whereas the hamlets of Killilan and Camus-luinie are. The lonely cottage at Maol-bhuidhe was the nearest neighbour to Pait Lodge and Strathmore five miles to the north-east on the shore of Loch Monar, two settlements made famous in Iain R Thomson's classic book about remote Scottish rural life *Isolation Shepherd*. Strathmore and around 60 other houses would be consumed by the development of Loch Monar for hydro-electricity in the 1950s.

In 1946 the house at Maol-bhuidhe was abandoned and uninhabitable and lay in this state until the late 1960s when the Mountain Bothies Association took over the upkeep of the cottage from Killilan estate. Ten children were born in the house between 1874 and 1893 when shepherd Halbert Renwick and his wife Mary lived at Maol-bhuidhe. I guess there wasn't much to do.

All too soon though, we must close the door of this cheery, welcoming cottage and strike on, back to the chilly, dereliction of Iron Lodge. The Allt a'Chreachail Mhóir, the stream immediately outside the bothy might well be difficult to cross in spate but a good landrover track continues beyond the ford. Once over the stream we continue, in the rain, on the landrover track, through heather, flagged white with tufts of bog cotton, in search of the third and final hill loch of the day, Loch na Maoile Buidhe. The rutted track climbs gently uphill. I stop at the top of the rise and look back down to the white cottage at Maol Buidhe and the rain sweeping over the grey surface of Loch Cruoshie and the low cloud flattening the top of Beinn DronaiG I wonder when the next people to visit the bothy will come. The little white cottage stands waiting in the mist.

A Monday morning, early in April: I was headed for Oban but thinking I'd check out some old haunts on the way. I was headed to Oban for a meet the author event, the second leg of my book tour. It was optimistically entitled 'The Making of Mickey Bell Book Tour.'

'Where are you appearing?' folk asked.

'Well, not exactly the SSE Hydro. I've got Aviemore Community Centre in June and I was supposed to be going to Loch Stooshie only they pulled out saying they wanted to concentrate on their community cheese making project instead. Only I suspect it's because they didnae like the rude bits in my books, the bits about willies going up bums if you ken what I mean.'

This happens quite often, you see. I'll approach an organisation somewhere remote in the Highlands, ask if they'd like me to come and talk about my book. The initial response, often from someone English and/or newly moved to the area, is enthusiastic.

'Oh yes we'd love you to come!'

But then there's a long gap between e-mails. I chase it up and there's now a problem about the dates. Or:

'We don't think they'll be much of a turn out.'

Or:

'It's a long way for you to come.'

Or:

'We can't afford your travelling expenses.'

You see, I know the signs now. They're trying to get out of it.

In these wee places there's always a committee that runs the book festival or the village hall or whatever and often the local minister or priest is on the committee and when it comes up at the meeting in the village hall that someone's invited that Kellan Macinnes it's like:

'Have you looked at his website Marjorie? Have you read his book? Well we can't have that kind of thing going on in Loch Stooshie now can we?'

Macrow: *Soon we found Loch na Maoile Buidhe—The Loch of the Yellow Promontory—a bare, heart-shaped pool.*

Hoods up in the rain, on we go, down past boulders capped with sphagnum moss and the lichen encrusted stones of a tumbled-down sheep fank. Out the far, far, farthest corner of my eye I can see my old dog Cuilean, a small, brown shadow following us down the hillside, a brown shadow in the corner of my eye that I can't quite see. But walking down the hillside I know she's there, an invisible presence, always at my heel.

Beside the track I see every one of the wild flowers Macrow described 75 years ago: 'the sundew... red and sticky among black peat...' the orchids, the saxifrage and the serpent grass. We cross the 'landslide of scree' mentioned by Macrow in 1946 before at last we see the tents and the white house of Iron Lodge.

1946: *In record time, I was down in the glen, across the bridge, over the threshold of the clean white house by the rushing fall. I was greeted by a welcoming smile from my hostess, a firm hand-shake from her husband, and a rapturous welcome from a collie puppy called Morag...*

Now I'm reading this and wondering what on earth the Munros

must have made of the mad Englishwoman who had descended upon them. Surely they must have been a bit anxious about what Macrow was getting up to on some of Scotland's highest and remotest mountains? Poor Mrs Munro probably had enough to do around the croft without worrying about whether the mad Sassenach had twisted her ankle on the top of Sgurr nan Ceathramhnan!

Though she didn't realise it, during the time Macrow spent at Iron Lodge with the Munro family, she was witness to a way of life that had existed in the Highlands for hundreds and hundreds of years. But that way of life was on the point of dying out. It would not be long before the Iron Lodge was abandoned. Once the nearby glens were flooded by the hydro, the support network that made crofting viable in remote areas (the neighbours to help out with shared community tasks like harvesting and sheep shearing) collapsed. Iain Mackay, in another life in the early 1950s, once lived at Pait Lodge at the head of Loch Monar. Writing in 2004 he called the flooding of the glens: 'The Last Highland Clearance.'

1946: *Supper followed—stew, oatcakes, scones and crowdie, with as much tea as I could drink. Jeannie was finally persuaded to take a dish of brose and some scraps of meat...*

The rain has stopped by the time we finally get back to the Iron Lodge and there is some evening sunshine while I crouch beside the tent preparing my standard backpackers meal. I'm not one of those folk who go in for complex cooking on a tiny, camping gas stove. You just know it's going to pour with rain halfway through or the wind will drop and clouds of midges gather and spoil your carefully laid culinary plans. Nope I always do the same basic meal:

Back Packers Banquet
Served Alfresco
Starter:
John West tinned crab with buttered oatcakes

Main Course:
Curry flavoured instant noodles from the Chinese supermarket, just add boiling water

Look What We Found Lancashire Hotpot in a foil bag. Snip the corner off and squeeze into pan. Ready in 2 minutes and far cheaper than Tiso's climbers' meals

Dessert:
Morrisons individual steamed pudding. Just prick the foil lid with a fork and boil* it for 5 minutes. It says like 25 minutes on the instructions but believe me if you're hungry after a day on the hills it'll be perfectly edible in five.

Dried apricots and mango strips with squares of Waitrose dark chocolate. Yum!

*save hot water to mix in with dried dog food for 'le doggie dinner.'

East

The King of Scotland

The hand of Progress is now upon Kintail, with the recent arrival of the Hydro-Electric scheme. The changes will be welcome, bringing added comfort to the Highland homes.
BGM, 1948.

Next morning, our third day at Iron Lodge, in Glen Elchaig raindrops glisten on every blade of deergrass. The path we're following begins to fade to a grassy track. Just tyre marks in the lush green grass where Mr Munro once grazed his sheep. On the north side of Loch na Leitreach. I can see the track we cycled up to reach Iron Lodge, the track Macrow rattled down the glen on her bicycle in 1946.

It must've been cold that July day. In photo 8370 L has got her woolly hat on. The path follows the east bank of the burn, a blue line through the twisting brown contours on the OS map. Now I'm in danger of straying into Macrow territory, finding myself about to type: 'Carnan Cruithneachd rises like a witch's hat at the end of the glen.'

L strides on ahead of me. Higher up the hillside opens out and we can see down to Iron Lodge and the old, birch tree and the stream. Iron Lodge looks lonely among the green mountains.

Macrow: *Mrs. Munro and I read, wrote letters, and did 'odd jobs' about the house. Towards evening, before the cows came up for milking, we went out for a short walk.*

Around the 400 metre contour line the track ends and it becomes a challenge to find the faint, old stalkers' path. The mist is right down on the high hills. L has her hood up too now.

I write with OS sheet 25 Glen Carron, the 1976 edition, open on the desk in front of me, the Inverinate Forest, the Attadale Forest, the Killilan Forest and the West Benula forest. In my mind I tramp the deep gashes of the glens and the scree strewn mountain tops with Macrow and Jeannie. Macrow with her old overcoat flapping in the breeze from the snowfields and the sole coming away from the cracked, leather uppers of her boots.

Confusion. Which way to go? Wooden pallets have been strategically placed to get an all-terrain vehicle across the peat hags. The stalkers' path is faint to non-existent but eventually I pick it up again and we follow its easy-angled, zig-zags up into the mist. A break in the cloud, the rain eases and sunshine catches the summit of Sgurr na h-Eige. The bulk of Creag Ghlas, one of the mighty arms of Sgurr nan Ceathramhnan looms out of the mist (Oops! Slipped into a Brenda-ism there again) and we reach a cairn, a little ruckle of stones in the heather. We push on, the old grassy path twisting between mossy, lichen crusted boulders. Mist on mountains on mist. The sunlight is gone and Glen Elchaig is disappearing again.

Macrow 1946: *We found Loch Sgurr na h-Eige at 2,250 feet... A fierce wind whipped round us and lifted the tufts on Jeannie's ears. We found shelter behind some rocks, where we had tea. Dark cloud was now bearing down on us from the west.*

It's freezing. I'm slurping coffee from my thermos and munching on a cheese roll and a packet of crisps. When I'm done I squat down at the edge of the loch and dip my hand in the peaty water. There's nae chance of going in the water today, not even a paddle. It's too cold.

1946: *My feet by this time were squelching in my boots, and Jeannie resembled nothing so much as a drowned rat.*

THE WILD SWIMMER OF KINTAIL

We contour around the shore of the loch heading for the summit of Sgurr na h-Eige, a little bump, a short distance north-east. In the black peaty soil of the hillside, tangled among the deer grass are cladonia, yellow mountain saxifrage and the cannabis-like leaves of alpine ladies' mantle. We slither over lichen-dappled boulders to reach the top of the Sgurr. The mist is all around us now but hundreds of feet below we can just make out a large body of grey water filling the glen.

'That must be Loch Mullardoch.'

L nods her head in agreement.

In my head, I'm back in 1946. From the crags of Sgurr na h-Eige Macrow looked out across a lost landscape. She knew it not, but hers was to be one of the last recorded descriptions of a landscape soon to be lost forever.

1946: *We could see beyond Loch Lungard to where the river widens into Loch Frith an Acha and Lochan na Cloiche, with a hint of blue Loch Mullardoch behind, set among blue-black hills.*

Macrow gazed out across a landscape that by 1951 would be gone forever. Soon the prophecy at the beginning of our tale, the second sight vision the young woman saw on the road in Glen Cannich ten miles to the east, 15 years earlier would be fulfilled. Even as Macrow and Jeannie climbed the crags of Sgurr na h-Eige, in the east of Scotland, in Edinburgh Tom Johnston was drawing up plans, shuffling papers, looking at maps, planning his industrial strategy for the Highlands, free electricity for factories. Soon Loch Frith an Acha and Lochan na Cloiche would be gone forever, swallowed up by the grey waters of a vastly expanded Loch Mullardoch.

For who today remembers Loch Lungard and Loch Frith an Acha and Lochan na Cloiche or the now forgotten, nameless river that linked the lost lochans? Soon the hand of progress would be upon Kintail and the lochans would be gone forever, lost to the rising waters of the Mullardoch mass gravity hydro-electric dam. Macrow saw natural beauty but the engineers of the Hydro-Board saw only glens and straths nursing lochs crying out to be dammed and cataracts begging to be harnessed.

Tom Johnston was both a socialist and an unrepentantly patriotic Scot. In February 1941 Johnston was summoned to Downing Street for an interview with Winston Churchill which he later described as being like a rabbit before a boa constrictor. When Johnston said he wanted to get out of politics to write history the PM snorted disdainfully and said Johnston should join him and: 'help... make history.'

It didn't take long for Johnston to realise he had been given a unique opportunity: 'to inaugurate some large-scale reforms... which... might mean Scotia Resurgent.' As Johnston strode down Whitehall after his meeting with Churchill he was already listing the projects he was keen to start and they included: 'a jolly good try at a public corporation on a non-profit basis to harness Highland water power for electricity.' And the wind stirred the deer grass by Loch Lungard. And the branches of the pines by Loch Mullardoch trembled in the breeze.

Johnston would come to be dubbed: 'the uncrowned king of Scotland.' At the peak of his popularity he would be approached by people on the streets of Edinburgh and Glasgow who wanted to shake him by the hand. Thirty-four of the Hydro-Board's dams were on a scale to be included in the World Register of Large Dams. But as the people who lived at Benula and Monar were evicted before the flooding of the glens, the socialist Johnston became, like the nineteenth-century, landed gentry he despised, the author of what has been called the last Highland clearance.

THE WILD SWIMMER OF KINTAIL

I reach for the OS map on the desk but I can see no Loch Frith an Acha marked nor Lochan na Cloich nor indeed a Loch Lungard. There is a Coire Lungard marked on the map and a stream called the Allt Coire Lungard but no Loch Lungard. Gone, vanished, swallowed up by the murky waters of Loch Mullardoch. The price of what Macrow called The Hand of Progress.

The price of electricity generated so I can make searches on Google, or look at Facebook or check to see if anyone has retweeted my tweet. But what it means is no-one can ever again stand on the sandy shore of Lochan na Cloiche or sit on the stones beside the River Lungard. Because it is gone, the true price of electricity, the lost landscape of Loch Mullardoch. You never think just a click of the mouse or a tap on your phone could make a landscape disappear. But it can. The hand of progress has been at work here.

Aw Naw Not the Bromide Again!

Our third day at Iron Lodge, in the evening while we are sitting outside the tents enjoying the evening sunshine and watching the cloud shapes on Aonach Buidhe, a pick-up truck comes up the glen. It stops on the road, at the end of the track that leads down to Iron Lodge. Two figures get out of the vehicle and stare across at the house and our tents. Janet from the estate office must have sent two of the Sheikh's men to check up on us.

L decides to play it cool and helps herself to another squeeze of wine from the foil bag. (She removes the cardboard packaging from a wine box to make it easier to carry when backpacking. She's a practical soul.) We decide to ignore them. We figure there's not much the Sheikh's men can do about us camping in the field beside Iron Lodge. I'm hoping they don't come down the lane and across the bridge to speak to us though since L has dragged two of the wooden chairs from the kitchen out to sit on and that way they'll know we've been inside the house. At least I haven't lit the campfire yet. In terms of the outdoor access code we're probably infringing it because we're wild camping within the curtilage of what could be considered the garden of Iron Lodge. So we ignore them, keep sipping the Merlot and after five minutes the Sheikh's men get back into their vehicle and the pick-up truck moves slowly off back down the glen.

Next morning it's a bright, sunshiny day and instead of crossing the bridge to the Glen Elchaig road we walk across the field behind Iron Lodge towards the waterfall. The house lies between two streams and the noise of water is always with you. The white waterfall is the feature that makes Iron Lodge unique, the feature that makes it one of Scotland's special places. We head past the waterfall with its clear pool, aiming for the track that climbs the grassy hillside behind the

THE WILD SWIMMER OF KINTAIL

Iron Lodge.

It tugs at my heart no-one lives here and that a foreign landowner is allowing this house and the neighbouring house at Carnach to fall into dereliction. They are good houses. I would love to live somewhere like this. I think of the homeless man in his red sleeping bag curled up in a doorway in South Clerk Street. It's so wrong there are empty houses in Scotland while people sleep on the pavement. It makes me think it's time the Scottish people said to the likes of the Sheikh and the rest of the English, Dutch and German landowners:

'No hard feelings pal but this is our country, you've got your country (your sand dunes, your desert, your polders or your shire) the whole Lawrence of Arabia bit but this glen is our land now.' And believe me, because that day is coming, sooner than you think.

Macrow: *We set out bright and early, emerging from the cosy house into a world glimmering with raindrops… We climbed up the flooded path behind the Iron Lodge into the sombre eastern hills…*

In 1946 this old right of way led from Iron Lodge over to Glen Cannich but today much of the path lies submerged below the waters of the vastly expanded Loch Mullardoch. As the track hairpins up the steep hillside, the Iron Lodge with its red oil tank and the two green tents pitched beside it slowly shrinks. From up here it just looks like a white painted house. You can't see the neglect and dereliction. From up here the Iron Lodge looks like Rivendell in JRR Tolkein's *The Lord of the Rings*, the last homely house west of the Misty Mountains.

I keep thinking of Macrow. Weary after Chapter XII 'The Longest Trek of All: Benula and Back.' tumbling down this track towards a wisp of smoke from the chimney of the Iron Lodge and the kitchen stove, roaring away. Not a cold, wet tent in the long grass and a chilly evening in the 'uninhabitable' kitchen.

Macrow: *Following the old right-of-way from Kintail to Glen Cannich, we came presently to Loch an Droma, a tiny ribbon of water at a height of about 1,000 feet.*

The loch is shallow and I crouch down among the reeds and splash water on my face. Hill loch number 20. Eight to go!

The path leads us on to the mouth of Gleann Sìthidh, the fairy glen. A simple bridge, with no handrail and wide gaps between the planks that form its deck, spans the Abhainn Sìthidh today. A rowan tree still clings to the rock beside the fast flowing stream. Could this be the very rowan Macrow clung to as she crossed the burn? The Labradoodle has a gun dog's skill at scenting. I wonder can a dog's almost psychic sense of smell detect the faintest trace at the base of the trunk of this old rowan tree, here beside the Abhainn Sìthidh where Macrow used to cross the burn, of a Syke Terrier in the long grass in 1946?

Macrow: *The Amhainn Sìthidh was still high, but I found a reasonably good crossing-place by a cluster of rowan trees… It was 3.30 in the afternoon when we reached Loch Lungard with its lonely shepherds' bothy and brown-and-white cattle grazing along the shore.*

My plan for the day is to tick off more of Macrow's hill lochans. We're playing the game by Macrow's rules as outlined in *Kintail Scrapbook*. Either visiting the lochans or if that isn't feasible or the weather turns against us, spotting them at a distance. Macrow approached the clutch of hill lochans that lie tucked in the corries of the sprawling mountain massif the Gaels called Sgurr nan

THE WILD SWIMMER OF KINTAIL

Ceathramhnan, (which vies with Seana Braigh and Carn an Fhidhleir as the most remote of the Munros) by tramping up Gleann a'Choillich and returning via Gleann Sithidh.

Macrow: *We crossed the Amhainn a' Choilich by a flimsy bridge which quivered beneath our weight. Before us, desolate Gleann a' Choilich curved away into hazy hills; the north-east ridge of Sgurr nan Ceathramhnan on one side; Beinn Fhionnlaidh, Mam Sodhail and Carn Eige on the other.*

Now I knew, from a previous attempt to climb Beinn Fhionnlaidh, that there is today no bridge over the Abhainn a' Choilich, a body of water best described as a wide river. A recent edition of *The Munros*, Scottish Mountaineering Club Hillwalkers' Guide states that this route 'involves at least one river crossing that may be difficult or impossible in spate conditions.' I'd read Macrow's descriptions of conditions underfoot in Gleann a'Choilich 75 years earlier, it wasn't encouraging either.

1946: *The glen seemed to go on for ever. We left the cattle far behind, crossed the burn again, and floundered into peat-bog and water-logged turf.*

I doubted things would have improved much in the seven decades since then. And then there was L. She had agreed to chum me to Iron Lodge, the plan being to bag some of the remote Munros around Iron Lodge at the same time as swimming Macrow's hill lochs. This was before we'd realised quite how far Macrow had walked on some of her stravaiges. We quickly realised just getting to the hill lochs was a major expedition, requiring all the hours of daylight July had to offer, let alone trying to bag remote Munros as well.

All this is a roundabout way of saying that L and I decided to take the high road that day. Instead of battling through the peat hags of Gleann a'Choilich we planned to climb the long north ridge of Mullach na Dheiragain, the hill that rises between the two glens. Its Gaelic name translates as the summit of the kestrels and from the mountain we would have a bird's eye of the hill lochans high on nearby Sgurr nan Ceathramhnan *and* we'd get a remote Munro ticked off.

From the hill of the kestrels, I hoped to be able to spy out my prey, the hill lochs of Kintail. From the summit of Mullach nan Dhearagain we planned to continue along the mountain's south ridge then drop down to the head of Gleann Sithidh, taking in Loch Coire nan Dearcag and Am Gorm Lochan on the way. It was quite an ambitious plan, I have to say in retrospect but it looked fairly straightforward on the map. Ah, but those fatal words, it looks straightforward, the words that tempt fate where mountains are concerned.

We enter the narrow, V-shaped Gleann an Sithidh, the Glen of the Fairies and strike up the hillside between clumps of spiky flat rushes. Though it is July, Sgurr nan Ceathramhnan, at the head of the glen, still wears four white slashes of snow. The climb up the flank of the Mullach from Gleann Sithidh is very steep. It feels even steeper than last time I came this way. I don't know what angle the hillside is. But there's very little white between the brown contour lines on the map, let's put it that way. Higher up, the steep grass begins to break out into crags and we steer a winding course upwards, squelching through wet flushes bright with red sphagnum moss and the purple-flowered starfish of common butterwort.

After 1,000 feet of steep ascent I'm thinking, it must be the last pull up to the ridge now. My heart's thumping in my chest. I'm gasping for breath, sweat running into my eyes. I could have a heart attack. But you know what? If it did happen it wouldn't really matter.

THE WILD SWIMMER OF KINTAIL

A flash of blinding pain then blackness and nothing, that's OK with me. Better that than lying in a hospital bed. Better that than a nursing home smelling of wee and having someone wipe my bum for me. Be a shame for L mind, stuck on a remote mountain side with my lifeless body. Grey-faced, on my back in the heather, eyes and cock bulging, mouth hanging half-open, deader than fuckin' hell, my story over.

Back in the present though and I'm still here and we've got onto the ridge at last. L and I walk on along the crest over shattered quartzite and between clumps of thrift trembling in the breeze. We stop and eat our sandwiches in sunshine at the summit of Mullach na Dheiragain.

'How many Munros is that now?' I ask L but she refuses to answer. She says she just likes to get out and insists she isn't countinG

On the far side of Gleann Sithidh, we can see the blue gleam of Loch an Fraoich-choire high on the north ridge of Sgurr nan Ceathramhnan, another tick, albeit, a long distance one. We've had enough for one day though. We're knackered from three nights wild camping and rough walking and not sleeping properly on tussocky ground in wet tents. We agree that Loch Coire nan Dearcag and Am Gorm Lochan will still be there another day. They ain't going anywhere. The blue hills stand all around as we turn back and begin the long descent down to Gleann Sithidh and the tents waiting for us in the meadow beside the Iron Lodge.

Macrow: *At 2,500 feet, we came so suddenly upon the loch that we almost walked into it. Cloud poured round and over us in great, wet billows… Jeannie sat and shivered, refusing to share the damp sandwiches and looking in horror at the flask of brandy.*

Jeannie: Aw naw! What's she got in the bottle? She's got the bromide with her. Aw naw! Not the bromide again please!

The Death of Granny's Tent

Now it was while we were camping outside Iron Lodge that the sad event that has become known as The Death of Granny's Tent occurred. I should begin this sorry tale by explaining that in my family, since the arrival of the first grandchild a quarter-of-a-century or so ago, my mother, for reasons that require no further explanation, has been referred to as Granny. Now Mum, or Granny if you prefer, retired from hillwalking a number of years back, having compleated the Munros in 2001 on Ben Dorain and gone on to tick off 100 of the Corbetts.

Following her retirement from hillwalking Granny was keen, as older folk often are, for her outdoor gear to go to a good home. When she heard about our plans to camp outside Iron Lodge she gifted L her 25-year-old tent, a veteran of many a backpacking expedition to Fisherfield with her pals in the Ladies Scottish Climbing Club. I was busy as usual and perhaps should have had a better look at the tent. I do recall it seemed to have some bits missing from the cursory glance I gave it but L had pitched it on the back-green of her tenement in Shandon and said it was fine.

Now some 20 years earlier Granny's tent had itself been present at the demise of an earlier family tent during a storm at Sligachan on the Isle of Skye. My ex was keen on Skye. Not from a mountaineering point of view it has to be said, more because he had spent all his childhood holidays at the campsite at Glen Brittle, driving up with his mum from Newcastle every Whit weekend.

There is a photo. The tree in the picture is still there to this day beside the toilet block at the campsite in Glen Brittle. In the photo my ex, aged nine and his cousin are playing on a rope swing hanging from its branches. There's another photo too. This time of my ex in red bathing trunks paddling in the sea and in the background, Sgurr Mhic Coinnich and the jagged peaks that surround the amphitheatre of Coire Lagan. A little boy jumping over the breakers, little suspecting the waves those mountains would cause in his adult life.

Anyway, like I say, my ex was keen on Skye. I wasn't, regarding it as being full of scary mountains and white van men bombing along busy main roads. And that's before you even get to the rain and the midges. But I was young and in love and we'd had a great week camping in Torridon the summer before so off we went to Skye.

The only car we could afford to hire was a tiny Fiat Cinquecento. I don't think they make them anymore. It was like the smallest car ever. After the five hour drive up from Edinburgh in the teeny-weeny Cinquecento with the mother-in-law /Granny sat in the back talking for Scotland, we'd just managed to get the tents pitched before the rain started.

Granny had brought her own one-man-tent she used for hillwalking, the one that was to meet its own demise at Iron Lodge almost two decades later. My ex and I though had arranged rather more luxurious accommodation for ourselves. We were using a large, canvas tent, a relic from my mother's married life, which we'd taken on family holidays to Mull and Argyll. It was hard to date, having been bought second-hand from friends Gill and Ian at some point in the early 1970s. But the system for closing the door flaps, which involved fastening dozens of brass curtain hooks, rather worryingly appeared to predate the invention of the zip fastener. Now, if you've ever tried to fasten two dozen brass curtain hooks while being eaten alive by a cloud of midges you will appreciate why the use of curtain hooks as tent door fasteners went the way of the Tilly lamp and Betamax video.

Needless to say my ex and myself to a lesser extent (I've never been that much of a fan of camping. It's OK in Spain or somewhere it's hot and disnae rain) we felt the faded canvas and brass hooks all added to the charm of the antique tent. Like I say we reached Sligachan and managed to put both tents up before the rain started and the wind really got up. My ex had the kettle going on the calor gas double-burner (circa 1974) and we were sipping tea from orange and blue plastic mugs I remembered from childhood.

My ex mother-in-law had baked a lemon cake for us to take on holiday. My ex was just offering Granny a slice of said lemon cake when a mighty gust of wind swept down from the black Cuillin and tore a huge hole in the thin, perished 40-year-old canvas. Suddenly there was just daylight (and a lot of raindrops) where the roof of the tent had been.

It was immediately clear the tent was a goner. My ex and Granny ran around in the lashing rain trying to pack the sleeping bags and other contents of the destroyed tent into the minute boot of the Cinquecento and we were forced to beat a soggy retreat to the youth hostel in Broadford. Meanwhile I had a huge strop and stormed off and sat in the passenger seat of the Cinquecento smoking roll ups and muttering I always knew something like this would happen if we went to fucking Skye. Oh dear!

Back at Iron Lodge, the demise of Granny's one-man tent is not to be as dramatic as the death of the family tent in the storm at Sligachan 20 years earlier. L. sleeps all right in the quarter-of-a-century-old tent on the first night (come to think of it Granny's one man tent died young compared to the family tent) but on the second night it rains… a lot. The absence and function of certain crucial guylines and pegs becomes apparent when L wakes up in the middle of the night in her sleeping bag, floating on a puddle. Next morning she declares Granny's tent not fit for purpose and announces she intends to sleep

THE WILD SWIMMER OF KINTAIL

in the Iron Lodge that night.

'Rather you than me,' I say, 'are you not worried about whoever it was left all those empty vodka bottles in the kitchen turning up in the middle of the night?'

'Well it's that or another night sleeping in a puddle.'

'And there's that lemonade bottle with the end cut off and all those dead matches on the worktop. Like somebody's been chasing the dragon. What if it's some crazed junkie?'

She just sticks her tongue out at me this time. Like I said she's the brave one.

I know for certain I'd be outside in the leaking 25-year-old tent rather than sleep in spooky Iron Lodge. It's not the ghosts of Macrow or Mr and Mrs Munro I'd be bothered about. What's worrying me is suppose whoever it is who's been smoking heroin in the kitchen where Mrs Munro once prepared the crowdie sandwiches to sustain Macrow on the long trek to Benula and back, turns up in the middle of the night. Now I'm really wishing we'd brought the Labradoodle with us. Not that she's got great guard dog potential (I'll lick you to death Mr Burglar) but she's very good at barkinG

But no, when I put my head round the door half-an-hour later L has swept up the fallen plaster and cleared a space for her camper-mat and sleeping bag in one of the ground floor rooms. The place smells of soot and damp plaster and it's such a long, long way from the circle of lamplight and the fire and Mr Munro coming in from the sheep. I drain the last of the Glenlivet from the plastic cup, get up from the table, go out to my tent and leave L alone with the ghosts of Iron Lodge.

1946: *Outside, the blue shadows gathered and fell across the quiet glen... Mr Munro came in from the sheep, and the three collies peered curiously round the door, their eyes yellow in the circle of lamplight.*

The Worst Chippy in Scotland

Back in the day when 'the three collies peered curiously around the door, their eyes yellow in the circle of lamplight' Macrow tramped the long miles up Gleann Sithidh to Loch Coire nan Dearcag and Am Gorm Lochan high on the remote Munro Sgurr nan Ceathramhnan. But nowadays with the Iron Lodge long abandoned, the 'easiest' way to approach these hill lochans is from Alltbeithe youth hostel in upper Glen Affric. Macrow herself did not discover Glen Affric until after *Kintail Scrapbook* was published, writing in 1946 that Glen Shiel was possibly 'the loveliest glen in the West Highlands.'

So we're going to leave Macrow and Jeannie back in 1946 for a little while as we approach the hill lochans of Sgurr nan Ceathramhnan from the east. I've written the 'easiest' way to reach these hill lochans is from Glen Affric but believe me, there's nothing easy about it. Limited in how many days I could survive wild camping at Iron Lodge, one hot July day I park the car at the end of Glen Affric. Even to get to this car park involves a long drive from Cannich, itself one of the remoter Highland villages. Glen Affric also happens to be one of the midgiest places in Scotland. Not quite on a par with Barrisdale Bay in Knoydart or Glen Brittle on Skye but headed that way. One morning I was so distracted being eaten by midges that when I got back to the car park having climbed one of the An Socachs, I found I had carefully locked the car but left the passenger window wide open! But then, I don't think anyone's going to nick stuff out your car in remote Glen Affric anyway.

On this hot July day, having taken a leaf out of Macrow's book, I've left the Labradoodle in the care of Senga, a Mark 2 leading high street department store fag-hag from my ex's days in small leathers. Small leathers? I see you raise an eyebrow. Small leathers, you ask? In reality working in small leathers proved to be a lot less interesting than many of our gay friends imagined. Small leathers in a department store meaning purses and bus passes rather than anything more exotic. Senga and her kids are great dog lovers so I know the Labradoodle will be in good hands splashing about in the River Spean while I continue with Macrow's hill lochan odyssey.

I check the panniers are fastened, put my helmet on and leaving the mobile homes and cars parked among the Scots pines and silver birches behind, rattle off down the hill and over the bridge across the River Affric. I'm headed for Alltbeithe. Yellow buttercups and purple foxgloves tangle in the long grass beside the track. Bump bump bump rattle rattle rattle. Midges and boneshaking track notwithstanding I love Glen Affric, so many memories of hill days and dog walks along the lochside. There's a great book by Duncan MacLennan, head stalker in Glen Affric for nearly 50 years. In a poignant section towards the end of the book he recounts how at the age of 70 he realised his hill days were coming to an end: 'I felt this might be the last time I would tread the heads of these majestic mountains; and in case it would be, as a gesture of farewell, I put a large stone on each of their summit cairns.'

New Year's Day in Edinburgh: I'm clicking through my photos. I'm writing, New Year's Day in Edinburgh, no lying on the sofa watching *Raiders of the Lost Ark* for me. Nope, the shop's closed so this is writing time. I want to re-assure you dear reader I do have a life. I did go out last night to see in the New Year. But writing time is hard to come by and I'm broke. This starving writer is going to have to work

THE WILD SWIMMER OF KINTAIL

every Sunday in January driving the van. But at least it's premium rate, time-and-a-half on the Sabbath. So I'll earn £94 for a six hour shift feeding the starving hordes of Morningside, because as I may have mentioned already I'm a Starbucks Scribbler me.

I click from the photos of Glen Affric to the BBC News homepage to check if the Queen's still alive. Last night in the pub someone said she didn't make it to the Christmas Day church service at Sandringham. When the page loads though, the Queen's still alive. I click on a photo of Alltbeithe and my mind turns back to that summer trip to Glen Affric. Back to the River Affric where Scots Pines shade white water foaming over sheets of grey rock. Heather, Scots pines, blaeberry bushes, blue water, high hills, this is all Glen Affric to me. Gripping the handlebars tightly I glance across at Affric Lodge, a grey, stone house among the pines by the lochside. Two white horses graze at the edge of the reeds on the shore of the loch and I wonder were Glen Cannich and Loch Mullardoch once as beautiful as Glen Affric (still is) today?

I pedal on past the house at Garbh Allt. God, I hate this fucking track. Below the crags of Na Cnapain, a green Scottish Rights of Way Society signpost points the way to Cougie. Ahead lies upper Glen Affric and I pedal on into the the blue July sunshine. The track stretches out ahead, a white ribbon through the glen, leading me on. A solitary Granny Scots pines stands by the track, the 75 years since Macrow wandered the hills of Kintail just a narrow segment of rings, beneath the gnarled bark of her trunk. She watched the hydro men come and she watched the hydro men go and still she keeps her lonely vigil by the loch, a *chaillich* guarding the glen.

The bike rolls on, freewheeling downhill towards the boundary of the parish of Kintail, through stands of rowan and silver birch. At the head of Loch Affric there is a narrow, sandy beach. On my way back from climbing the Corbett Carn a' Choire Ghairbh I swam here 1 October. In warm sunshine, I ran naked along the beach. The Labradoodle snapped at my heels, barking excitedly. My footprints drew a line in the sand, from where my rucksack, shorts, T-shirt, boots and socks lay scattered across the beach. A line of dog paw prints running parallel to my footprints, led straight into the loch.

When I reach Athnamulloch the cottage looks as if it's floating on a sea of waving, thigh high grass. Its walls need whitewashing and its red, corrugated-iron roof is rusting. I wheel my bike across the wooden planks of the bridge over the River Affric, the water beneath my feet is black and slow flowing. Beyond Athnamulloch, where the river flows in lazy curves, I remember the track deteriorates but I persist in cycling for a couple of kilometres further. You always end up cycling a bit further than you should. It's like in winter when you always put your crampons on about ten minutes after you should have.

The path skirts along the foot of the hillside, above the wide flat floor of the glen. Near a marshy lochan, I leave the bike in the heather and continue towards Sgurr nan Ceathramhnan on foot. At a wooden bridge over the Allt Coire Ghadheil there is a metal sign cemented to a rock: *National Trust for Scotland West Affric*.

I stop on the bridge over the stream and look over the wooden parapet at the little waterfall and the black peaty pool below. I smile to myself. A while back, before I came to know Affric and Kintail so well, one scorching day I was on my way back from climbing a remote Munro. Hot and sweaty I stripped off, stepped across the white, lichen-covered rocks and slid into the pool of peaty water under the bridge. What I didn't know at the time is that the bridge is on the track to Alltbeithe youth hostel, which along with Loch Ossian, vies for the title of remotest youth hostel in Scotland.

I thought I was in the middle of nowhere floating happily on my back in the stream stark bollock naked, when suddenly three young guys, backpacking into Alltbeithe from Cannich crossed the bridge above me. The young guys gave me a wave and a cheery hello but five minutes later two young women arrived. The first one stepped onto the bridge then stepped back off it, with a little shriek and a look of terror on her face! The expression on her face said something like: 'Hide Your Shame Young Man!' I swam across the pool and skulked at the far side of the burn until they finally summoned up courage and ran across the bridge. I felt like shouting after them: 'It's only a willy!'

The track draws close to the river for the final straight stretch along to Alltbeithe. In the grass beside the white stony track, field scabious, buttercups and cat's ear, all the flowers of the grasslands and meadows pages of the flower book. By my side the River Affric hurries on down to Cannich over rounded boulders and banks of white shingle. At last I reach the green, corrugated-iron (well at least the modern version of corrugated-iron) clad buildings at Alltbeithe. The door is open but there is no sign of the warden. I smile to myself again.

The first time I climbed Sgurr nan Ceathramhnan was with my mate J. We drove up from Edinburgh, parked near the Cluanie Inn and walked into Alltbeithe along the valley of An Caorann Mor beneath the mountains Am Bathach, the barn and Ciste Dubh, the black coffin. Our rucksacks were heavy (J was carrying a winebox and a curry she had pre-cooked in Edinburgh). I as ever had my usual plastic drinking bottle half-full of whisky.

Like many remote places in the Highlands, Alltbeithe has no radio reception and no mobile phone coverage and like many wild places in the world it is all the better for that. During the long walk in I had been telling J about Ronnie Burn, the second (or possibly the first Munroist, but that's another story) and how he fell in love with the daughter of the farmer at Alltbeithe in the second decade of the twentieth century when the youth hostel was still a farm. In the days before radio and TV, Ronnie Burn used to carry the news to the remote houses and crofts he visited while climbing the Scottish peaks over 3,000 feet.

The hostel was quite busy our first night at Alltbeithe and in the long, light summer evening we were all sat round the table in the kitchen. The other guests staying at the hostel had been there for a couple of days. Deprived of their phones and the internet, they asked us eagerly:

'What's been happening in the world?'

'Well… ' I replied, after a suitably dramatic pause, and feeling every bit like Ronnie Burn, the crippled, itinerant priest carrying news of the outside world into the wilderness: 'Michael Jackson's dead!'

The youth hostel stands in the long, lush, green grass that was once Angus Scott's grazing. The fire-assembly-point sign with its stylized diagram is bolted to the side of the old farm buildings where Ronnie Burn once fell in love with Angus's daughter, Katie. The wind turbine that supplies the hostel with electricity is stationary. There is no wind. Two silver birches lean drunkenly over the burn as I stomp past low ruins in the long grass, headed up to the corrie behind the hostel, this sunny July morning. And I see Macrow, typing: *the hill-road mounted swiftly up the brown brae.*

I'm out on my own in the Highlands. Like the time my ex sat on the top of Scald Law, 24-years old, arms folded round his knees as he took in the vista of the Pentlands and the city and the distant mountains and cried, 'Come and get me Mum!' freedom intoxicating his 24-year-old self. I can't believe now my ex was ever 24, was ever the same age as Sam at work, Sam who's so fresh-faced, so cheery. Can't believe the tired, stressed-looking 40-something who comes to collect the Labradoodle for the weekend was the boy I went to La

THE WILD SWIMMER OF KINTAIL

Caleta with.

I look back down on the farm buildings at Alltbeithe, just as Ronnie Burn once did. It is Burn's shadow with me today in the green, grassy corrie. But I know Macrow and Jeannie are waiting for me, up there, high on the ridge. I hear the clack clack clack of Macrow's typewriter on the path behind me: *the hill-road mounted swiftly up the brown brae.* And then I'm back in that summer of 1946 and Macrow's sweeping the white blossom out the door of the cottage because the most beautiful things in life are always the shortest lived.

I like this path, this grey-white seam in the long grass. My boots like this path. This path that leads me up to the long, east ridge of Sgurr nan Ceathramhnan, the peak of the quarters. Quarters of what I wonder as I climb up between grey, schist rocks? Splashes of white lichen on boulders and now I'm heading north into the peaty, upper corrie, climbing onto the ridge which marks the southern boundary of the Parish of Kintail, within which lie all 28 of Macrow's hill lochs.

Below me lies Gleann a' Choillich. To the west the rounded lump of An Socach, the snout (as translated by Macrow's Gaelic dictionary in 1946) and in front of me, Sgurr nan Ceathramhnan, a green triangle on a blue backdrop. Ahead the ridge narrows, a staircase in the sky, climbing up to the pointed summit of the Sgurr. The white flags of bog cotton mark the way along the misty ridge, leading me back to Kintail. Drops of sweat on my forehead, a damp circle on the front of my T-shirt as I climb on up, drawn into the spell, drawn back to Kintail.

And now here's Macrow and Jeannie battling through the mist and over the scree. When I read it later, sitting in a deckchair outside the caravan, watching for the black flash of porpoise fins on the blue waters of Loch Duich, there's something of the eighteenth-century traveller in Scotland about Macrow's description of the approach to

KELLAN MACINNES

Loch Coire nan Dearcag.

1946: The head of Gleann a' Choilich, when you finally reach it, presents scenery of appalling wildness and desolation. Riven grey rock—black peat—fierce crags, and great, dark peaks... It was now 7 p.m., and I was tired and hungry, but still quite a distance from the lochan.

A patch of yellow Alpine saxifrage, another twist in the ridge, another squeeze between grey schist boulders and then far below, at the foot of the green triangle that is the Sgurr: Loch nan Dearcag.

Macrow 1946: *At length—a gleam of vivid green—and there was the tiny lochan, covered with young weed, hiding in a hollow among steep grey cliffs and loose scree. Before us, the highest of the four summits of Sgurr nan Ceathramhnan, 3,771 feet, rose clear against a patch of blue sky. But we were again racing the cloud, which was pouring like a torrent over from Glen Affric, billowing and belching silently to our undoing...*

Big Munros stand all around, guarding the glen, Mullach Fraoch Coire, A'Chralaig, Ciste Dubh, as I plod on up towards the summit of the Sgurr. Moss and lichen-covered slabs of grey schist are scattered across the upper section of the ridge. A cairn of mossy stones marks the top of Stob Coire na Cloiche. Now in my photos the mist is rolling in across the ridge, just like in 1946.

From the summit of the Sgurr I catch a glimpse of Am Gorm Lochan and feel myself coming over all Brenda: 'a dark jewel nestled in the bosom of the mountain.' No! No! No! Score that bit out. What is it that Andrew Greig says in *The Return of John Macnab*? The bit when Neil Lindores arrives in a fictional Highland village which bears more than a passing resemblance to Braemar: 'He looks up at the hills that circle the town, sees the upper slopes are purple with heather and reminds himself he mustn't say so. Certain things about his country invite clichés. Certain things about his country are true.'

Macrow: *There was no time to take notes, much less a photograph… We headed for the still-clear north-east ridge, tired and breathless, and it seemed that we would never make it! At last, we were past the 3,000ft. level… We plunged down, without pause, to the welcome gleam of the Amhainn Sithidh… Whatever happened now, we were safe at last from the treacherous cloud.*

Intermission, now it's back to the computer, typing again. The fire's lit. I've been to Morrisons for the shopping, put the tea on. Feel I've gone a bit Alan Bennett's diaries here. Back to Kintail then and like Macrow, I had hoped to continue some way along the south ridge of the Mullach then scramble down to Am Gorm Lochan. I had already visited Loch Coire nan Dearcag the time J and I walked into Alltbeithe carrying the news about the death of Michael Jackson. That day we climbed Sgurr nan Ceathramhnan, Mullach na Dheáragain and finally reached An Socach at 6.30pm. We sat by the summit cairn of An Socach in the early evening sunshine and I peeled my clammy, sweaty T-shirt off.

J looked at my bare chest.

'I'll take my top off too,' she giggled, 'that'll scare you.'

'Go on then…'

Actually I wouldnae have minded if she had taken her top off. Don't tell anyone this, by the way, but even though I'm gay I still quite like breasts. Don't know why. Doesn't make me any less gay,

I guess. Anyway, she didn't take her top off in the end but I wish she had, because a few minutes later a bloke appeared coming up the path from Alltbeithe. The sight of J with her Sgurr na Ciches out would probably have cheered up his day no end, putting the other mighty peaks in the vicinity in the shade.

Back to the present: as I say, I had intended visiting Am Gorm Loch rather than gazing at her longingly from a distance but by the time I reach the summit of Sgurr nan Ceathramhnan there just isn't the time to go any further into the wilderness. The cycle back from Alltbeithe along the hateful, stony track pursued by clouds of midges and clegs looms large in my mind not to mention the drive back from Cannich. But according to Brenda's rules, it still counts as a tick. Five hill lochs to go! So I turn back at the summit of Sgurr nan Ceathramhnan, turning back from Kintail, returning into Affric.

Macrow 1946: *I left the Iron Lodge at 1 pm, and stopped for only fifteen minutes during the whole tramp. Nevertheless, I did not reach ' home ' again until a quarter to eleven—and that in a state of near-exhaustion. Mrs Munro confessed herself on the verge of organising a search-party of one...*

On the way back I have the second-worst fish supper I've had ever had. I have to say at the risk of the Independent Scottish Publisher being sued for libel that I cannot, I'm afraid recommend the chippy in D_____. It's run by Scots Asians who tend in my experience to be better at samosas than Scotch pies, it doesn't appear that clean, though there is a queue. But even after a long, hungry wait I can't finish the heavy, greasy batter that peels away in soggy strips from the chewy, white fish. It's like the ones from the R_____, a chippy located on a certain street in Edinburgh's Georgian New Town, well the bit of the New Town near the top of Leith Walk that is. My pals

THE WILD SWIMMER OF KINTAIL

D&G swear they switch the hot cabinet containing the fish, pies and sausages off overnight then switch it back on in the morning to reheat anything left unsold from the night before. Aw fuck even writing about it's making me feel a long, skittery *(my bottom's just been sick!)* sit on the toilet coming on.

As I say the chippy in a certain village on the shores of Loch Ness is where I've just had the second-worst fish supper I've ever eaten. The first/worst (if you get my drift) I've ever eaten (or not eaten to be more accurate) was from a chippy attached to a hotel near Fort William. The chippy in question was located in one of several outbuildings in the car park of the hotel. A large blue and white banner tied to the railings outside proclaiming *Freshly Cooked Fish and Chips* was to prove woefully inaccurate.

On entering the establishment there was a heated cabinet but it was empty. Now sometimes this can be a good sign in a chippy, suggesting as it does that everything is cooked to order, *Freshly Cooked* in the words of the banner in the car park. I stood and waited at the heated cabinet, which I now noticed was switched off and cold, not a good sign. After a couple of minutes an Eastern European dumpling of a girl in a whitecoat appeared behind the counter. Her blond hair scraped back in a bun.

'Vat vould you like?'

'I'll have a white pudding supper please.'

'Vite pudding vith chips?'

'Yes,' I replied.

There's a regional variation in white puddings I never knew about until I went to university in Aberdeen. When we were kids and then teenagers we used to run down the tenement stairs from the sunny top flat on the corner of Arden Street and Spottiswoode Road just across the street from where Ian Rankin's fictional detective Inspector Rebus would take up residence in the early-90s. The white pudding suppers at the chippy on the corner of Marchmont Road had a firm, sausage-like consistency and weren't dipped in batter. That was a great chippy by the way. It's still there today, still feeding the students of Marchmont.

Poor old Marchmont: the magnificent, baronial sweep of Warrender Park Road with its splendid, heavily corniced, high-ceilinged flats. Poor old Marchmont, she's like a dowager duchess fallen on hard times. Her tenement stairs littered with fag ends and rusting bikes. Her plastic entry-phones smashed, their wire entrails hanging out. Tatty curtains and Scotland flags hang from her wide bay windows and her back-greens lie overgrown and abandoned. Poor old Marchmont, a grand old lady fallen on hard times, laid low by the curse of the HMO, the house in multiple occupation. The tenements of her scruffy cousin Leith often better maintained than the stairs of Marchmont these days.

When we were kids and went to the school at the end of the street, there were families in every flat on our stair. The Miss Macdonalds on the first floor, Russell Stewart and his mum and dad on the second floor and Caroline and her family opposite, the Stevens in 3F3. On the ground floor were two retired schoolteachers, with a mad barky dog, who sat in the garden drinking gin all day and chain-smokinG But we didn't have much to do with them because they had the main-door flat with its own separate front door.

As I was saying though, at least poor old Marchmont still boasts a good chippy. Now when I went to Aberdeen to be a student I discovered white puddings north of the central belt were something quite different. They came coated in batter and were soft in the middle. When me and my pal Al Mac had had a heavy weekend on the wacky backy, the amphetamine and the drink, on a Sunday night we'd go for our tea in the canteen at Hillhead Halls of Residence. I'd have a white pudding, chips and beans with a sachet of brown sauce.

THE WILD SWIMMER OF KINTAIL

The kindly wifies who worked behind the counter with their *Fit like? Faur ye been?* Aberdonian accents used to pile the chips high on our plates, taking pity on me and Al because we looked so thin and skinny and wasted. I can still taste those chips and the oat-mealy white pudding and crispy batter dipped in brown sauce. All washed down with a mug of tea.

But to get back to the story, some of this is what was going through my mind in the chippy in the car park of the Highland hotel when I said:

'I'll have a white pudding supper please.'

The Eastern European Dumpling behind the counter shuffled towards a freezer and took out a white pudding, still frozen solid. Heart sinking now, I'd had my doubts about visiting this establishment I have to say, I watched as she proceeded to dip the frozen white pudding into an orange, plastic bucket of gloopy, white batter. The deep fat frier spat and hissed as the Dumpling dropped the pudding in. This isn't going to be good, I thought. And it wasn't. Outside sitting in the car, the chips were just about passable but the white pudding was luke warm at both ends but still cold, only just thawed out in the middle. Most of the chips and all the white pudding went in the bin in the car park. Even the Labradoodle turned her nose up at it. Like I said, the worst chippy in Scotland.

The Wild Swimmer of Kintail

One morning in late summer: I'm heaving my bike out the back of a hire car near Killilan at the mouth of Glen Elchaig. In the course of researching and then writing this book, which in my mind, for now at least, has the working title and may or may not be published as 'Macrow and Me', I have become very familiar, I could almost say have fallen in love with the remote and beautiful Glen Elchaig. Just as Macrow did 75 years ago. Though I don't know it now, as I heave my bike out the back of the car, trying not to damage the trim or scratch the paintwork, by this evening I'm going to be even better acquainted with Glen Elchaig.

The way in to the glen begins at Dornie with its hotel and pub and *romantische* Eilean Donan castle on its island guarding the place where three lochs meet. Glen Elchaig, it's not a Glencoe among glens, it's not a glen of weeping. It feels like a friendly sort of a glen, a homely sort of a glen, perhaps that's because of the many generations of Highland folk who lived and worked and travelled through the glen at least until a few decades ago.

Like I say I've got to know Glen Elchaig well. From the flat fields at the mouth of the glen, where the salt water of Loch Long laps the pebbles and black seaweed, to its leafy, lower reaches of birch, rowan and oak. I know the strange little model village built in the 1930s by a tobacco tycoon at Killilan at the foot of the glen and the large agricultural shed which stands where the big house stood when Macrow came to the glen. All that is left of the big house, the only clues that a shooting lodge once stood here are the trees and low stone walls enclosing what was once the garden.

I've got to know Glen Elchaig well through all its length. From the smooth, tarmac estate road at the start of the glen to the rough, stony potholed track higher up, past the red-painted, iron gate where

THE WILD SWIMMER OF KINTAIL

the fields and woodland of the lower glen give way to the heather and rocky outcrops of upper Glen Elchaig.

I've got to know the long climb up to Loch na Leitreach and the gentle descent along the lochside to Carnach. Like Macrow before me I've got to know Carnan Cruithneachd standing guard over the green chasm that leads to the Falls of Glomach.

There are houses and homes, families living at Killilan and across the mouth of the glen at Camus-luinie but today upper Glen Elchaig is deserted, the houses at Carnach and Iron Lodge falling into ruin.

I've got to know the River Elchaig, from its wide slow pools beneath the broad leafed trees at Killilan, to its outflow from Loch na Leitreach and the narrow gorges and side streams that feed into it in the upper glen.

I've got to know the head of the glen where the lonely house at Iron Lodge stands between the waterfall and the river. From Iron Lodge the traveller has a choice of three ways through the hills. A steep hill path climbs the brae over to Loch Mullardoch, a second path between the mountains will take you to Pait Lodge on the shores of Loch Monar and the third path takes you to the remote bothy at Maol-bhuidhe. Whichever way the wanderer chooses will lead deep into the heart of the wilderness.

I've got to know the glen well during six months walking in Macrow's footsteps. I first got to know this glen even before I had ever heard of a poet by the name of Brenda G Macrow. I've tried to paint a picture in words of the glen because it played such a central part in Macrow's wanderings through Kintail.

One morning in late summer: like I said I'm heaving my bike out the back of the car at the parking place near Killilan. My plan: to cycle eight kilometres up Glen Elchaig as far as the abandoned house at Carnach and then follow an old stalkers' path up to the remote Coire Lochan. To grasp the remoteness of Coire Lochan you need to understand this hill loch lies just a few hundred metres below the west top of Sgurr nan Ceathramhnan. A Gaelic mouthful of a mountain, Sgurr nan Ceathramhnan, as well as being something of a pronunciation and spelling challenge. Believe me I should know, I've typed the name often enough – a scene in my novel *The Making of Mickey Bell* takes place on the mountain's summit. The east top is the Munro for the anoraks out there (just kidding! I'll be needing to get my anorak on too now on account of knowing all these obscure facts and figures) and is also one of the remotest of the Munros, that elite group of Scottish mountains the altitude of which exceeds 3,000 feet. Don't take my word for it (though I did just slip on a quilted windproof jacket.) Here's what the 2006 edition of the *Scottish Mountaineering Club's Hillwalkers' Guide The Munros* has to say about the Sgurr: 'This remoteness adds to its character and makes it one of the great prizes for the hillwalker.'

So like I say Coire Lochan is just a wee bit remote. In fact you could say Coire Lochan put the R in Remote. OK, got it. It's a long way away then. Yip and that's why I one morning in late summer I'm clicking the car shut, clipping my pannier onto my bike (more of that later) and heaving a lycra clad thigh over the crossbar of my Revolution Cuillin. I've brought my Edinburgh bike with me. I used it a couple of days earlier to cycle into the remote Corbett Beinn Vuirich from Loch Moraig near Blair Atholl. Got tae be another book in that. *Kellan's Corbetts*? It does have a bit of a ring to it? Shut up! One book at a time Sweet Jesus to paraphrase Lena Martell.

In 1946 Macrow approached Coire Lochan from Iron Lodge while she and Jeannie were staying with the redoubtable Mrs Munro and her husband and the three collies Fred, Jack, Sheila and Morag the puppy. Like Macrow seven decades before, L and me had cycled down the rough road from our tents pitched at Iron Lodge to the abandoned house at Carnach and left our bikes before taking the hill path up Sgurr na h-Eige. Although it was June the weather was that kind of Scottish weather that could be any month from March to November, intermittent driving rain and cloud blanketing the hills around the 650 metre contour line. We found the old stalkers' path that leads up to Loch Sgurr na h-Eige and crouched among the rocks at the summit. Then following in Macrow's footsteps we climbed up onto Creag Ghlas, a minor peak at the start of the four kilometre long north ridge of Sgurr nan Ceathramhnan. But somewhere between Creag Ghlas and Stùc Fraoch Choire the photos I always take on walks end abruptly in a grey smirr of rain and mist.

The weather was similar but a wee bit worse than Macrow and Jeannie endured in 1946 and wet to our pants and with no means of drying them in the abandoned ruins of Iron Lodge, no Mrs Munro cheerily tending the Rayburn for us twenty-first-century visitors we turned back. I do though have one photo with a grey-blue blur in the distance (a pause now while I check my photos, it'll be under Iron Lodge pics I'm guessing, yip!) which we ascertained was Coire Lochan.

Coire Lochan and nearby Loch an Fhraoich-choire (well nothing's nearby on Sgurr nan Ceathramhnan, but kind of over the other side of the ridge) were two of the hill lochs that Macrow approached from above and appears to have ticked off her list after having spotted them from a distance, rather than getting within paddling distance. So, at the time, as L and me retreated soggily off the mountain to try and dry our pants at chilly Iron Lodge, we both convinced ourselves that a sighting of Coire Lochan (albeit at a distance of some 2,500 metres) did constitute a bona fide hill lochan ticked off the list. And, if you check the rules as laid out by Macrow, I think you'll be compelled to agree that, on a technicality at least, we did 'bag' Coire Lochan.

Back at the caravan in Dornie though, Coire Lochan began to

bother me. I felt like I was cheating myself. It felt like not getting to the top of a mountain.

To cut a long story short and I'm good at them! Both *Caleb's List* and *The Making of Mickey Bell* ran to over 100,000 words and a glance to the right of my screen as I type this shows a word count of 108,241. But I'm gonnae go back through this one when I've finished and cut it back, cut out the boring bits like. Boring bits? In a Kellan MacInnes book? Surely not, I hear you say. But no, I want maximum readability, less *Caleb's List* more Muriel Grey's *The First Fifty*.

So, as I was saying, to cut a long story short I decided to go back to Coire Lochan. I'd pick a better route, try to choose a good day and I planned to swim in it. So that dear reader, is why I'm free-wheeling off down the estate road heading for Killilan and the long pedal up Glen Elchaig..

Eight kilometres of potholed, stony track later and I'm locking my bike to the bridge at Carnach. The house looks just as sad and neglected as before. Something bad has happened to the flashing. The slates all along the gable end of the roof have fallen off exposing the wooden sarking beneath to all the winds that blow down from Carnan Cruithneachd. Not that the plight of one sad, neglected old house in Glen Elchaig will concern the Sheikh with the upkeep of all those palaces to keep him busy. Such is the way we seem happy to have our country run for us. So stands Scotland at the end of the second decade of the twenty-first century.

I stand on a flat rock at the side of the road and peel my mountain bike shorts off, baring my big, white arse to the family of sparrows who live in the roof of the house at Carnach today. Having completed the transformation from mountain biker (well kind of) to hillwalker, I press the button on the side of the GPS and head for one of the waypoints I noted down for this walk when I did it previously. That time I was following in Macrow's footsteps going up to Loch Lòn

THE WILD SWIMMER OF KINTAIL

Mhurchaidh and the Falls of Glomach. This time I can check if my directions actually work.

It turns out they do and I find the crossing place on the burn easily and remember to avoid the fallen down wooden footbridge leading to nowhere. So far, so good, pausing on the path across the steep hillside I glance back down to Glen Elchaig thinking how green the glen looks in its summer clothes. A wisp of cloud brushes the top of Carnan Cruithneachd. The sky is overcast with streaks of blue, the day could go either way.

The old stalkers' path climbs up beside the waterfall where the Allt Coire Easiach cascades over the edge of the flat, heather moorland below Sgurr nan Ceathramhnan and down into Glen Elchaig.. It rained in the night so the falls look spectacular, a kind of mini Falls of Glomach with the bonus of being a lot easier to see.

The old path cuts a thin line across the hillside below the waterfall. The upward movement of a head catches my eye. A stag and four hinds are grazing beside the path. They watch me approach, a four-legged-figure with walking poles, then move lazily off down the corrie. I watch the deer splash through the burn below the waterfall, the stag leading the way. My scalp tingles as I watch them cross the burn below the waterfall and make their long-legged way through the bracken up the far hillside. Next time I look they are gone.

The old path zig zags up the steep hillside well to the left of the waterfall, just like I remember. In a couple of places the steep hillside has burst open spewing gravel and pebbles and sand down the hillside. I teeter across steadying myself with my walking poles and soon pick up the line of the Victorian path again, on the far side of the landslip.

Where the path tops out onto the flat, heathery plateau above Glen Elchaig I'm in for a shock. Since my last visit, when I cycled from Shepherd's Cottage, an ugly, poorly constructed, vehicle track has been bulldozed along the line of the faint, old Victorian stalkers' path that led to Loch Lòn Mhurchaidh. The old path Macrow followed across the moorland is gone for ever, in its place an ugly scar of peaty mud. Even by the standards of bulldozed tracks this one looks poorly constructed. It has turned the delicate moorland into a morass of black mud. Boulders that had lain undisturbed since the Ice Age have been ripped out the ground and lie heaped by the side of the track.

When I reach Loch Lòn Mhurchaidh it gets worse. Whoever built this track bulldozed it right along the side of the loch. Wooden pallets have been dumped beside the shoreline to stop the ATVs getting stuck in the mud of their own creation and all this within a stone's throw of the Falls of Glomach, one of Scotland's great (and protected) wild places.

Macrow 1946: *I came to Loch a'Mhurachaidh* [sic]... *I followed the well-defined path along the western shore. At the edge, the water was deep amber, with a hint of sand underneath.*

The miniature, sandy beach where I splashed in the loch is still there but there are streaks of what looks like white paint on the sand. The churned up mud and boulders and wooden palates make the loch an uninviting place to swim now. I walk on thinking, what other country on the planet would let a rich man from halfway across the world scar our land, our infinite Scotland like this? And the Sheikh doesn't even need planning permission to do this, just some spurious agricultural reason to bulldoze a track. Because remember he lives in Dubai and he owns the land, not we who live in Scotland.

I walk on along the muddy ATV track dodging between puddles and then I have an idea. I'll write to the Sheikh, address c/o Janet at the Inverinate Estate Office. I will ask him why, as landowner,

THE WILD SWIMMER OF KINTAIL

he has allowed this ugly track to be bulldozed across one of the remotest areas of wild land in Scotland. My mind's really birling now. I'll enclose an extract of Macrow's writing, a paragraph about the natural beauty of Loch Lòn Mhurchaidh. I'll ask the Sheikh to explain his actions. As I walk on I feel sure Macrow would approve of my plan. And maybe I'll send a copy of my letter to *The Herald* and *The Scotsman* too.

The bulldozed track goes all the way to the banks of the Allt Coire-lochain which means it actually crosses land owned by the National Trust for Scotland. Now I climbed Beinn a' Bhuird on the NTS owned Mar Lodge estate in the Cairngorms a while back. I saw the painstaking work carried out by the Trust to remove the dirt track road, high on the south-western shoulder of the mountain, constructed by two Swiss brothers who owned Beinn a' Bhuird back in the '60s. The road was the first stage of a plan to develop a ski resort on the mountain. Swiss brothers, Sheikhs, maybe you're beginning to see a bit of a pattern emerging here?

The NTS went to great lengths and spent a considerable sum of money restoring the dirt track road on Beinn a'Bhuird back to a footpath. So I think they'll be less than delighted to find an ATV track bulldozed across their property near the Falls of Glomach.

Still fulminating against the Sheikh and the fact that fewer than 500 people own more than 50 per cent of Scotland's land I leave the ATV track and begin to follow the left bank of the Allt Coire-lochain, heading for the elusive Coire Lochan. Map and GPS are both telling me it's over two kilometres to the lochan so I'm relieved to find the going easy over short deer-cropped grass beside the burn. Two kilometres across peat hags or thigh deep heather can be a very long way. Short sections of deer paths and tyre tracks help too. Every so often I pause and look back down towards Glen Elchaig and crooked Carnan Cruithneachd hunched over the Falls of Glomach. The waters of the burn I walk beside, the Allt Coire-lochain, destined to join the waters of the Abhainn Gaorsaic in a 370-foot plunge over the Falls of Glomach, the quickest route back down to Glen Elchaig.

Grey-white cloud blankets the heights of Sgurr nan Ceathramhnan and I reckon the mist will be just brushing the surface of the water in Coire Lochan. The burn tumbles out the corrie, down a staircase of white-water steps and dark, boulder-fringed pools. I'm beginning to rather regret not having told anyone where I was going. I know! What were you thinking of? A remote area like this and all, but I just thought of the walk to Coire Lochan as being a walk up to a loch. But now as I approach the cloud level I register what I already know, that Coire Lochan lies at 770m, at an altitude higher than some Corbetts*. When I'm climbing a Corbett alone or with the Labradoodle I always send a text or leave a note with details of my route so someone knows where I'm going. But now I'm thinking no-one ever goes up to Coire Lochan except, judging by the tyre tracks on the ground, during the stalking season. Ninety-nine point nine per cent of Munro baggers are gonnae approach Sgurr nan Ceathramhnan from the Glen Affric side. Aw fuck, dinnae break yer ankle up here! Could be days before anyone realises I'm missing. Aw naw, remember those bits about 'Safety on the Hills' I included in the appendix of *Caleb's List*. Think of the headlines: 'Writer of Mountaineering Guidebook Rescued After Failing to Follow Own Advice.'

I'm a born worrier me. On the other hand though, there is always, on the few occasions I've walked on my own in the mountains without anyone knowing where I am, a sense of freedom, a sense of self reliance. It's all down to me now so I'd better not fuck up. It adds a certain frisson. If I break my leg, will I get a signal on my phone and be able to call mountain rescue from up here in Coire

---

*The Corbetts are the Scottish mountains over 2,500ft/762m.

THE WILD SWIMMER OF KINTAIL

Lochan? Almost certainly not. I do carry an emergency shelter, a tiny one man tent without a groundsheet so I reckon I could last a few days up here. Hamish Brown didn't tell people where he was going when he made the first ascent of the Munros in one expedition. Sure he had pre-arranged rendez-vous points with friends and family and if he'd failed to show up they would have alerted mountain rescue but his rendez-vous points were days apart. Likewise no-one knew where Macrow was when she headed up into the hills around Glen Elchaig in 1946. But then if you'd just survived working on a USAF base during World War Two, the risks of climbing Sgurr nan Ceathramhnan in an old overcoat with some crowdie sandwiches stuffed in the pocket and a Skye terrier for company probably doesn't compare with dodging bombs and V2 rockets.

I plod on up towards Coire Lochan having resolved to walk very carefully and not slip and twist my ankle. Looking north I realise I am almost level with the summit of 730m high Carnan Cruithneachd. The loch must be here somewhere. No, there is another rise waiting to be climbed, leading to an upper, upper corrie. I tramp on, passing a little gorge with a whitewater burn which seems to flow down out of the cloud from the very summit of Sgurr nan Ceathramhnan. The gorge is like the Falls of Glomach made in miniature, high up on the mountainside. The climb up into the corrie is turning out to hold far more interest than I had expected. Looking at maps in the caravan at Dornie, I'd expected a tedious plod through heather and peat hags up to a dreich, wee loch. But the climb up to Coire Lochan is proving to be anything but and on a hot summer day I think it would be fun to explore the little gorge with the waterfall and swim in the pools.

Then suddenly, in a grassy hollow, I come upon death on the mountain. One of the saddest sights I have seen in nature. I catch a glimpse of a hoof and a leg, sticking up out the long grass. A dead hind, not unusual in the hills, at least she'd died high on the mountainside, not hit by a car on the A87. Up here in the corrie just below the west summit of Sgurr nan Ceathramhnan would not be such a bad place to die. I can think of many worse places to die than up here. But something draws me on to look into the hollow and there I see the saddest of sights. The hind, I realise with a twisting in my stomach, must have died while calfing. The hind must have climbed up here, to this remote corrie, to give birth. The head and neck of a calf protrude from between the back legs of the hind. The dead calf's mouth still open, a red orifice frozen in its first and last gasps for breath. I turn my face away and walk blindly on up the hillside.

Macrow: *We found the elusive Coire Lochan (2,500 feet) tucked cunningly away in a cloud-filled cleft—a little pool almost the shape of a star...*

I'm nearly into the mist when, at last, at the top of a final grassy rise, there in front of me, like a sheet of rippling grey steel lies the elusive Coire Lochan. The mist hangs just 50 feet above the water but there is a brightness, sunlight, cutting through the low cloud. Boulder-strewn slopes of grass and scree sweep up to the west top of Sgurr nan Ceathramhnan, somewhere up in the clouds. Three sets of antlers watch me from high up on the east face of the corrie. The lochan lies at 770m, higher than the summit of Suilven and it feels about the same temperature as on a Scottish mountaintop. I take off my rucksack and walk to the edge of the lochan. The water is black and peaty but I can see smooth stones on the bed of the lochan. It looks about two feet deep here at the edge.

'Got to do it, mate,' says a voice in my head, 'It's why you climbed all the way up here.'

Effectively I'm on a mountain top. The temperature is what... five degrees? I'll get hypothermia. A new headline flashes in front of my eyes: 'Little Known Scottish Writer Froze to Death Skinny Dipping on Remote Munro.'

'Got to do it mate,' says the voice again and I bend down and begin to unlace my boots.

The short, deer-cropped turf feels cold under my bare toes as I pull my fleece and T-shirt off then unbuckle the belt on my Rab trousers. I'm wishing I'd worn a better pair of pants though. These ones are definitely not 'pulling pants.' They're definitely 'caravan pants.' Caravan pants I hear you ask? Yip I keep a separate set of clothes at the caravan. My caravan wardrobe consists mainly of Umbro T-shirts from Sports Direct and hoodies from Primark. The idea is to minimise the amount of stuff I have to take with me. There are caravan shoes and socks too and of course caravan pants. The problem with caravan pants is that they're a collection of like all those pants you bought that weren't quite the right size but the shop refused to take back. Or those ones that shrank in the wash or those leopard skin CKs that were briefly fashionable about eight years ago or those cheapie blue Lonsdale ones from Sports Direct you never really liked. You know what I'm talking about guys!

So now I'm stood there on the shore of Coire Lochan in a pair of black Calvin Klein briefs that are kind of washed-out and faded and a bit small for me. What the fuck! It's pretty unlikely I'm gonnae meet some handsome climber up here. It's only the deer over there among the boulders and scree who can see them and they're coming off now anyway. Woo hoo! I wade across the smooth, weed-coated stones and stand there in the water and raise my fists and shout: 'Yes!'

Naked under the mountain, I crouch down in the icy water. I just typed that but actually it wisnae too cold. I kick my legs and do a few splashy strokes of back crawl. Then I stand up. The mist drifts across the north ridge of Sgurr nan Ceathramhnan. I look down. My willy looks very small and shrivelled.

'Got to get your hair wet, mate,' says the voice.

So I swim a couple of strokes on my front with my head under the water. Then I wade back out and stand on the grass. I feel brilliant. I've always been into a wee swim in a Highland burn on a hot July day coming down from a mountain. I knew other folk went swimming on days when it wasn't sunny, on days when it was grey and cloudy and cold, raining even, but for me it had to be a hot day. But standing there naked with the mist swirling over the west peak of Sgurr nan Ceathramhnan I totally get it now. I totally get why they do, why they go wild swimming. I raise my clenched fists again then reach for my paramo jacket and start drying myself.

The sun has come out. The mist has lifted from the tops. Dressed, sitting on a flat boulder beside the lochan, eating a sandwich and a bag of crisps. I've got my furry hat with the ear flaps on because I'm worried about getting hypothermia. But I'm not cold. My skin tingles under my down jacket and I feel great, rejuvenated, refreshed, ready for the long tramp back to Carnach and my bike. Unfortunately the karma wisnae set to last. If only the karma could have lasted a wee bit longer...

Bloody Buggery Brenda

I walk the six kilometres back to Carnach very carefully and having managed not to sprain my ankle, am pleased to get back to the bike about 4.30pm. Just the eight kilometre cycle down Glen Elchaig now, should be back in plenty time for scampi and chips and a pint in Dornie, I think to myself as I clip my bike pannier on and rattle off down Glen Elchaig. At 5pm, about two kilometres beyond Carnach, near the path that leads to the Falls of Glomach I pass a couple with a Golden Labrador on a lead

'Excuse me,' the woman asks, 'But are we being stupid? Is this the way to the Falls of Glomach?'

I stop and put the bike on its kickstand.

'Yes,' I answer pointing towards the River Elchaig, 'You go across the bridge down there.'

'Oh, but we've just come from there and we couldn't find the path.'

Trying not to sound *too* patronising, I explain that the route to the Falls of Glomach from Glen Elchaig involves traversing a narrow path above precipitous drops along a steep-sided gorge. I think about saying the legendary Scottish mountaineer W H Murray described it as 'exposed and dangerous' but manage to stop myself in time.

'I don't think my dog would like it along there,' I say instead before fishing my map out and explaining how to get to the Falls of Glomach by the (much) easier Bealach na Sroine route. Standing there I'm feeling every bit the mountain man from my Jack Wolfskin T-shirt to my wrist mounted Garmin GPS. Even though they can't see I'm wearing a pair of frayed old pants that only cover half my arse.

'We've been looking for the Falls since one o' clock,' the woman says as I get back on the bike and I pedal off thinking about what a long way they've got to walk back down the track to the car park at Killilan and how smart I was to do it by bike. Poor dumb touristas. I'm still in smug, self-congratulatory, poor English people mode and have rattled another three kilometres further down the glen before I glance down to my right and think: Aw fuck, where's my pannier?

Bollocks! It must've fallen off just after I spoke to the dumb touristas with the dog. Well never mind it'll be lying in the road. I just need to cycle back up the road to get it. After two kilometres of rough, unsurfaced road I pass the poor English tourists again. They look a bit bemused to see heading back up the glen again. I'm feeling a lot less smug and self congratulatory about bringing the bike now.

'I've lost my bike pannier,' I say, trying to effect cheery nonchalance between clenched teeth as I pedal slowly uphill past them.

By the time I've cycled (and pushed the bike up the steep bits with the sweat dripping off my cycle helmet) the whole five kilometres back to Carnach where I started and still haven't found the missing pannier I'm feeling a lot less FUCKIN'nonchalant! Especially now I've started to remember what was in it. The contents of the missing-in-action pannier include an old Montane down jacket (I could do with buying a new one anyway), my Rab trousers (they cost £80 aaaarghh!) as well as a paramo jacket (ancient but serviceable nonetheless.) Also my good camera I bought with some of my grant money from Creative Scotland (with the photos of today's walk on it, my aide memoire, like Macrow with her notebook.) The keys to the caravan and of course being borderline OCD I know for certain I locked all the windows and the door. Last but not least, the pannier contains the two spare innertubes and the bike pump so I'm gonnae have to pray I don't get a puncture.

Bloody buggery Brenda!

At this point I spot a pick-up truck, the only vehicle I've seen all day, coming up the track towards me. The driver is wearing a

THE WILD SWIMMER OF KINTAIL

deerstalker and as he slows down to pass me I make a 'wind the window down' gesture.

'I've lost my pannier.'

Nope the stalker hasn't seen it and he's just been speaking to the people with the dog and they didn't mention it. I tell him I'll phone the estate office in Inverinate next week in case someone hands it.

'My camera's in it,' I explain pathetically as he drives off.

So I start again, cycling back along the way I just came. I'll have cycled this section of Glen Elchaig three times today. You can do the maths. And all this on top of a hillwalk to near the summit of one of Scotland's remotest Munros. By this point most of the refreshment and rejuvenation I was feeling as I emerged naked and dripping from the loch has worn off. In fact I'm just fucking knackered.

Bloody buggery Brenda!

So now I'm going to have to cycle five kilometres, with my head twisted round, looking in the ditch at the right hand side of the road. My reasoning is that since I kept to the right-hand side of the track all the way from Carnach, the pannier *must* be in the ditch on that side of the track. Why for? How do I know this? Because, I always keep to the same side of the track on a bike ride on the way out and on the way back. Why for? Well, this eccentric behaviour is born out of a belief it reduces the likelihood of punctures. I know. You think I'm crazy now. Well maybe I am, but you don't go through the stuff I've been through in my life without ending up a little crazy I guess. The pannier couldn't have bounced on the road and rolled into the ditch on the left hand side of the road goes my reasoning. It's just too far. It would have been lying in the road. It wasn't. Therefore, I reason, the pannier is somewhere in the five kilometres of ditch between Carnach and the point where I noticed it was missing. By now it's 6pm and the pint and the scampi and chips in Dornie are rapidly receding over the horizon.

After one kilometre of staring into the ditch I'm starting to develop a serious crick in my neck, a case of a real pain in the neck. Bloody buggery Brenda!

After three kilometres I've begun contingency planning. The owner of the campsite has spare keys for the caravan. I could use some of my Airbnb money to buy new waterproof trousers and a down jacket. Maybe my ex still has that old digital camera he'll never use because he's got an iPhone. After four kilometres I'm thinking how fortunate it was my wallet and (Oh God!) the key to the hire car (with its fob which has printed on it Dodgy RentaCar.com will charge £400 for a replacement) were in my rucksack and still on my back. After four-and-a-half kilometres and about 500 metres from where I first noticed it was gone, I spot the missing pannier in the ditch by the right hand side of the track as per my hypothesis. Seldom have I been so glad to see an inanimate object again. I plucked it from the ditch and I may have kissed it, tears in my eyes. I don't remember I was too shattered by then. I pedal the remaining four kilometres slowly back to Killilan. No sign of the couple with the dog. The poor dumb English touristas are probably back at their car by now I reflect, a good hour-and-a-half before Mr Mountain Man on his bloody buggery bike. In fact they're probably having a pint and scoffing the last portion of scampi and chips to be had in Dornie. Bloody buggery Brenda!

The Starbucks Scribblers Part II

Now I personally haven't delivered Ian Rankin's shopping, but my best buddy at work Paul has. He told me about the boxes of books stacked in the hall of the house in Merchiston.

I'm sitting, on my swivel chair under the glare of strip lights behind mainbank checkout number seven when I'm seized by a sudden, desperate longing to be striding along the narrow traverse path between Mullach Coire Mhic Fhearchair and Beinn Tarsuinn in Fisherfield. In Fisherfield, 200 miles to the north-west as the osprey flies, in Fisherfield, where bog asphodel pricks the hillsides with yellow candles in summertime.

BEEP goes the till. Misread item. Rescan needed. Some days there aren't enough deliveries for us drivers and you have to work in the shop or even worse you get 'put on checkouts.' I usually manage to avoid it and some of the drivers refuse point blank to do it. They seem to regard working on a till as being a slur on their masculinity. I'm not bothered like. It's just that the time passes so so slowly. I find if you talk to every second customer it helps your shift go quicker. You can't work in a supermarket and not end up on a checkout at some point. There's no point being precious about it. There's no point moaning. Everyone who works in the shop has to be till-trained and no matter how obstinate you are they'll get you on a checkout in the end.

Halfway through my six hour shift now and I'm pushing a tracker along aisle four. The display on my handset is giving my picking rate as 77.77ppm which is really slow. Elena who runs Deliver admin can do close to 200ppm. That's when I spot Ian Rankin, in an overcoat clutching a shopping basket. He looks older than in his publicity pics and has a bit of a belly. He's a best-selling writer though and I'm still just a Starbucks scribbler, scrawling lines on the back of sundry scraps of paper, *Sorry We Missed You* cards and even parking tickets.

Sometimes after three cans, I get purple patches of writing. Like Christopher Isherwood, drinking Pils in the café on Brandenberg Strasse, World War Two only a few short years away. Sometimes, I think writing is like having HIV. It's inside me and it takes over in the same way. I found a career but lost a family. Books are like wars, you see. Your next book has its roots in the last one you wrote.

Several members of my family have had books published. Back in the seventies my uncle penned *A Song for the Disco*, in a genre known today as young adult fiction. My uncle's books are still available, though last time I checked, his tome entitled *Wordsworth and Education* was ranked 7,939,562 on Amazon.

I'm writing this book, just like I wrote *The Making of Mickey Bell* while house-sitting a flat in the same Edinburgh street where J K Rowling wrote *Harry Potter and the Philosopher's Stone*. And while I write, I dream a little of that magic will rub off on me and my book.

One Friday Night

A guy in a pub asks me,
'What do you do?'
I've had a few pints.
I'm feeling a bit cocky.
I'm buzzing like.
'I'm a writer, I reply,
'I sprinkle stardust on words.'

I pull the gear lever back and left, the engine grinds down from third to second as the van bangs over the speed bumps on the corner of Kilgraston Road and Grange Terrace. I push the greasy button on the left of the dashboard.

'And now Desert Island Discs and our castaway this week is the writer Kate Atkinson.'

Kate Atkinson! I've delivered her online supermarket shop too. I didn't realise the customer was The Kate Atkinson until my mate Paul at work told me she was a writer. I'd never met the lady so I was in incognito mode when I delivered her shopping. Wearing a high-vis makes you practically invisible anyway, I've found. Even people you know sometimes don't recognise you. Kate Atkinson was nice (big house, much posher than Andrew Greig's place up at Greenbank) but she didn't give me a tip. Middle-class people living in big hooses please take note. Tips make a big difference to folk on the minimum wage. If every customer gave us just one pound it would make a huge difference to us and no difference at all to them.

Bang over another speed bump. The crates in the back of the van crash from side to side. Huh, a successful writer, on Desert Island Discs no less, not a Starbucks Scribbler like me, oot in a smelly, dented old van delivering other people's gin and toilet rolls.

As I was saying Kate Atkinson was nice. But delivering online shopping to a minor celebrity during the Edinburgh Festival turned out to be a real eye-opener. The celebrity in question, an English comedian famous mainly for presenting the then prime minister with a P45 during the Tory party conference, had brought his family with him to Edinburgh. I'll be charitable. It seemed like the stress of having young children and appearing in a Fringe show every night was getting to the 'right on' TV prankster. He was renting a place in Newington. His delivery slot was 7-8pm. Carrying the first of several heavy crates of groceries down the greasy steps that led to his basement flat, I gave my usual cheery, 'Hi! delivery for you!' as I banged the plastic crate down on the kitchen floor.

The celebrity appeared with a face like thunder and hissed, 'Could you try and make any more noise, do you think?' Well that's charming, I thought, coming from the *Guardian*'s favourite comedian. How was I to know his rug rats were asleep? I just blanked him after that, as I do with rude customers. I didnae say another word while I unpacked the remaining five crates (the comedian had bought enough food to keep a family of Syrian refugees going for six months.) As I held out the handset for him to sign, I think he realised his mask had slipped and he'd been rude to someone on the minimum wage. But it was too late by then. I'd seen what he was really like. A bad celebrity and a D lister to boot, it doesn't do to be rude to folk on the minimum wage when you're on the telly. But at least if I'm ever famous enough to go on a TV chat show, I'll have a good sofa story to tell.

Then I think of Ronnie Burn sitting on the pavement in the Grassmarket in Edinburgh, his grubby overcoat wrapped around his knees. A man in a trilby drops a farthing at his feet. Burn looks up at the man and smiles. Jessie Kesson, emptying the yellow and brown contents of the bedpan into the sluice, pushing her trolley along the carpeted corridor of the nursing home even as she imagines the opening lines of a new book: *There would be no gathering in of the corn today. The rain that had swept across Inveraig blotted out the firth itself.*

But then I pause and (metaphorically) put my pen down (in reality my fingers hover momentarily over the keyboard) as the realisation dawns that I, Kellan MacInnes, have most likely already joined that motley crew of legendary Scottish hill characters. Perhaps the 'eccentric survivor of AIDS who went on to compleat the Munros' will one day feature in the climbing books of the future alongside the likes of Ronnie Burn, Ben Humble, Syd Scroggie and their ilk. Now that would be something.

The Lodge Under the Loch

Neart nan Gleann, the power of the glens.
Motto of the North of Scotland Hydro-Electric Board

The guy cutting the grass has stopped the motor mower. The sound ceases. Silence fills the air and the gap is filled by the sound of the river, the water pouring over the stones, the birdsong and the distant lowing of cattle.

I open the frayed, linen-bound book and turn the page. Chapter XII of *Kintail Scrapbook* has the title 'Benula and Back: The Longest Trek of All.' It is Macrow's account of a two day expedition from Iron Lodge in Glen Elchaig to four remote hill lochans located high on Sgurr na Lapaich and on Carn Eige which is the highest mountain north of the Great Glen. The paths Macrow walked to reach these hills, today lie deep beneath the waters of the vastly expanded Loch Mullardoch. Reaching these Munros from the west involves many miles of very rough walking so I opt, like most twenty-first-century hillwalkers, to approach Sgurr na Lapaich and Carn Eige from the village of Cannich in the east.

I pull the handbrake on. The Labradoodle sits up looking out expectantly. It's summer still. A van and several other cars are parked here where the road ends at the head of Glen Cannich. I tie the laces on my boots, pull my rucksack on, the Labradoodle jumps out the car and we set off along the track heading for Loch Mullardoch. Past spikey clumps of soft rush and yellow buttercups in the grass and a grey bleached stump of Scots pine, like a wooden anchor. At the edge of the track the bracken and grass ends abruptly giving way to bare rock, washed clean, bleached by the constant change of the water level in the reservoir. The rise and fall of the water over 70 years has created a steeply shelving beach of grey sand, gravel and boulders.

THE WILD SWIMMER OF KINTAIL

Two green, mildew-covered, fibreglass rowing boats lie beached beside the road. They won't ply the loch again.

Clegs and midges buzz in the air. This is an ugly, despoiled place now. Poor Mullardoch will never grace the pages of the Scotsman calendar or get her pic on the VisitScotland website. In 1947, Glen Cannich and Glen Affric were part of a proposed national park but the plan was never progressed. This is a place few tourists will see, the plaques erected beside the loch by the Clan Chisolm Society Nova Scotia speak bleakly of Scotland's diaspora. A glance at the map in my hand on shows half a dozen footpaths that now end in the reservoir where once they led to the lodge under the loch.

Where the track dwindles to footpath there's an ugly concrete boathouse with a rusty, corrugated-iron roof and several small motor boats in varying states of disrepair. In the 70 years since the old ways were submerged beneath the grey waters of bloated Mullardoch, a rough walkers' path has developed along the northern shore of the loch. It's a muddy, slippery, rocky walk over boulders, heather roots, bracken and bog myrtle.

I can see a square windbreak of conifers ahead. I wonder what it is, a building, a ruin perhaps? I pull the map, folded neatly inside its clear plastic bag, out the side pocket of my shorts and glance at it. There are no buildings marked on the map. It must be a ruin. I'm walking through the flooded glen, walking back in time, walking back to Kintail.

1946: *Then I went out into the cold wind, and plodded along the road towards the ridge of Br*àigh a' Choire Bhig. *It was then 10.30 am*

In the photo the Labradoodle is standing at the fork in the path looking like she's wondering which way to go. The skirts of the hills along Loch Mullardoch are hemmed by the grey-white, scree shoreline of the reservoir. At the waterline, what was hillside in 1946 is thick with a jungle scrub of bracken, heather, reeds and woody bushes of bog myrtle.

Cloud brushes the top of 1,063metre high Toll Creagach on the southern shore of the loch. I get closer to the trees. They're a stand of fine old Scots pines, pre-dating the dam, part of the lost world of Kintail 1946. I unzip the top pocket of my rucksack and fish out the 1934 edition of Bartholemew's Revised Half-Inch Contoured Map of Central Ross, Sheet 20. The map Macrow used back in 1946. The topography of the glen lost beneath the loch is confusing. I reckon I'm approaching the site of Cozac Old Lodge, drowned by the waters of Mullardoch in 1951. Marked today only by the lonely windbreak of Scots pines, waiting forlornly at the water's edge.

When at last I reach the stand of old pines, I see three have fallen during some long ago winter storm. They lie heaped like giant matchsticks. Ahead I can see crags where the ridge of Bràigh a' Choire Bhig, an outlier of the Sgurr na Lapaich massif, curves down to the lochside. Sgurr na Lapaich and its high altitude hill lochans being my objective this overcast day in late summer.

1946: *I took off my heavy rain-coat and fixed it with a complicated system of straps over my shoulder. Just before Cozac Old Lodge, I cut off the road to the north and began to climb the ridge.*

I'm aiming to pick up a path marked on the OS maps of today as running straight into the loch but which I guess in Macrow's day ran along the now flooded floor of the glen. The Labradoodle and I brush through waist-high bracken, trying not to think about the ticks perched on the end of the ferny fronds, waiting for the opportunity to insert themselves onto a passing dog ear, snout or my hairy calves.

THE WILD SWIMMER OF KINTAIL

There is a ruin beyond the trees. The remains of an old but-n-ben drowning in bracken but no trace of the building that the stand of old pines must once have sheltered.

Past the ruined cottage where the Allt Taige empties into Loch Mullardoch, there's another ugly bay of bleached boulders and black peaty mud. This is a landscape damaged by electricity. The contrast with Loch Affric just over the hills, in the next glen is stark. I don't want to think about the bay of white sand at the head of Loch Affric where I swam last October. No-one would want to swim in the murky waters of Mullardoch, to slither over the boulders and black mud.

1946: *Loch Mullardoch, with its tree-covered islands, had the appearance of a tropical lagoon under a blue sky. Outcrops of rock and mica began to gleam silver on the hills.*

Once there were two sisters, Affric and Mullardoch. Both were possessed of great beauty but Mullardoch was destined to pay the price to save her sister Affric's looks. By the time plans for a hydro-electric scheme in Glen Affric were announced people had begun to raise serious concerns about the damage being done to the Scottish landscape by the construction of dams, power stations and pylons in once pristine Scottish glens. To assuage the protesters, prominent among whom was the legendary Scottish mountaineer W H Murray, the North of Scotland Hydro-Electric Board devised a scheme whereby the scenic gem that was Glen Affric would be spared the ugly artificial tidelines caused by the constant rise and fall in the level of reservoirs as electricity was generated. A tunnel carrying water from Loch Mullardoch ensures that Loch Affric and Loch Beinn a' Mheadhoin are kept topped up and spared the ravages of the ugly, artificial tidelines of bare rock and boulders that scar other glens dammed by the Hydro Board. But to save Affric the great beauty that was Mullardoch was lost forever. A concrete cliff of a wall built across Glen Cannich, her blue Scots pines torn down and the natural, sandy shoreline replaced by a 100-foot-wide strip of ugly, eroded grey scree all around the loch.

I find the old path marked on the map on the east bank of the Allt Taige. It's as clear as old stalkers' paths always are, a thin grey thread, taking a good line up the east bank of the Allt Taige, always finding the drier ground. As the path climbs higher, Loch Mullardoch and the bleached boulders and gravel and black mud of the arid canyon-like, eroded lower section of the Allt Taige, are left behind. Rowans and silver birches still grow beside the stream just as they did before the Hydro came. The burn tumbles into a deep gorge between green, mossy rocks. Scented bog myrtle and yellow candles of bog asphodel brighten the heather by the path. Above the gorge, on the open hillside the burn gurgles down the grassy hillside, a Highland stream free again.

Cloud drifts across the hills on the far side of the loch. I'm looking across to the long ridge that runs from Beinn Fionnaidlh to Mam Sodhail. Beinn Fionnlaidh, rendered inaccessible today by the swollen waters of Loch Mullardoch, was the hill that once rose up behind the lodge under the loch. I'm looking across at the mountain and I'm thinking how much easier it was in Macrow's day, when you could stop the night at Benula Lodge and then climb Ben Fionnaidlh next day. The expansion of Loch Mullardoch has completely changed the geography of the glen making the Munros and tops far more inaccessible and remote than they were in 1946.

There's something about the flooded lands and the stories of the people who once lived there. A wistful sadness hangs over the empty glens. Only the mountains stand as they have always stood, silent witnesses to the rape of Mullardoch. Isolated, sparse rural communities were powerless to do anything against the power of the office of the secretary of state for Scotland. In his headquarters in the city on the hill, the secretary of state Mr Tom Johnston had a plan. He wanted to harness the power of the glens, *Neart nan Gleann*. You see the words yet, among the dripping branches and wet leaves on the rusty gates of the power station at Invergarry. *Neart nan Gleann*, the power of the glens was the plan, free electricity to power new industries in towns and villages across the Highlands. This was Soviet style five-year economic planning and all that stood in the way of building this new world, bringing electricity to the Highlands was the beauty of Mullardoch. *Neart nan glean*, ah but it was a glorious vision, a Scottish economic miracle bringing electricity to the remotest clachans. The loss of the beauty of Mullardoch and a handful of remote crofts swept away by the Hand of Progress must have seemed but a small price to pay.

And tens of fathoms below in the peaty water, foot-steps echo in the empty corridors of the lodge under the loch.

And Macrow's boots drying by the range.

And Macrow setting off along the dusty road in the Highland morning that will never come again.

1946: *At last, I stopped for a brief rest by a stream. Something white was moving along the winding road far below. With the aid of my glasses, I saw it was a white horse, carrying its rider swiftly in the wake of a lorryload of logs.*

'We'll need to tell the lawyers about the caravan,' my ex announced at one point well into the protracted divorce negotiations. By now I'd already paid 50 per cent of the new for old value of the ten-year-old sofa, the nine-year-old PC and the one-year-old dishwasher.

'Listen,' I said, 'If you want to go asking a firm of snooty Edinburgh lawyers how much they think a very small eleven-year-old caravan is worth and how we should divide it up, you go right ahead but I'm just not going there...'

'But they're ten grand new,' he protested.

I ended up phoning Freedom Caravans in Stafford. The conversation went something like this:

'Hi, I'm splitting up from my ex... er... getting divorced and I was wondering if you could give me an idea of how much our Freedom Caravan is worth?'

'I'll put you through to Dave in sales, just popping you on hold for a sec.'

While I was on hold I it occurred to me I could possibly turn the caravan situation to my advantage. I'm like that, you see.

'Hi is that Dave in Sales? I've got an eleven-year-old Freedom caravan and I was wondering how much you'd give me for it, secondhand like...'

Then the inspiration kicked in:

'I've done a lot of cooking in it and my ex was a heavy smoker and we've got two long-haired dogs.'

'Does it have a fridge,' said Dave in sales.

'No.'

'I'll give you twelve hundred quid for it, mate.'

Job done!

I step across the burn, glancing down at the shiny, rounded pebbles beneath the clear, peaty water. Leaving the stream behind I strike up the ridge of Bràigh a' Choire Bhig. Looking back with the gain of height I can see the great bowl of Mullardoch, the waters held back,

THE WILD SWIMMER OF KINTAIL

cradled in the giant concrete arms of the mass gravity hydroelectric dam.

The ridge leads on. The summit of the Sgurr is hidden in the mist, I step over the blackened stump of a long dead Scots pine still embedded in the black peat. I see no-one, no people, not a living soul climbing this Munro. For no climbers today approach Sgurr na Lapaich by the old ways, by the paths that lead from the drowned lands.

I click the mouse. I see I stopped here on the summit of Mullach a' Ghlas-thuill, the whaleback of the grey hollow, caught my breath, had a slug of water, reached in my pocket for a dog biscuit, patted the Labradoodle's furry coat, felt the solitude of the empty hills.

Pink cross-leaved heath shines in the grass. My boots trample yellow spears of bog asphodel and white flags of bog cotton. The Labradoodle pauses and stares ahead. An erratic boulder stands on the skyline, bearded with black lichen flecked with white. A survivor from the last ice age perched on the hillside, standing guard high above the flooded floor of the glen. Sentinel in 1946, the rock watched Macrow come and it watched Macrow go.

From my vantage point, up on the mossy ridge beside the erratic boulder, I look down on the glassy, black waters of Mullardoch 800 metres below. Now I can see along the length of the long glen that cuts almost across Scotland from Cannich in the east to Killilan in the west. The ridge is furrowed with solifluction terraces and I imagine how cold it gets here in winter. I remember reading how the concrete froze before they could pour it, when they built the dam at Monar in the 1950s. And in typing that, I see in my photo taken at the end of July, there is still a snow patch just below the summit of Sgurr na Lapaich, the memory of winter.

Suddenly, up there on the wide shoulder of the Sgurr, a hind and calf, deer running across the wide, grey gravel solifluction terraces.

I've captured it on a little movie. I'm sat at the kitchen table, warmed by the Rayburn, grey January sky outside, watching the deer running high on Sgurr na Lapaich.

The Labradoodle looks like she's up for chasing them but a stern look from master and a quick: Sit! Biscuit! Clip the lead on puts a stop to any nonsense. The Labradoodle takes the opportunity of being on the lead to hold up progress by rolling in the deer grass for a good back scratch every ten paces. Hmmm. Cantakerous Labradoodle? Yip!

Green cushions of mountain thyme lie scattered across the ridge, crinkled leaves of cloudberries and yellow petals of cat's ear are tucked in among the grass and sphagnum moss. I'm just about to type: 'and now I can't see Loch Mullardoch, the mountains have closed in hiding the scars of the glen' But then I wonder why I took this photo and I zoom in a bit and then I see why. Over the next line of hills, beyond Glen Affric the turbines of the Millenium wind factory near Invergarry march across the hillside. Today a new wave of renewable energy, even greater than the Hydro in 1946, is breaking over the Scottish hills. Twenty-first-century despoilation of the landscape just so teenagers can get fat and spotty and depressed, spending all day looking at their phones. I don't have a problem with wind turbines, no, honestly I don't. I have no problem with three wind turbines on the hillside above a Highland village providing efficient, environmentally friendly power for the local community. But what I do have a problem with is greedy land-owners pocketing government subsidies to construct giant wind factories, spoiling the landscape. I'm sorry but the German and Dutch tourists, the folk I take on the bike tours round Edinburgh come to Scotland to see, 'oor bens and glens' Not rows of dumbly spinning turbines and lines of super pylons transmitting the electricity yes, but losing around seven per cent of it from cables and substations en route. And all

THE WILD SWIMMER OF KINTAIL

so teenagers can grow fat and spotty and depressed sitting in their bedrooms looking at Facebook and porn all day.

Wind 'farms' sprouting up across the hills and a hydro-electric dam on the every burn, suddenly this remote area feels under threat, a fragile landscape: a landscape under pressure, a landscape threatened by the human race's insatiable demand for electricity. Like who needs air conditioning units in Scotland? *Please*?

Home, where I live, is a Victorian tenement in Edinburgh, in one of the streets at the foot of Arthur's Seat. This Victorian flat I purchased jointly with my ex used to be home to three old ladies. They'd lived there all their lives, been born there I think. Their father bought the flat. I'm only the second owner since the flat was built in 1906, around the time Caleb sketched cup and ring mark boulders in the countryside around Aberfeldy.

When we purchased the flat we realised the old ladies must have been struggling with mobility issues. In every room extra sockets had been installed at waist height to save the old souls from having to bend down to plug in the hoover. When we first moved into the flat 15 years ago we thought: there are so many sockets. But now I struggle to find somewhere to charge my phone, my laptop, my digital camera, my Kindle, my hair clippers, my bike lights, my power pack, my electric toothbrush. Now it seems like every socket has some electrical device I probably don't really need plugged into it. How much of this electronic junk that crams our homes do we really need? I mean really need to be happy. Because you know for sure the best things in life are free, like Cuilean, my first dog.

The fallen stones of an old drystone wall run along the edge of the broad ridge. In the next photo the Labradoodle is peering into a cairn, a little ruckle of weathered stones on the hillside.

Macrow 1946: *I reached a cairn. There, just below... shone Loch a'Choire Bhig, 2,500 feet up, with its two tiny islets and cloud-filmed ridge behind.*

Macrow's right about the islets. I zoom in on them and there they are. Seen from above the lochan is a star-shaped mountain pool and I sense it was once part of a glacier, like the erratic boulder on the ridge, a survivor of the ice age. I stand beside the cairn high on the ridge of Sgurr na Lapaich and take a series of digital images of the lochan. See Macrow lying flat in the grass in her old overcoat holding the brownie box camera out over the edge of the crags on that day in late summer long ago.

1946: *But of the other loch I could see nothing. So now I must walk along the ridge. What a day!*

Then, in among the boulders, a pair of ears and a head, horns and a long snout, the Doodle sniffs the air, a flock of mountain goats. The Labradoodle inhales their scent, carried on the wind. Afterwards, back in my tent at Cannich, I count 20 goats in a photo I took. All horns and beards and shaggy coats dappled grey and white with patches of black, descendants of the domestic goats kept by the people who once farmed the glens before the Clearances and the Hydro, wandering over the mountains for the rest of time.

The tops of Carn Eige and Beinn Fionnlaidh on the north side of Mullardoch are in cloud but the peak of the bogland, Sgurr na Lapaich stands clear now. I tramp across a desert of grey rock dotted with white quartzite. Mist blows across the green mossy ridge. And then at last there it is below us, Loch Tuill Bhearnach. Macrow's account is a bit confused, maybe a little heat adled, at this point for she writes about Loch a' Choire Bhig with its two tiny islands but she must mean Loch Tuill Bhearnach. But all Macrow had was a notebook shoved in the pocket of her old raincoat. She didn't have the luxury of 120 digital photos of the climb up Sgurr na Lapaich to help jog her memory six months or a year later when it came to writing up her notes, writing her book.

1946: *And, at last, following the long line of Coire Glas Liath, I found it, an oval expanse of shining water on the great shelf between high hills... Loch Thuill Bhearnach, or the Loch of the Notched Hollow. It is much more trouble to reach than one would imagine from the map—*

Ah poor Brenda, it was ever thus in the hills, it was ever thus. I walk on into the mist, heading for the summit of the peak of the bogland. I check the 1930s edition of the map, for there is no Coire Glas Liath marked on my 2017 map. Macrow refers to one of the summits of Sgurr na Lapaich as Sgùrr nan Clachan Geala, the peak of the white stones. As I walk along the ridge, across ground white with quartzite boulders, I realise that the hill's old name, as recorded by Macrow, must be its true name.

The rocky edge of the crags is padded with green cushions of alpine ladies-mantle and there are cowberries among the boulders. A flattening, the cliffs draw back and then we're up, standing on the summit of Sgurr na Lapaich. There's another hillwalker here too, from Inverness. He stands at the edge of one of my summit photos, giving a little perspective to the view.

Macrow: *Then I sat down and devoured the tomato-sandwiches. .*

We talk, the Labradoodle barks until I shush her with a biscuit. I munch one of my (as taken on the hill by Macrow in 1946 style) tomato sandwiches. They're actually OKish but not a patch on tuna.

I slither about on mist-coated rocks exploring the summit. I find a well-constructed stone shelter and then in a little hollow, protected from the prevailing wind, gable end and fireplace still standing, the ruins of a second building. The summit was an important survey station during the primary triangulation of Scotland in the 1840s and I think of the men up here with their limelights, firewood and stock of provisions. All carried up by pony. The ground carefully levelled where the men of the Ordnance Survey sheltered from the weather, the mapmakers leaving their mark on the landscape.

As I turn to leave the summit, I reach into the side pocket of my rucksack for the digital camera. The Labradoodle's head is in many of my pictures quickly snapped as an *aide memoire*, to be written up over the winter in Edinburgh with the dog curled up at my feet waiting patiently for it to be four o'clock and time to go to the park.

1946: *I photographed Loch a' Choire Bhig across the scree-slope, then plunged on down to Benula.*

Heading back down the broad shoulder of Braigh a' Choire Bhig, I can see the mudflats at the head of Loch Mullardoch, where Macrow took the path from Iron Lodge that warm summer's day in 1946. The eroded shores of Loch Mullardoch, white when seen from up here at over 3,000 feet, cut east through the glen. The reservoir is low and I can see the shadowy outline of Loch Frith an Acha and Lochan na Cloiche, the lost lochans. I can see the faint ghostly twists of the lost river that once wound its way along the the glen down past Benula Lodge. A glimpse of a lost landscape, a glimpse of the land as Macrow knew it in 1946.

1946: *Now I could see over the lower slopes to where the river widened into two swirling pools—Loch Frith an Acha and the*

THE WILD SWIMMER OF KINTAIL

slightly larger Lochan na Cloiche. Beyond this, it swirled over a shallow fall into Loch Mullardoch. Nestling against a dark triangle of pines, the gracious white lodge of Benula shone in fitful sunlight. Through my glasses, I could see signs of great activity—carpets lying on the lawn, painters wandering in and out of the French doors, and a tiny cairn terrier which seemed to be in charge of the entire proceedings!

Above the muddy, stony tideline, I can see a path. It emerges straight out of the loch and climbs the grassy hillside in a faint Z shape. Like a childhood scar on a man's leg. The path that starts in the loch, another 75 years and it will be gone.

1946: *Down. Down into the darkening valley... Then across the bridge... up the gravel road, and through the iron gates of Benula Lodge... I stumbled round to the back door and rang a bell. Within, the sound of voices and laughter ceased. An attractive, dark-haired girl came to the door. Yes, I could come in; but I must excuse the muddle, as the place was being redecorated in preparation for the 'family's' summer visit...*

I have the strangest feeling that round the next bend in the track out the corner of my eye I might find a lost path back to 1946. I might slip through a tear in the folds of time and see the dark murky waters of Loch Mullardoch receding, the pine-clad islands re-emerging. See the swirling pools of Loch Frith an Acha and Lochan na Cloiche and the waterfall and the river winding past the lodge down to the white bridge at Benula.

At last I reach the rough, muddy path that struggles its way along the south shore of Loch Mullardoch today and head back to the car. I have swum in, washed my face, dipped my hand in or glimpsed at a distance 26 of the 28 hill lochs on Macrow's List. There are still two lochans left on the list. But I can't follow in Macrow footsteps any further. Too many kilometres of rough terrain and the raised level of Loch Mullardoch bar the way. The old paths that led to Benula Lodge lie deep beneath the loch. I can go no further.

1946: *They found me a bed. Mrs Forbes, the English-born house-keeper; Janet, the cook; the dark-haired maid, Lily—all excelled themselves in kindness to the untidy and grubby stranger who had dropped into their midst, as it were, from the summits of Càrn Eige.*

I zoom in on the loch and its eroded artificial shores, its level raised and lengthened by the dam and I wonder where exactly beneath the steel grey surface lie the ruins of Benula Lodge, the lodge under the loch. I think about snorkelling Loch Mullardoch but it's an unattractive idea, full of fears of becoming entangled in unseen debris lying beneath the black peaty waters of the loch. No, there's only one thing for it, if I want to keep walking in Macrow's footsteps and go back, all the way back to Benula and find the lodge under the loch. If I want to follow in Macrow's footsteps, if I want to follow Macrow's route to the last two hill lochans high on Carn Eige, it looks like I'm gonnae have to walk on water.

1946: *After a goodnight cup of tea, I retired to the pleasant, airy room placed at my disposal. There were two hot-water bottles in the bed. The blue mountain night closed in. Outside, the wide river sang dreamily among the great, scarred hills.*

Water

The Lost World

'Mind you, boy, the light in the byre is handy but all the power in the world couldn't replace the pleasure of a fine day on Loch Monar.'
      Kenny Mackay, cleared from Pait Lodge, 1959.

'What's his name again? The guy with the boat?'

L is peering over the steering wheel of her black VW Golf. We're driving along the single track road up Glen Cannich through the dripping bracken. The Labradoodle barks as the car rattles over a cattle-grid.

'He's called Angus. I think he's the stalker *and* he works behind the bar in the Slater's Arms in Cannich.'

Desultory electricity cables are strung across the hillside above the dripping birch trees and the whole glen is swathed in dense mist

'And why are you making me go on a boat?'

'Because Benula Lodge is where Brenda... remember her?'

L nods her head. 'Totally obscure female poet and mountaineer you're writing a book about?'

'That's her! Brenda stayed the night at the lodge but the footpath she followed from there to the foot of Carn Eige is underwater now. So that's where Angus and his boat come in.'

'And I'll get a Munro ticked off on the way to these hill loch thingees right?'

'You'll get a tick,' I assure her.

Mist: over the green bracken, beyond the white lichen smattered boulders, Loch Mullardoch is lost in the mist. A bank of fog hangs at treetop height over the Scots pines on the shore of Loch a' Bhana where in 1930, at the beginning of this tale, the young woman, the stalker's wife halted on the dusty road and heard the sound of hammering and wooden boards being thrown down.

Suddenly out of the mist there looms the vast, gloomy, concrete edifice of the Mullardoch mass gravity hydro-electric dam. It appears out of the mist like some concrete fortress, like the ramparts of Skaro. Maybe there are Daleks within.

Half-a-dozen cars are parked on the short, sheep-cropped turf beneath the louring concrete wall of the dam. The sinister edifice stretches from one side of the glen to the other. The 70-year-old concrete is black with moss and streaked with white drips. I pull my rucksack on and we walk the last 100 metres of steep single-track road up to the dam.

I stand at the start of the walkway that runs out along the top of the dam. Behind the concrete wall of the dam a steep bank, a wave of black sand and grey boulders shelves steeply down to the leaden waters of Loch Mullardoch 150 feet below. Weeds and moss sprout out of cracks in the concrete below the grey painted handrail. A hundred yards away the first tower of the dam is veiled in mist. It's like the edge of a time portal. I feel like a spy on a foggy bridge on the border between East and West Germany in the 1960s during the Cold War. Anyone, anything could emerge out of the mist, I think, as I stand there.

Here on the top of the dam, 150 feet above the floor of the glen on one side and the waters of Loch Mullardoch on the other, I remember a photo in a book on the shelf of Scottish books back home in my flat in Edinburgh. The book tells the story of the hydro boys who built the dams. In the photo, a barechested workie is carrying a pile of planks on his shoulder, while walking along the top of the dam. In the black and white photo he stares cheekily back out of the page at me, no safety rope, no harness, no scaffolding, trusting to his balance alone. He looks so cocky with his smile brimming with life and confidence and surefootedness. Then I think, the photo, it's sort of a metaphor for life. One minute you're strutting along the top of the dam with your top off carrying a load of planks in the sunshine, next minute you're sliding down the concrete into the murky loch below.

A beam of sunlight cuts through the mist. Maybe if I walk a hundred paces along the top of the dam to where the concrete fades into the fog and the mist particles dance in the sunlight, maybe there I'll step through the mist and back into Macrow's lost world of 1946 and find the blue loch and the pine-clad islands still shimmering in the sun.

We're onboard Angus's boat now. It's not exactly the pride of the fleet I have to say. It's like about 30 years old. L is crouched in the front looking dubious and I'm holding tight onto the Labradoodle's collar. Angus sits precariously balanced on an upturned plastic crate steering the boat. There's not a life jacket in sight. The grey surface of the loch looks thick and viscous and oily. The wake of the boat scoops a shallow trough through the foaming, white bubbles. The dam lies behind us now, a darker grey wall against the grey mist, holding back the waters of the loch. The towers on the dam stand like a Roman wall in the fog. Bright white patches above where the sun will break through and melt the mist and make the lost world disappear.

I'm grasping the chrome handrail of the boat. An island, it must have been a hill once, I figure, appears out of the mist, skirts hemmed by artificial shores of scree. Grey on darker grey, the shores of the loch lost in the fog, cloaked by the mist. The boat alone, throbbing, its wake like a guttit haddie, like a whale's fin, like a tail, like one of the kelpies of old.

The sun is beginning to melt the bank of fog, curls of grey mist, a tear of blue sky now between the grey, scree shore of the loch and the top of the green hillside. Grass and rocks and a miniature artificial beach of white sand glimpsed through a break in the low clouds of mist. The dam has gone, vanished. The light through the mist catching the white foaming whale tail of our wake, a glint of sunlight is reflected in the black plastic cover of the rattling, throbbing, outboard hanging from the stern of the boat.

I stare ahead, looking over Angus' shoulder watching the mountains along the shore of Loch Mullardoch appear then disappear out of the mist. Then I look behind me. At the end of the white, bubbling, roaring, foaming, white whale tail of a wake, the sun, a brilliant white orb suspended in the mist six feet above the surface of the loch. Like a strange new planet hanging in the grey mist of space.

And then we enter the lost world. A low grey shore appears out of the mist. How can Angus possibly find the bay I pointed to on the map in this fog, I wonder? But he seems certain of where he's going. This is like the fog of time. I'm travelling back through the mist to the lost world of 1946.

Macrow: *Loch Mullardoch, with its tree-covered islands, had the appearance of a tropical lagoon under a blue sky.*

Slimy, black branches reach withered arms out of the oily water to snatch us, the rotted remains of the pines that once glistened under a blue sky on the tree-covered islands.

We jump down from the boat onto a black beach of peaty mud and sand, washed into tidelines by the rise and fall of Loch Mullardoch. As the demand for power, for electricity, for *neart nan gleann*, for power from the glens, to spin the turbines rose and fell, it washed the sand and peaty mud into gently curving tidelines across this strange beach, like the rings on a tree stump.

Where are the cheery young tradesmen from Glasgow? Where is the white horse on the dusty road? Where is the housekeeper frying freshly caught trout for breakfast? Where are the rugs spread out to

THE WILD SWIMMER OF KINTAIL

air on the grass? Where are the iron gates of Benula? Where is the Cairn terrier playing on the lawn in the sunshine? Where is the white house at Benula? All gone, all drowned, deep beneath the turgid grey waters of Loch Mullardoch, all gone, sunk beneath the loch. And with our Goretex and phones and GPS we step ashore like spacemen from another planet, like aliens from outer space, visitors from the future.

The Black Beach of Benula

So sad—the days that are no more. So strange—the beautiful things of the world, that are always the shortest-lived...
                                                  BGM, 1948.

To either side of the strange alien beach are 30-foot-high outcrops of schist. Not the familiar mossy-grey they once were when they were on the hillside. Now, since the glen was flooded, bleached white, washed clean by the rise and fall of Loch Mullardoch as electric kettles, microwave ovens, laptops, phone chargers and a multitude of electronic gadgets make their incessant demands for power from the lonely glen.

Where the strange black beach, like the volcanic beaches of Tenerife ends there is just black peaty mud, 300 feet of it and we climb up onto the bleached white schist outcrops to avoid it. In the black mud there are dozens of tree stumps. The stumps of Scots pines felled before the glen was flooded to prevent branches and debris choking the hydro tunnels and turbines. These rotting, grey stumps all that remains of the pine trees that once gave Mullardoch her great beauty.

The grey mist drifts across the artificial scree shoreline and the islands that were once hills on the floor of the glen. The scree, the bleached schist, the mud, the grey stumps of felled trees, Mullardoch's ravaged face, a great beauty has been lost.

I take a compass bearing, aiming to find a path that now starts 50 feet beneath the loch, the path that led from the back door of Benula Lodge where a tired and bedraggled Macrow rang the doorbell to ask for shelter for the night.

But maybe its faint outline is still there beneath the water. Winding across the muddy bed of the loch where once the white ponies followed it through the bracken. A drowned path, still there under the grey waters of Loch Mullardoch. If I look round, over my shoulder, it's not hard to imagine a ghostly stalking party making their way along the bed of the loch, following the lost path to Carn Eige. If I look round, over my shoulder, a spectral stalker in dripping tweeds with pondweed in his hair leading a ghostly white horse will emerge from the loch and through the banks of fog.

I glance down at the Garmin GPS on my wrist, it concurs with the compass bearing and we set off through the mist. Behind us the chug chug chug of Angus' boat fades as it vanishes into the mist between two islands leaving great concentric ripples in its wake. The little waves spread out and wash over the slimy branches protruding from the loch and break gently on the black beach of Benula.

And then the sun breaks through. The hot July sun burning the mist off just as we reach the edge of the bleached scree shoreline and step over the last rotting tree stumps. Suddenly there are green birch trees and tall Scots pines and yellow deer grass and we're back on a Scottish hillside, the lost world of Benula and the black beach and the mist all burned off by the hot July sun. The green birch trees beside the stream there, this burn must be the Allt a' Choire Dhomhain. Angus has piloted us through the mists of time and dropped us off at exactly the right place. At the exact spot I showed him on the map before we set off in the boat from Mullardoch Dam. Ahead the hills are grey-green against a sky of blue. The mist is lifting all around us. In the bright sunshine I can see a track climbing uphill beside the stream.

1946: *The hill-road mounted swiftly up the brown brae.*

Looking back over my shoulder the mist still lies along the surface of the loch and over the strange black beach of Benula. But ahead are only bright sunshine and the promise of a day on the hills.

The track fades to a faint footpath. Yellow flames of golden rod cut through the deer grass and bell heather. In the photo L looks back at me over her shoulder. I must have stopped to take the picture. There's a half smile on her face and I wonder what she's saying to me. Behind us the long, flooded trench of Loch Mullardoch and Glen Cannich, now the mist has lifted I can see the level of the loch is low. The white scar of the 30-foot-high artificial shoreline runs all around the foot of the mountains. From up here on the hillside the islands in the loch are white, like desert islands topped with a few scrubby green bushes and birch trees.

1946: *Now I looked along the whole sun-chequered length of Glen Cannich, with its string of lochs stretching away into cloud-filled distance.*

The old stalkers' path climbs the hillside in hairpin bends and makes easy going of the steep hillside and we're glad of it because though it's only half ten in the morning it's already hot. There are blue petals of milkwort and white thyme among the sphagnum moss and deer grass. I'm looking at the photo I took from high up on on the steep flank of Carn Eige looking across the glen to An Riabachan. And when I look down at Loch Mullardoch I see the waters of the loch are blue now the mist has gone.

The path is faint but it's there. A narrow shelf cut into the steep hillside, its edges blurred by moss and long grass. But we can still follow its ghostly line up the hillside. How many people a year walk this path I wonder? There can't be more than a handful. Nobody climbs Carn Eige from this side now. Not since the 1940s when the glen was flooded. Munro baggers approach Carn Eige by first climbing Mam Sodhail in upper Glen Affric. Angus the boatman

THE WILD SWIMMER OF KINTAIL

knew the path though so maybe the stalkers' still use it sometimes.

Beyond the point where Angus dropped us off at the black beach of Benula, the present day Loch Mullardoch narrows into an ugly gorge of bleached white rock and artificial shoreline squeezed between the steep flank of Beinn Fionnlaidh and Coire Lungard. A gouged out channel of bleached white rock and scree, an ugly place, the kind of place you could have filmed an episode from a 1970s series of *Doctor Who*. Set on another planet, set in the ruins of Skaro. In this blazing heat it doesn't even look like Scotland. I'm looking down on a lost landscape. A lost landscape that Macrow was one of the last people on earth to see.

There's L in the picture again, stomping up the track ahead of me in her skort and sunhat with a hot looking Labradoodle trailing along at her heel. In my photo she casts a long shadow on the green hillside. The angle of ascent eases as we approach the Bealach na h-Eige and the path fades and becomes harder to follow. I remember Angus telling me something on the boat as he steered us through the mist on Mullardoch, comfortably seated on his upturned plastic crate. If you're not sure of the line of the path he'd said, look for rocks set on edge. That's how the ghillies marked the line of these old paths when they built them. So they could find their way in the mist, he explained. Sure enough as we climb onto the bare shoulder of Carn Eige a line of upended flat rocks carefully set in to the scrub heath shows us the way.

Up here we're on the broad whaleback of the mountain. It falls away on either side in crags and grey scree. The July sun beats down on and sparkles on the glistening white quartzite. In my pictures of that day the hills once again have a look of the mountains of Paros seen across the Aegean Sea from the Island of Naxos.

This July day in the sunshine up here on the ridge the hills stretch away to the horizon like waves on the ocean. Beinn Fhionnlaidh,

An Riabhachan, Sgurr nan Ceathramhnan, Sgurr na Lapaich, the mountains and blue ridges reach all the way to the horizon. At my feet among the shoots of deergrass and the mossy stones there are red cloudberries. Away over to our right a sheet of blue glass lies in the corrie below Beinn Fhionnlaidh, another Coire Lochan, number 27 on Macrow's list, my second last hill loch.

1946: *The lochan I was seeking lies on the top of a shelf of grass-grown rock. I climbed above it to the left, and looked down to where it nestled darkly in the hollow.*

Boots clinking through the white scree we plod on along the ridge towards the summit of Carn Eige. For the last ten minutes I've been aware of a cloud of flies round my head. I fish my red and white buff out the side pocket of my rucksack and try to swish the flies away. When I look over my shoulder at L she has a cloud of flies over her head too. White scree in cloud shapes on the green hillside mirrors the white cannon puffs of cloud in the azure sky above. There are gravel solifluction terraces up here on the mountainside, like ripples in the sand on a beach. Alpine club moss sprouts in cracks in the rocks. Angus's faithful line of upended stones leads us on across the bare plateau.

The broad ridge becomes more defined, develops a bit of an edge and then, there in the shallow grassy corrie below, at the foot of a grey scree slope lies Loch a' Choire Dhomhain. Situated at a height of 927 metres or 3,041 feet I've saved the highest of all the hill lochs of Kintail until last. My last hill loch! I've completed Macrow's List! But we don't stop for long to celebrate, L has her tick to get too plus we've got a boat to catch so we push on, up the ridge heading towards the summit of Carn Eige. Over to the left I can see the 'cruel precipices of Tom a' Chòinich [sic]' that, as she would later write,

THE WILD SWIMMER OF KINTAIL

turned Macrow's heart over.

1946: At last, spent and breathless, I attained the summit of the ridge, and looked down the sheer crags of Càrn Eige on to Loch a' Choire Dhomhain... it lies among great pinnacles of scree and rock, surrounded by weirdly-shaped crags and boulders—some having a strangely human appearance, like the inhabitants of a lost world.

There's a picture of me here, on the screen standing in the sunshine in front of my last hill lochan. Maybe L suggested taking it to celebrate reaching the last of Macrow's hill lochans. Hands in pockets, hair neatly trimmed. I stare diffidently back at the camera and looking at the picture now I think I look younger in it.

Far below us, close by the lochan, a line of deer drift across the plates of rock and boulder fields on the corrie floor. The pinnacles and strange outcrops on the crest of the ridge are closer now and I think of Macrow up here, alone, seven decades ago, clambering through the scree to get her last hill lochans. Cushions of sea pinks are scattered across the ridge among the boulders and pinnacles. The great bowl of Coire Domhain and Loch a' Choire Dhomhain with its lochan lies far below us now. Looking at the photo I took and reading the pages Macrow wrote in her book *Kintail Scrapbook*, I have the certain feeling that it was right here she lay on her stomach trying to get a photo of the dramatic mountain amphitheatre.

1946: Lying flat on the top of the precipice, I looked over, feeling faintly sick from the height...

I click the right arrow and move onto the next photo from that day: L striding up the ridge, a distant figure on the skyline ahead of me. She's in a funny mood that day, I reflect, but it doesn't go any deeper than that and I brush the thought aside. At last sweating in the heat of the July day we reach the dome like summit of Carn Eige. When we reach the top L props herself up against the cairn and using her rucksack for a pillow takes a nap in the sunshine. She's got her tick.

1946: *I got my photograph and finished my crowdie sandwiches. Then, down, down... Past the grey crags and precipices—over the shining quartz, where a flight of sea-gulls rose into the air at my coming, white wings against the white drifts of powdered stone.*

Just below the summit, on the ridge on the way back down the hill, in a gravelly hollow in the flank of the mountain at around the 1,000 metre contour line a 20-foot by six-foot, arrow-shaped snow patch has survived from last winter, an oasis of cold in the sweltering July day. Drip by clear freezing drip the ice melts. Drip by clear freezing drip the ice melts from the point of the arrow.

1946: *Down towards the darkening valley, the silver curve of waters below. Down to the far gleam of Loch Mullardoch with its pine-clad islands and rocky hummocks along the shore.*

The surface of the snow patch is a pitted with little ripples where the sun has melted its surface. It is grubby and pock-marked with fragments of heather and flecks of soil. No longer pristine, white newly fallen snow, no, this snow fell long ago during last winter. In fact I call it a snowpatch which is how it would appear seen from a distance but in reality it's more like ice. At the point of the arrow the snow patch is melting in the hot July sun, drip by clear freezing drip. The icy cold drips feed a little trickle of a stream. I take my water bottle and place it among the starry saxifrage at the point of the arrow and allow the trickle of icy water to fill it. It is the best water I've

THE WILD SWIMMER OF KINTAIL

ever drunk on a mountain, icy, cold, refreshing in the sultry heat of the July afternoon. I raise the half-full, plastic water bottle to my lips and toast my compleation of all 28 hill lochs on Macrow's List with ice cold melt water.

1946: *Back on the road, I lay flat in the dust beside a small clear burn and drank deeply of the sunlit waters.*

As I watch the plastic waterbottle fill up again, drip by clear freezing drip I wonder if this is how all streams and great rivers begin, how the glaciers melt. And standing 3,000 feet up on the hillside I think about all the strange paths I've trodden to find the hill lochs of Kintail. I think about leaving London in the faint drizzle of the blue night, lying under the sheet and scratchy blanket in my underpants in the darkness on the night train north. I smile as I remember the sulphurpous Doodle farts on the train to Kyle of Lochalsh and Donnie's taxi waiting to pick us up. And the old fashioned bath in the Dornie Hotel and staying at Shepherd's Cottage and towing the smallest caravan in the world up to Dornie, Lachie pushing the boat clear of the seaweed by the old jetty below the bridge at Dornie, Eilean Donan Castle and the throngs of tourists. Walking from Totaig and coming to sad Ardintoul and the fish farm and the burnt out farmhouse. And I remember sitting round the table at Iron Lodge telling a ghost story. And skinny dippping in Coire Lochan below the west peak of Sgurr nan Ceathramhnan. And all the miles the Labradoodle has walked with me, the Labradoodle following in Jeannie the Skye terrier's pawprints. I think about all the miles I've walked. How many tens of thousands of paces have I taken following in Macrow's footsteps? And all the walks, across rock, across heather and all the ground I've covered. And all the tarmac roads I've cycled and the forest tracks and the faint old lost paths and Angus steering the motorboat through the mist on Mullardoch. And Angus telling me to follow the line of up-ended stones across the hillside. And all the puddles and marshy pools and peathags and heather moorland I've crossed in my search for Macrow's hill lochs. And all the streams I've crossed and the burns and the rivers. And the swallows and the swifts and the sparrrows and the buzzards and the dotterel on Carn Eige. And the deer splashing through the stream in Glen Elchaig.. And the birch trees I've walked beneath and the oaks and the rowans. And all the times I cursed bloody buggery Brenda and my lost pannier. And all the compass bearings I've taken and all the GPS waypoints and all the maps I've studied. And the non-existent paths at Camus-Luinne and the Russian boys working at the Cluanie Inn and the scampi and chips after walks and the pints. And L in her skort and sunhat. And the midges and the ticks. And the sun and the rain flying on the hills and the mist on the loch. And all this to follow in Macrow's footsteps. And all this because of one Highland summer long ago. And all this to find Macrow's hill lochs. And so that's why I went back to Kintail. And that's the story of Macrow and me.

Macrow and Me

Beautiful Benula has completely vanished from the face of this earth... Iain MacKay, *The Last Highland Clearance*, 2004.

When he returns to collect us, Angus has brought the Polish girl with him. The girl sits in the prow of the beat up fibreglass boat as it bangs across the waves. The girl clutches her light summer dress down over her knees and her hair blows in the wind as the gleaming, crystal droplets of water sparkle in the sun.

Before he takes us back to the dam at Mullardoch I ask Angus if he can take the motorboat over the exact spot where the lodge under the loch – Benula Lodge – once stood. Still comfortably seated on his upturned plastic crate Angus turns the boat in the direction of the far shore. The outboard motor roars and we go banging across the little white waves with silver droplets of spray shining in the sun. About 100 yards from the shore Angus puts the outboard into neutral and we drift as he points out a small brick-built, water tank just above the shoreline. He says this structure was the header tank for Benula Lodge and he explains that in 1946, before the glen was flooded, the tank would have stood high up on the hillside behind the house.

1946: *Everywhere was the pleasant smell of new paint. Young men from Glasgow, singing merrily, came in and out of the kitchen while I was having supper. I was told they were all living in the house until the work was finished.*

As the little waves break against the bow of Angus's boat and we float on the water over the drowned ruins of Benula Lodge my mind drifts back to something that happened a few weeks back. And now it seems to me that something that began one Tuesday night in a bar in Edinburgh a long, long time ago has finally come to an end here on the blue waters of Loch Mullardoch.

I'd gone to pick up the Labradoodle from Corstorphine where my ex has bought a house with his new partner. I'm glad he's got a house again. In the heat and bitterness and inevitable acrimony of the break-up it didn't feel like it at the time, but he was generous to me in the divorce settlement. His lawyer had wanted to force me to sell the flat we both owned. I wasn't jealous at all when he told me he was buying a place with his new partner, relief was the main emotion I felt. Relief that the 20 years he'd spent slaving in a department store and paying into the mortgage for my flat wasn't going to be wasted.

My ex-mother in law looks genuinely pleased to see me as I open the garden gate and she surprises me with a hug and a peck on the cheek. The Doodle wags her tail enthusiastically and approvingly. While we're chatting at the garden gate a couple in their seventies in tennis whites greet the Ladradoodle. They must be from the tennis club my ex paid £700 to join. This is all very suburban is what I'm thinking. This must be what he wanted and it's making Abbeyhill where we used to live look positively bohemian.

My ex asks solicitously about my mum who's not been keeping so well recently. This is all very grown up and modern. We're not good at this kind of thing in my family. On one occasion in the 1980s, my mother hid behind a parked car when she saw her ex-husband and his new wife coming along the street. I too can be prone to Bette Davis type revenge fantasies. But this is much better. We are where we are. There's enough trouble in the world without me and my ex being at each other's throats. The dog share has worked out remarkably well, particularly from the Labradoodle's point of view as she now gets twice as many holidays as she did before the divorce. Over the last few years of our relationship, I'd hated to see someone I loved so tortured and unhappy. I'm genuinely glad my ex has found happiness and stability with his new partner even if he has, in the words of Jean Brodie, ended up:'in a suburb like Corstorphine.'

The sun shines down, the blue waters of Loch Mullardoch sparkle and we drift with the waves lapping gently against the fibreglass hull of Angus's boat, floating there, over the ruins of Benula on the bed of the loch 50 feet below the hull of the boat, we drift over the lodge under the loch.

We're floating there on the surface of the loch, me and L and the Labradoodle. Floating over Mrs Forbes the housekeeper and the workies from Glasgow and the Cairn terrier and the white horse and the bridge at Benula and the empty corridor Macrow awoke to in a grey dawn light. All gone, sunk beneath the waters of the loch now.

Where are the cheery young workies from Glasgow? Where is the white horse on the dusty road? Where is the housekeeper frying freshly caught trout for breakfast? Where are the rugs spread out to air on the grass? Where are the iron gates of Benula? Where is the Cairn terrier playing on the lawn in the sunshine? Where is the white lodge at Benula? All gone, all drowned, deep beneath the blue waters of Loch Mullardoch, all gone, sunk beneath the loch, all gone.

My phone buzzes, charged that morning from electricity generated by turbines spun by the waters held back by the dam at Mullardoch. It's a WhatsApp from James my buddy the ex-van driver now backpacking round Australia with his girlfriend. He's replying to the (alcohol-fuelled) message I sent him last night. The one about being over my ex and thinking I was happy being single but maybe I'm not and I've decided to stop wasting my time chasing straight boys at the supermarket and I'm going to try and get a new bf off Grindr. And I think the price of James' WhatsApp message is the lodge under the loch submerged and the glen drowned beneath the waters of Mullardoch.

Then Angus twists the throttle and turns the boat east in the direction of Mullardoch Dam. The Labradoodle barks and we go banging across the waves again, silver crystal droplets of water sparkling in the sunlight, leaving the lost world of Benula deep beneath the loch.

> Macrow 1946: *The room was full of a cold grey light when I awakened. Foot-steps echoed with a bleak hollow sound among the empty corridors downstairs .I dressed and went stiffly down to a breakfast of freshly-caught trout.*

I lean over the side of the motorboat, watching as a wisp of cloud brushes the top of Sgurr na Lapaich and think of Macrow setting out from Benula Lodge that morning in 1946. Loch Mullardoch, she wrote, had the appearance of a tropical lagoon under a blue sky. A few weeks later Macrow and Jeannie left the cottage at Dornie for the last time for 'the inevitable journey south' and a life lived in England.

One year later the lorries, bulldozers and engineers of the North of Scotland Hydro Electric Board moved into Glen Cannich. Teams of joiners and carpenters set to work constructing hundreds of giant wooden boxes. Boxes filled with concrete to build Mullardoch Dam at the very place where, back in 1930, at the beginning of our story, the young woman, the stalker's wife heard the sound of hammering and boards being thrown down and the shouts of workmen.

That afternoon Macrow will leave Benula Lodge for the last time. She will never return. Five years will pass and then Mr Tom Johnston, the Secretary of State for Scotland will open the Mullardoch-Affric hydro-electric scheme. Loch Mullardoch will double in size and Loch Lungard, Loch Frith an Acha, Lochan na Cloiche, the waterfall, the pools, the pine covered islands and Benula Lodge will all disappear beneath the black, peaty waters of the reservoir forever.

As Macrow walks through the gates of Benula for the last time and takes the dusty track back to Iron Lodge and Jeannie, she leaves the Kintail of 1946 behind her and walks down the brae, off the page and into the future.

'Spring comes again,' he said, 'and summer and the fires of autumn, and then the silence of the deep snows. But never the same. Never twice the same.'

> BGM, *The Amazing Mr Whisper* 1958.

South

THE WILD SWIMMER OF KINTAIL

Dennis grasps the black plastic sacks of rubbish in one hand as he pushes open the door of the conservatory. The door with its peeling white paint sticks on the uneven floor tiles. The cold wind off the Downs has stripped the last of the leaves from the hawthorn trees on the patch of wild land at the end of the garden. Then he sees the fox. It stands halfway down the garden path, red-brownish fur, staring straight back at him. And the light from the back bedroom of Myrtle Cottage falls in a yellow shaft across the bare twigs of the gooseberry and redcurrant bushes at the edge of the path. Through the leaded window panes, where the faded watercolour of Sgurr na Lapaich hangs on the wall and Macrow sits hunched in a frayed armchair, a book resting in her lap. Arthritic stabs of pain at the end of her fingers like little jaggy needles as she turns the page, eager to begin the next chapter.

APPENDIX I

The Life and Times of Brenda G Macrow

3 June 1916: Brenda Grace Joan Barton born. Her family lived at 86 Inderwick Road in Hornsey, North London.

1921–28: at boarding school in England.

1928: Brenda Barton started writing stories, aged 12.

c1928: her father Joseph William Barton, a company secretary, moved to Chicago in the USA for work reasons, taking his family with him.

1928–39: The Barton family lived in Chicago during the era of prohibition and were resident there when 'Machine Gun' Jack McGurn, a gangster involved in the St. Valentine's Day Massacre was shot dead in 1936.

Brenda Barton attended high school in Chicago. Determined to become a writer she collected 370 rejection slips from publishers: enough to cover a three-panel screen on both sides.

1934: Brenda Barton had first poem published at age 18.

c1939: BB and family returned to England.

1939–45: during World War Two, Brenda Barton worked as a farm-worker, a nurse for the Voluntary Aid Detachment and the Red Cross and was the librarian on a USAF base.

May 1941: aged 24, BB married Herbert John Macrow, an Englishman of Scottish descent. Brenda G Macrow visited Scotland for the first time on her honeymoon. Stayed at cottage in Coylumbridge. Climbed Cairn Gorm, walked to highest point of Lairig Ghru and visited Ryvoan Pass.

THE WILD SWIMMER OF KINTAIL

1942: acquired Jeannie, a Skye terrier puppy. September: climbed Arthur's Seat while visiting Edinburgh.

1942–45: visited Loch Lomond, Glencoe, Glen Etive, Dornie, Skye, Glenfinnan, explored the Cairngorm Mountains, and climbed Braeriach, Ben Avon, Lochnagar and Ben MacDhui (several times.) Also visited Glen Clova, Glen Ey, cycled up Glen Einich, walked through the Lairig Ghru, visited Loch an Eilean, the Shelter Stone and Loch Morlich.

1944: March: slept in remote bothy, probably in Braemar area and visited Inverey.

1946: marriage to Herbert Macrow ended. *Unto the Hills* published by Oliver and Boyd. April–late August: aged 30 spent six months at Nostie in Kintail researching a book later published as *Kintail Scrapbook*. BGM visited all 28 hill lochs in the Parish of Kintail over 1000 feet. She also travelled to Gairloch and Stornoway.

1947: BGM and Jeannie travelled from London to Lairg by train and then mail bus to Lochinver and finally car to a remote croft at Rhegreanoch near Inverkirkaig where they stayed for the summer with a shepherd and his wife. The journey took 27 hours. While based at Rhegreanoch BGM acquired an autocycle (possibly from Glasgow or Edinburgh) and rode it back to Lochinver via Dunblane, the Trossachs and Oban (from where she visited Staffa and Iona.) BGM also travelled to Kylesku, Altnaharra and Tongue by autocycle. Stayed with friends in cottage at foot of Ben Loyal for two days. Climbed Ben Loyal. Travelled on to Durness and visited Smoo Cave. Stayed at Cape Wrath Hotel. Returned to Lochinver via Brora and Golspie. Climbed An Teallach and the Five Sisters of Kintail and visited Glen Affric around this time. BGM took the autocycle to Braemar where she met Cambridge school-master George Thomas who told her: 'Whatever you do, you mustn't miss seeing Torridon!'

BGM took his advice and travelled from Strathpeffer to Torridon in a day on the auto-cycle and later climbed Liathach, Beinn Eighe and Beinn Alligin. Wrote her best known poem 'Climb in Torridon—Liathach, 1947.'

1948: April: spent week in Edinburgh. April–October: rented cottage by Loch Torridon. Researched and made notes (a suitcase full) for book later published as *Torridon Highlands*. August: spent three weeks hill walking with George Thomas. They climbed the Black Carls of Beinn Eighe. September: backpacked around the SYHA hostels at Applecross, Kyle of Lochalsh, Craig and Opinan. *Kintail Scrapbook* published by Oliver and Boyd. October: rented thatched cottage at Thorley near Bishop's Stortford, Hertfordshire. Met Dennis E Prior who lived next door and who helped her do up cottage.

1949: *Hills and Glens* published by Oliver and Boyd. November: Aged 33 Brenda G Macrow married Dennis Prior with a service of blessing at Thorley Church.

1950: August: cycled from The Dell, Rothiemurchus then climbed Braeriach while six months pregnant. November: Brenda G Macrow's only daughter, Lesley Denise Hampshire (née Prior) born.

1950–55: BGM suffered intermittent bouts of thrombosis and arthritis which forced her to give up hillwalking before she was 40.

c1952: while BGM was working on the final draft of a book about Torridon, Brian Vesey-Fitzgerald, the nature writer and editor of Robert Hale's Regional Books, invited her to contribute a volume on Scotland to the series.

1953: *Torridon Highlands* published by Robert Hale.

1954: 'Land of Enchantment' article published in *The Scottish Annual and Braemar Gathering Book*.

1955: January: BGM completes final draft of *Speyside to Deeside* at age of 38.

1956: *Speyside to Deeside* published by Oliver and Boyd.

1958: *The Amazing Mr Whisper* published by Blackie & Son. *Field Folk* published. *The Amazing Mr Whisper* published in the USA and transcribed into Braille.

1959: *The Return of Mr Whisper* published.

1960: *Bumbletown Tales* published.

1962: *Babies of the Wild* published by Blackie & Son. BGM aged 45.

1982: 'Climb in Torridon—Liathach, 1947' appears in *Poems of the Scottish Hills,* an anthology selected by Hamish Brown.

1984–93: exchange of letters with the journalist and illustrator Colin Gibson.

1985: April: David Foster interview with BGM published in *The Scots Magazine*. BGM makes nostalgic return visit to Torridon at the age of 68.

1989: BGM and Dennis Prior celebrated their ruby wedding anniversary.

1992–2011: BGM regularily had poems published in *The People's Friend* magazine.

2001–11: correspondence with Gillian Zealand, daughter of Colin Gibson.

2004: Dennis Prior dies.

2007: poetry anthology *A Red, Red Rose* self-published by BGM.

2011: BGM continued to write poems for *The People's Friend*, too numerous to list in this volume, until she died at the Abbas Combe Nursing Home at the age of 94.

APPENDIX II

The (known) Published Works of Brenda G Macrow

The Scottish Books

MACROW, B G, *Unto the Hills*, Oliver & Boyd, Edinburgh, 1946.*

MACROW, B G, *Kintail Scrapbook*, Oliver & Boyd, Edinburgh, 1948.*

MACROW, B G, *Hills and Glens*, Oliver & Boyd, Edinburgh, 1949.*

MACROW, B G, *Torridon Highlands*, Robert Hale, London, 1953.*

MACROW, B G, *Speyside to Deeside*, Oliver & Boyd, Edinburgh, 1956.*

* With photographs by Robert M Adam

Prose

MACROW, B G, *Wolf in Sheep's Clothing,* Chamber's Journal, W & R Chambers, Edinburgh, Eighth Series, Vol. XIII, January–December 1944, pp 393–399.

MACROW, B G, (Letters to the Editor), SMT Magazine and Scottish Country Life, Vol. XXXVI, No.3, Edinburgh, September 1945, p1.

MACROW, B G, *Over the Hills to Ballater*, SMT Magazine and Scottish Country Life, Vol. Vol. XXXVI, No.3, Edinburgh, March 1946, pp 26–29.

MACROW, B G, *In Trust for Scotland*, SMT Magazine and Scottish Country Life, Vol.XXXVIII, No.4, Edinburgh, October 1946, pp 13–17.

THE WILD SWIMMER OF KINTAIL

MACROW, B G, *Return to the Cairngorms*, Scotland's SMT Magazine, Vol. 39, No.4, Edinburgh, April 1947, p26.

MACROW, B G, *The Spell of Sutherland*, Scotland's SMT Magazine, Vol. 40, No.1, Edinburgh, July 1947, pp36–39.

MACROW, B G, *Birth of a River,* The Scottish Annual & Braemar Gathering Book, The Herald Press, Arbroath, August 1947, pp 201–207.

MACROW, B G, *The Hill-lochs of Kintail*, The Scottish Field, Vol. XCV, No.538, Edinburgh, October 1947, pp14–15.

MACROW, B G, *Western Wonderland*, Scotland's SMT Magazine, Vol. 41, No.4, Edinburgh, April 1948, pp22-26.

MACROW, B G, *The Two Loch Brooms*, Scotland's SMT Magazine, Vol. 42, No.2, Edinburgh, August 1948, pp33–36.

MACROW, B G, *Mountain Music Club*, Scotland's SMT Magazine, Vol. 43, No.2, Edinburgh, February 1949, pp36–40.

MACROW, B G, *Quaint Tales of Torridon*, The Scots Magazine, Vol. LI, No.2, Dundee, August 1949, pp358–364.

MACROW, B G, *The Sanctuary of Applecross*, The Scottish Field, Vol.[Unknown], Edinburgh, March 1950, pp20–21.

MACROW, B G, *Discovery of Glomach*, The Scots Magazine, Vol. LI V, No. Dundee, November 1950, pp128–135.

MACROW, B G, *My Favourite Chain of Hostels*, Scotland's SMT Magazine, Vol. 48, No.5, Edinburgh, May 1952, pp30–33.

MACROW, B G, *Loch of Legends*, Scotland's SMT Magazine, Vol. 49, No.10, Edinburgh, October 1953, pp32–35.

MACROW, B G, *Land of Enchantment*, The Scottish Annual & Braemar Gathering Book, The Herald Press, Arbroath, August 1954, pp 135–143.

MACROW, B G, *A Never-ending Song*, The Scottish Annual & Braemar Gathering Book, The Herald Press, Arbroath, August 1963, pp 125–131.

Children's Books

MACROW, B G, *The Amazing Mr Whisper*, Blackie, London, 1958.

MACROW, B G, *Field Folk*, Blackie, London, 1958.

MACROW, B G, *The Return of Mr Whisper*, Blackie, London, 1959.

MACROW, B G, *Bumbletown Tales*, Blackie, London, 1960.

MACROW, B G, *Babies of the Wild*, Blackie, London, 1962.

Poetry

MACROW, B G, *The Hills Waited*, Chamber's Journal, W & R Chambers, Edinburgh, Eighth Series, Vol. XII, January–December 1943, p 367.

MACROW, B G, *Mountain Day*, Chamber's Journal, W & R Chambers, Edinburgh, Eighth Series, Vol. XII, January–December 1943, p 613.

MACROW, B G, *For All Things Green*, Chamber's Journal, W & R Chambers, Edinburgh, Eighth Series, Vol. XIII, January–December 1944, p246.

MACROW, B G, *Arthur's Seat*, Chamber's Journal, W & R Chambers, Edinburgh, Eighth Series, Vol. XIII, January–December 1944, p 477.

MACROW, B G, *Heart's Haven*, Chamber's Journal, W & R

Chambers, Edinburgh, Ninth Series, Vol. VIII, January–December 1944, p336.

MACROW, B G, *Glenfinnan*, Chamber's Journal, W & R Chambers, Edinburgh, Eighth Series, Vol. XIV, January–December 1945, p 477.

MACROW, B G, *Song of the Vagabond*, Chamber's Journal, W & R Chambers, Edinburgh, Eighth Series, Vol. XIV, January–December 1945, p477.

MACROW, B G, *The Heather Blowing*, Chamber's Journal, W & R Chambers, Edinburgh, Eighth Series, Vol. XV, January–December 1946, p192.

MACROW, B G, Reflections on Deeside, *The Scottish Annual & Braemar Gathering Book*, The Herald Press, Arbroath, August 1951, pp 153-157

MACROW, B G, *The Hills above the Dee, A Sonnet Sequence,* The Scottish Annual & Braemar Gathering Book, August 1955, pp 179-185.

MACROW, B G, *Hill Haunted,* The People's Friend, DC Thomson, Dundee, No. 6373, March 14 1992, p18.

MACROW, B G, *Primrose Poem,* The People's Friend, DC Thomson, Dundee, No. 6376, April 4 1992, p14.

MACROW, B G, *Road to the Hills,* The People's Friend, DC Thomson, Dundee, No. 6392, July 25 1992, p23.

MACROW, B G, *Mountain Pool,* The People's Friend, DC Thomson, Dundee, No. 6401, September 26 1992, p21.

MACROW, B G, *The Witching Hour,* The People's Friend, DC Thomson, Dundee, No. 6404, October 17 1992, p13.

MACROW, B G, *Mountain Magic,* The People's Friend, DC

Thomson, Dundee, No. 6410, November 8 1992, p 16.

MACROW, B G, *Highland Burn,* The People's Friend, DC Thomson, Dundee, No. 6419, January 30 1993, p 40.

MACROW, B G, *Sundown Poem,* The People's Friend, DC Thomson, Dundee, No. 6421, February 13 1993, p 4.

MACROW, B G, *Highland Colours,* The People's Friend, DC Thomson, Dundee, No. 6425, March 13 1993, p44.

MACROW, B G, *A View of Islands,* The People's Friend, DC Thomson, Dundee, No. 6428, April 3 1993, p48.

MACROW, B G, *Noonday Dream,* The People's Friend, DC Thomson, Dundee, No. 6435, May 22 1993, p32.

MACROW, B G, *The Hills I Love,* The People's Friend, DC Thomson, Dundee, No. 6442, July 10 1993, p8.

MACROW, B G, *Daybreak,* The People's Friend, DC Thomson, Dundee, No. 6442, July 10 1993, p26.

MACROW, B G, *Bewitched, The People's Friend,* DC Thomson, Dundee, No. 6454, October 2 1993, p41.

MACROW, B G, *Lovely Lochnagar,* The People's Friend, No. 6461, November 20 1993, p12.

MACROW, B G, *Timeless Torridon,* The People's Friend, DC Thomson, Dundee, No. 6511, November 5 1994, p12.

MACROW, B G, *Morning Mist,* The People's Friend, DC Thomson, Dundee, No. 6511, November 5 1994, p 18.

MACROW, B G, *Remembered Beauty,* The People's Friend, DC Thomson, Dundee, No. 6515, December 3 1994, p28.

MACROW, B G, *Abiding Beauty,* The People's Friend, DC Thomson,

Dundee, No. 6523, January 28 1995, p54.

MACROW, B G, *My Cat,* The People's Friend, DC Thomson, Dundee, No. 6525, Feb 11 1995, p33.

MACROW, B G, *Winter Scene,* The People's Friend, DC Thomson, Dundee, No. 6526, February 18 1995, p52.

MACROW, B G, *Spell of the Sands,* The People's Friend, DC Thomson, Dundee, No. 6529, March 11 1995, p 52.

MACROW, B G, *First Snow,* The People's Friend, DC Thomson, Dundee, x, No. , December 1995, p 7.

MACROW, B G, *Torridon Dream,* The People's Friend, DC Thomson, Dundee, No. 6625, January 11 1997, p53.

MACROW, B G, *Bright and Beautiful,* The People's Friend, DC Thomson, Dundee, No. 6625, January 11 1997, p57.

MACROW, B G, *Mirrored Beauty,* The People's Friend, DC Thomson, Dundee, No. 6625, January 11 1997, p64.

MACROW, B G, *Silent Splendour,* The People's Friend, DC Thomson, Dundee, No. 6627, January 25 1997, p20.

MACROW, B G, *Dreams of Summer,* The People's Friend, DC Thomson, Dundee, No. 6627, January 25 1997, p53.

MACROW, B G, *Spring Song,* The People's Friend, DC Thomson, Dundee, No. 6632, March 1 1997, p53.

MACROW, B G, *Spring Dusk,* The People's Friend, DC Thomson, Dundee, No. 6633, March 8 1997, p47.

MACROW, B G, *Signs of Spring,* The People's Friend, DC Thomson, Dundee, No. 6636, March 29 1997, p31.

MACROW, B G, *Singing Waterfalls,* The People's Friend, DC

Thomson, Dundee, No. 6636, March 29 1997, p31.

MACROW, B G, *Springtime Glory,* The People's Friend, DC Thomson, Dundee, No. 6637, April 5 1997, p45.

MACROW, B G, *Sutherland Scene,* The People's Friend, DC Thomson, Dundee, No. 6639, April 19 1997, p43.

MACROW, B G, *Abiding Grandeur,* The People's Friend, DC Thomson, Dundee, No. 6640, April 26 1997, p39.

MACROW, B G, *Maytime Magic,* The People's Friend, DC Thomson, Dundee, No. 6642, May 10 1997, p11.

MACROW, B G, *Road of Dreams,* The People's Friend, DC Thomson, Dundee, No. 6646, June 7 1997, p51.

MACROW, B G, *Golden Hours,* The People's Friend, DC Thomson, Dundee, No. 6647, June 14 1997, p14.

MACROW, B G, *Magic Moments,* The People's Friend, DC Thomson, Dundee, No. 6652, July 19 1997, p10.

MACROW, B G, *Impressions,* The People's Friend, DC Thomson, Dundee, No. 6652, July 19 1997, p36.

MACROW, B G, *Holiday Welcome,* The People's Friend, DC Thomson, Dundee, No. 6654, August 2 1997, p20.

MACROW, B G, *Sunrise,* The People's Friend, DC Thomson, Dundee, No. 6657, August 23 1997, p21.

MACROW, B G, *Sunset Serenade,* The People's Friend, DC Thomson, Dundee, No. 6659, September 6 1997, p56.

MACROW, B G, *Autumn Glory,* The People's Friend, DC Thomson, Dundee, No. 6663, October 4 1997, p53.

THE WILD SWIMMER OF KINTAIL

Collected Works

MACROW, B G, *A Red, Red Rose*, Brenda Prior, Chichester, 2007.

Unpublished Poetry

MACROW, B G, *Highland Scrapbook* *

MACROW, B G, *The Wild Places and Other Poems*

* With illustrations by Colin Gibson

APPENDIX III

How to Find the Hill Lochs of Kintail

Loch nan Ealachan
Grade: **
Map: OS Sheet 33
Distance/Ascent: 12km/428m
Starting Height: 15m
Time: from Camus-Luinne 4h+breaks
Start/Finish: Camus-Luinne

1. Park where road ends at Camas-luinie NG 94204 28640. From car park cross wooden bridge and follow LH fork in track for 50m to gate.
2. Go through gate and follow footpath marked on map. Ignore sign reading *Riverside Walk*.
3. After 1.5km follow footpath through area of woodland enclosed by deer fence(gates) and across field to reach house.
4. Turn L at house and follow track across bridge over River Elchaig then turn R along unsurfaced road at shed.
5. Follow road for 1.5km passing two fenced-in areas of woodland to bridge NG98299 27298.
6. Leave road and turn L onto faint footpath that initially follows LH bank of stream. Path becomes clearer higher up and can be seen from road zig zagging up hillside to L of Allt an Daimh
7. Follow path to Loch nan Ealachan (413m) NG99701 28375
Navigation: be careful to stay on path.
Dogs: cattle, sheep and deer in Glen Elchaig.

Beinn a'Mheadhain Hill Lochs

Loch Beinn a' Mheadhain and Loch Dubhach
Grade: **
Map: OS Sheet 33

THE WILD SWIMMER OF KINTAIL

Distance/Ascent: 7km/484m
Starting Height: sea level
Time: 4h+breaks
Start/Finish: Bundalloch near Dornie

1. From Dornie Hotel walk/cycle/drive 1.5 km along by-road on S side Loch Long to Bundalloch. Limited space to park where road ends NG89597 27662. More parking spaces 500m before road ends in front of houses NG89055 27298.
2. At road-end cross wooden bridge over River Glennan and turn R. Follow muddy track beside river past ramshackle barn to gate. Go through gate.
3. Walk 5om to sheep-fank then strike NE up Beinn a'Mheadhain aiming for flat ground at about 200m NG90581 28117.
4. Avoid crags by climbing steep grass on L. Note top of gap in crags NG90692 28128 for return.
5. From unnamed top (371m) NG91271 28346 walk to outflow Loch Dubhach (332m) NG91629 28471.
6. From Loch Dubhach walk to summit Beinn a' Mheadhain (414m) NG91830 28830.
7. From Beinn a'Mheadhain walk SE to Loch Beinn a' Mheadhain (305m) NG92065 28585 then W to outflow of Loch Dubhach and then return by route of ascent.

Navigation: combination of confusing terrain/proximity of steep crags make this a walk best saved for a clear day.
Dogs: Cattle and sheep by River Glennan

Boc Mor Hill Lochans

Loch a'Mhuillin, Loch na Faolaig, Loch na Craoibhe-caoruinn, Loch Gorm Mor and Loch Bhuic Mhoir
Grade: **
Map: OS Sheet 33
Distance/Ascent: 12km/680m

KELLAN MACINNES

Starting Height: sea level
Time: 5h+breaks
Start/Finish: Dornie Hotel

1. Walk/drive 25m along road that leads to A87 from behind Dornie Hotel.
2. Turn L at signpost for *Carr Brae*.
3. Walk/drive 2km to high point on road where viewpoint is. Park 50m further along beside ramshackle animal pens NG90564 256414.
4. Continue short distance on foot and cross stone bridge over small burn NG 89817 24613. Immediately after bridge turn L at lay-by sign and follow faint/grassy track N through bracken.
5. Follow track to 250m contour line and just after sheep fank go L at junction near NG 89742 25264 heading N below the crags of Creag Reidh Raineach.
6. Pass ruin NG89736 25550 on R as track begins to climb.
7. Follow track to height of 400m. At double gate NG89772 25838 leave track and head E to flat top of Creag Reidh Rainich (503m).
8. Walk to higher SE top of Creag Reidh Rainich (525m).
9. From SE top Creag Reidh Rainich head NE towards Boc Mor past Loch a'Mhuillin NG90795 25110, Loch na Faolaig NG90564 25641, and Loch Gorm Mor NG91314 25361. Loch na Craoibhe-caoruinn NG90750 25795 lies 500m NW.
10. Climb fence at foot Boc Mor (631m) then bear R to avoid small crags and gain summit NG 91727 25891. Loch Bhuic Mhoir NG92244 26056 lies 500m E of Boc Mor.
11. Return the same way.

Dogs: deer.

Loch nan Eun
Grade: **
Map: OS Sheet 33
Distance/Ascent: 12km/609m
Starting Height: 90m

THE WILD SWIMMER OF KINTAIL

Time: 5h+breaks
Start/Finish: Inverinate

1. From Dornie drive 4km south on A87. Just past 40mph road signs turn sharp L onto by-road to Carr Brae.
2. Drive 1km along road to NG90715 23367 and park at waterworks (space for 2 cars).
3. Go through gate and past byre and follow track high above An Leth Allt to Coire Dhuinnid for 3km.
4. On the way it is possible to scramble down the steep sided glen and swim in the pools of the An Leth Allt.
5. Where track ends abruptly at height 315m continue E for 50 metres to rusty iron gate NG93045 24926(if you come to large cairn/ruin you've gone too far).
6. From gate head N following line of iron fence-posts up hillside to find footpath marked on map which follows E bank of unnamed burn. Footpath very faint. Keep burn on L to avoid problems.
7. Where ground levels off at 500m contour NG92985 25980 head E for 1.75km passing point 599m NG93610 26200 to reach Loch nan Eun NG94735 26300.
8. Return by same route.

Loch an t Sabhail
Grade: **
Map: OS Sheet 33
Distance/Ascent: 10km/380m
Starting Height:90m
Time: 4h+breaks
Start/Finish: Inverinate

1. From Dornie drive 4km south on A87. Just past 40mph road signs turn sharp L onto by-road to Carr Brae.
2. Drive 1km along road to NG90715 23367 and park at waterworks (space for 2 cars).
3. Go through gate and past byre and follow track high above An Leth

Allt to Coire Dhuinnid for 3km.

4. Track ends abruptly at height 315m. Continue E for 50m to rusty iron gate NG93045 24926 (if you come to large cairn/ruin you've gone too far.)

5. Continue to follow traces of path for 1.25km along N bank An Leth allt.

6. At height 400m NG 94450 24660 leave An Leth allt and follow unnamed burn NE to trio of unnamed lochans just below 500m contour NG95130 25100.

7. Continue NE for 600m to Loch an t-Sabhail (469m) NG95815 25552.

8. Return by same route.

Dogs: goats in Coire Dhuinnid.

Loch Lòn Mhurchaidh
Grade: **
Map: OS Sheets 25 and 33
Distance/Ascent: 28km/459m
Starting Height: 7m
Time: 6h+breaks
Start/Finish: Killilan car park

1. From Dornie drive N across bridge following A87 for 1km then turn R onto by-road along N shore Loch Duich for 8km (signposted *Conchra Sallochy Killilan Camas-luinie*.)

2. About 2km before road ends cross Belford bridge over river then at sharp bend keep straight on through white iron gates. Park here NG94100 30300.

3. Continue on bike along estate road through stone gateposts with notice *Inverinate Estate No Vehicle Access*.

4. After 4.5 km tarmac ends NG96972 27971. Continue along unsurfaced road.

5. Leave bike at Carnach NH02589 28188 (house at NE end Loch na Leitreach.)

6. Turn R along track past house. Cross wooden bridge over river and

THE WILD SWIMMER OF KINTAIL

continue along track for 500m.

7. At NH03131 27820 (160m) leave track and cross burn below waterfall on boulders between two pools (no bridge). A faint footpath strikes up hillside here following L/E bank of the Allt Coire Easaich.

8. Don't cross dilapidated footbridge on R.

9. Higher up steep hillside small landslides have eroded away sections of path but are easily bypassed. Be careful not to lose line of path.

10. Ignore developing path leading towards waterfall. True line of path goes well to L of waterfall.

11. Path reaches flat moorland NH03444 27323 (350m.) Turn R along muddy track. Note this place for return.

12. Follow track as it goes first to Loch Lòn Mhurchaidh NH03296 26403 (370m) and then onto unnamed lochan NH03080 26000 (380m.)

13. From unnamed lochan leave track and descend SW across moorland to Allt a' Ghlomaich. Follow riverbank to Falls of Glomach (330m) NH01879 25572.

14. Return by route of ascent.

Dogs: sheep, cattle and deer in Glen Elchaig.

Navigation: beyond Carnach path is hard to follow in places so navigation needed to find the Falls.

Loch Sgurr na h-Eige
Grade: ***
Map: OS Sheets 25 and 33
Distance/Ascent: 28km/650m
Starting Height: 7m
Time: 7h+breaks (2h 30mins to Sgurr na h-Eige from Carnach)
Start/Finish: Killilan car-park, Glen Elchaig

1. From Dornie drive N across bridge following A87 for 1km then turn R onto by-road along N shore Loch Duich for 8km (signposted Conchra Sallochy Killilan Camas-luinie).

2. About 2km cross Belford bridge over river then at sharp bend with signpost reading Camas-luinie 1½ miles keep straight on through white

iron gates. Park here NG94100 30300.

3. Continue on bike along estate road through stone gateposts with notice *Inverinate Estate No Vehicle Access*.

4. After 4.5 km tarmac ends NG96972 27971. Continue along unsurfaced road.

5. Leave bike at Carnach NH02589 28188 (house at NE end Loch na Leitreach)

6. Turn R along track past house. Cross wooden bridge over river and continue along track for 500m.

7. At height of 160m NH03131 27820 track becomes faint but stay on L(N) side of stream parallel to fence. Track becomes clearer higher up.

8. At around 400m leave track and bear L onto very faint stalkers' path NH04021 28009. If you come to old wooden pallets used as bridges across peat hags you've gone too far up track.

9. In clear weather it's fun to try and follow line of old path as it zig zags up hillside but in misty weather a compass bearing will be needed to find Loch Sgurr na h-Eige (620m) NH04882 27176.

10. Walk to NE end of loch then continue 200m NE to reach Sgurr na h-Eige (657m).

11. Return by route of ascent.

Dogs: sheep, cattle and deer in Glen Elchaig.

Navigation: the footpaths marked on OS sheet 33 around Carnach are very difficult to find and non-existent in places. Careful navigation required to find Loch Sgurr na h-Eige.

Loch a' Chleirich (A' Ghlas-bheinn)
Grade: ***
Map: OS Sheet 33
Distance/Ascent: 13km/975m
Starting Height: 5m
Time: 7h+ breaks
Start/Finish: Morvich NTS car-park
1. From Dornie drive south on A87

THE WILD SWIMMER OF KINTAIL

2. After 9km at S end of causeway at head Loch Duich take L turn signposted *Morvich* and park at NTS Kintail Ranger Service car-park NG96050 21065.

3. Follow signposts to Falls of Glomach then after 2km reach waymarker and bear L to cross Abhainn Chonaig at footbridge. Once across bridge turn R onto unsurfaced road NG98079 22336.

4. At edge of forest just before footbridge over Allt an Leoid Ghaingamhaich leave road (turn R) and head SE up ridge of A'Mhuc following line of iron fence posts up steep, grassy hillside.

5. Follow broad ridge to where crags start just below 750m contour line NH00185 23065.

6. Take compass bearing then traverse SE below summit ridge of A' Ghlas-bheinn for 15 mins to reach Loch a'Cleirich (756m) NH00603 22662.

6. From Loch a'Cleirich climb NE aiming for gap in crags around 875m NH00956 22785.

7. On reaching ridge head N(L) for 500m to reach A' Ghlas-bheinn (918m) NH00800 23095.

8. Descend W from summit to rejoin uphill route at 750m contour. From here return by route of ascent.

Dogs: deer, goats and field of cattle. To avoid the cattle: start walk from Dorusduainn forest car-park near Lienassie, as described on page xx . Follow signposts for *Falls of Glomach* as far as edge of forest, just before footbridge over Allt an Leoid Ghaingamhaich to join route described above at point 4.

Loch Mhoicean, Loch Cruoshie and Loch na Maoile Bhuidhe
Grade: ***
Map: OS Sheet 25
Distance/Ascent: 44km/640m
Starting Height: 7m
Time: 12h
Start/Finish: Killilan car-park, Glen Elchaig

KELLAN MACINNES

1. From Dornie drive N across bridge following A87 for 1km then turn R onto by-road along N shore Loch Duich for 8km (signposted *Conchra Sallochy Killilan Camas-luinie.*)
2. About 2km before road ends cross Belford bridge over river then at sharp bend keep straight on through white iron gates. Park here NG94100 30300.
3. Continue on bike along estate road through stone gateposts with notice *Inverinate Estate No Vehicle Access.*
4. After 4.5 km tarmac ends NG96972 27971. Continue along unsurfaced road.
5. Leave bikes 500m NE of Iron Lodge at head Glen Elchaig and take RH fork in track.
6. Walk along track to Loch Mhoicean NH07099 31512 (420m).
7. Continue to high point on track marked by cairn NH07845 32291.
8. Leave stony track here (it soon peters out.) Cross small stream and look for grassy old stalkers' path NH07866 32380 that continues N down glen on E (RH) side Allt Coire nan Each.
9. Continue for 2km. Below An Cruachan path marked on OS map fades. Pick up rough track that continues beside Allt Coire nan Each.
10. Cross Allt Lòin-fhiodha near NH07785 36188. This may prove impossible in wet weather.
11 Continuation of path after crossing Allt Lòin-fhiodha is not obvious. Head W, away from the river to pick up path which runs along foot of hillside at 270m contour-line, well away from very boggy ground beside river.
12. Once found path from Allt Lòin-fhiodha to Maol-bhuidhe is faint but followable and becomes clearer closer to Maol-bhuidhe bothy NH05240 35958 at W end Loch Cruoshie (254m) NH05529 36266.
13. Cross stream beside bothy (may be difficult in wet weather – no bridge.) Walk S along track for 6.5km back to Iron Lodge taking short diversion en route to view Loch na Maoile Buidhe (375m)NH05054 34481.
14. Crossing of An Crom-allt NH04377 31132 about 1.5km north of

THE WILD SWIMMER OF KINTAIL

Iron Lodge may be difficult in wet weather.

15. Cycle 12 km back down Glen Elchaig to car park near Killilan NG94100 30300.

Notes: Best to tackle walk anti-clockwise in case you have to turn back because Allt Loin-fhiodha in spate. One to do after a long spell of dry weather.

Maol-bhuidhe bothy: Why not take two days over this walk and spend the night at the remote Maol-bhuidhe bothy?

Dogs: Cattle, deer and sheep in Glen Elchaig. Dogs allowed in Maol-bhuidhe bothy.

Coire Lochan
Grade: ***
Map: OS Sheets 25 and 33
Distance/Ascent: 32km/770m
Starting Height: 7m
Time: 7h+breaks
Start/Finish: Killilan car-park, Glen Elchaig

1. From Dornie drive N across bridge following A87 for 1km then turn R onto by-road along N shore Loch Duich for 8km (signposted *Conchra Sallochy Killilan Camas-luinie.*)

2. About 2km before road ends cross Belford bridge over river then at sharp bend with signpost reading Camas-luinie 1½ miles keep straight on through white iron gates. Park here NG94100 30300.

3. Continue on bike along estate road through stone gateposts with notice *Inverinate Estate No Vehicle Access.*

4. After 4.5 km tarmac ends NG96972 27971. Continue on unsurfaced road.

5. Leave bike at Carnach NH02589 28188 (house at NE end Loch na Leitreach.)

6. Turn R along track past house. Cross wooden bridge over river and continue along track for 500m.

7. At NH03131 27820 (160m) leave track and cross burn below waterfall

—334—

on boulders between two pools (no bridge). A faint footpath strikes up hillside here following L/E bank of Allt Coire Easaich.

8. Don't cross dilapidated footbridge on R.

9. Higher up steep hillside small landslides have eroded away sections of path but are easily bypassed. Be careful not to lose line of path.

10. Ignore developing path leading towards waterfall. True line of footpath goes well to L of waterfall.

11. Path reaches flat moorland plateau NH03444 27323 (350m.) Turn R along muddy track. Note this place for return.

12. Follow track as it goes first to Loch Lòn Mhurchaidh NH03296 26403 (370m) and then onto unnamed lochan NH03080 26000(380m.)

11. Leave track at Allt Coire Lochain and follow L bank of stream for 2.5km up to Coire Lochan (780m) NH04687 23571. Deer and vehicle tracks make going easier.

12. Return by route of ascent.

Dogs: sheep, cattle and deer in Glen Elchaig.

Navigation: beyond Carnach path is faint and hard to follow so navigation needed to find lochs.

Loch Thuill Easaich, Loch Gaorsaic and Loch a' Bhealaich

Grade: **

Map: OS Sheets 33

Distance/Ascent: 12km/620m

Starting Height: 57m

Time: 5h+ breaks (add one hour if starting from Morvich)

Start/Finish: Dorusduain Forest Enterprise car-park

1. From Dornie drive south on A87

2. After 8km leave A87 just N of causeway at head Loch Duich and take L turn signposted *Morvich*.

3. After about 1 km ignore sign with arrow reading *Falls of Glomach Car Park*. Instead bear L at sign reading *Private Road*. Where tarmac ends there seems to be no objection to continuing along unsurfaced road past houses/farm buildings at Ruarach and Lienassie.

THE WILD SWIMMER OF KINTAIL

4. Open gate at start of forest and drive to Forest Enterprise car-park at NG97769 22225. There is a locked red barrier and sign *To Falls of Glomach*.

5. There is a height barrier along here: if you are driving a mobile home/van you will need to park at Morvich NTS car-park NG96050 21065 marked on OS sheet 33. (Follow signposts to Falls of Glomach then after 2km reach waymarker and bear L to cross Abhainn Chonaig at Innis a' Crotha footbridge. Once across bridge turn R onto unsurfaced road to join route described below at NG98079 22336. Add one hour if parking at Morvich.)

6. From Dorusduain car-park take unsurfaced road for 2km following signposts *To Glomach Falls*.

7. At edge of forest where unsurfaced road ends cross footbridge over Allt an Leoid Ghaingamhaich and continue E on footpath that climbs up to Bealach na Sroine.

8. Path is marked with cairns over high point at Bealach na Sroine NH00384 24339. From here Loch Thuill Easaich, Loch Gaorsaic and Loch a' Bhealaich can be seen.

9. From Bealach na Sroine follow path downhill to Falls of Glomach (330m) NH01879 25572.

10. Return by same route.

Dogs: sheep and deer, cows at Morvich.

Navigation: Path signposted/cairned but if misty be careful to keep on path.

To Swim Loch Thuill Easaich, Loch Gaorsaic and Loch a' Bhealaich:
Grade: ***
Map: OS Sheets 25 and 33
Distance/Ascent: 15km/583m
Starting Height: 57m
Time: 6h+ breaks (add one hour if starting from Morvich)
Start/Finish: Dorusduain Forest Enterprise car park
1. From Dornie drive south on A87

2. After 8km leave A87 just N of causeway at head Loch Duich and take L turn signposted *Morvich*.
3. After 1 km ignore sign with arrow reading *Falls of Glomach Car Park*. Instead bear L at sign reading *Private Road*. Where tarmac ends there seems to be no objection to continuing along unsurfaced road past houses/farm buildings at Ruarach and Lienassie.
4. Open gate at start of forest and drive to Forest Enterprise car-park NG97769 22225.
5. There is a height barrier along here: if you are driving a mobile home/van you will need to park at Morvich NTS car-park NG96050 21065 marked on OS sheet 33. (From there follow signposts to Falls of Glomach. After 2km walk reach waymarker to join route described below at NG98165 22210. Add one hour if parking at Morvich.)
6. From Dorusduain car-park continue E along unsurfaced road for 400m then at forest clearing bear R to cross Abhainn Chonaig at Innis a' Crotha footbridge NG98195 22323.
7. At waymarker turn L and follow footpath E along Gleann Chòinneachain.
8. At NH00640 21383 turn L and follow path over Bealach na Sgàirne to Loch a Bhealaich (380m) NH02490 20703.
9. Walk N over rough ground following W shore of loch to reach Loch Gaorsaic (380m) NH02265 22383.
10. Continue N on W bank of Abhainn Gaorsaic to Loch Thuill Easaich(380m) NH02760 23178.
11. Return by same route.
Dogs: sheep and deer, cows at Morvich.

Loch Droma and Loch a'Fraoich Choire
Grade: ***
Map: OS Sheets 25 and 33
Distance/Ascent: 38km/800m
Starting Height: 7m
Time: 9h+breaks

THE WILD SWIMMER OF KINTAIL

Start/Finish: Killilan car-park, Glen Elchaig

1. From Dornie drive N across bridge following A87 for 1km then turn R onto by-road along N shore Loch Duich for 8km (signposted *Conchra Sallochy Killilan Camas-luinie*.)

2. About 2km before road ends cross Belford bridge over river then at sharp bend with signpost reading Camas-luinie 1½ miles keep straight on through white iron gates. Park here NG94100 30300.

3. Continue on bike along estate road through stone gateposts with notice *Inverinate Estate No Vehicle Access*.

4. After 4.5 km tarmac ends NG96972 27971. Continue along unsurfaced road to Iron Lodge NH04300 29400.

5. Leave bikes at Iron Lodge and take track that climbs hillside beside waterfall behind house.

6. Follow track for 1.5km to Loch Droma NH05899 28711 (307m.) About 500m E of Loch Droma look out for indistinct track on R (NH06635 28790) and follow this S to reach Allt an Fhraoich-choire near NH06812 28287.

7. Walk along W bank of Allt an Fhraoich-choire for 3km to Loch an Fhraoich-choire (757m) NH05727 25107.

8. Return by same route.

Dogs: cattle, sheep and deer in Glen Elchaig.

Sgurr nan Ceathramhnan Hill Lochs

An Lochan Gorm and Loch Coire nan Dearcag
Grade: ***
Map: OS Sheet 25
Distance/Ascent: 36km/1,150m
Starting Height: 250m
Time: 9h+breaks
Start/Finish: Glen Affric car-park

1. From Cannich drive 18km to car-park (toilets) at head Glen Affric NH20113 23337.

2. From car-park follow unsurfaced road downhill and bear L across bridge over River Affric.

3. Go through gate and walk/cycle along unsurfaced road on S side Loch Affric for 7km to Athnamulloch.

4. Cross bridge over River Affric and follow rough track for further 5km to Glen Affric hostel NH07992 20100.

5. Walk around back of hostel and take footpath past water tank that leads uphill to E side Allt na Faing.

6. Go through deer-gate NH08266 20558 and follow path up into Coire na Cloiche.

7. Above 650m contour line where footpath becomes faint look out for cairns that mark way to bealach at head Coire na Cloiche (800m) NH07924 22886.

8. From bealach turn left/W and follow long, undulating ridge for 2km to reach summit Sgurr nan Ceathramhnan (1151m) NH05707 22839.

9. Descend narrow/rocky NE ridge Sgurr nan Ceathramhnan to Bealach nan Daoine NH06584 23463 (840m) unnamed on some maps. Scramble down to reach An Gorm-lochan (890m) NH05769 23381 which lies 400m to W of bealach.

10. Climb back onto ridge and continue for 3km over Càrn na Con Dhu (967m) to reach Mullach na Dheiragain (982m.)

11. Return over Càrn na Con Dhu to Bealach nan Daoine NH06584 23463 (840m).

12. Walk 650m SE from bealach to Loch Coire nan Dearcag (735m) NH07158 23006.

13. From loch make rising traverse across steep, rocky ground to reach bealach at head Coire na Cloiche.

14. Take footpath down to Alltbeithe and return by bike to Glen Affric car park.

Glen Affric Hostel: £25 per person per night. Open mid-April to mid-September. No dogs. hostellingscotland.orGuk

THE WILD SWIMMER OF KINTAIL

Sgurr na Lapaich Hill Lochs

Loch Thuill Bhearnaich and Loch a'Choire Bhig
Grade: ***
Map: OS Sheet 25
Distance/Ascent: 24km/1060m
Starting Height: 230m
Time: 8h+breaks
Start/Finish: Mullardoch Dam near Cannich

1. Drive to car-park at head Glen Cannich where road ends at Mullardoch dam. Continue on foot to dam.
2. Go through gate where tarmac ends and at boat-house follow faint footpath along N shore Loch Mullardoch. Path follows 250m contour line most of the way.
3. Ignore R fork near memorial cairn.
4. About 1km W of dam reach bridge over Allt Mullardoch NH 20644 31838 near shed/ruined cottage.
5. Continue on faint path along lochside aiming for small windbreak of trees.
6. From trees walk 750m along lochside to next major stream, the Allt Taige and take footpath marked on map on E bank of stream NH18767 31114.
7. Cross stream below waterfall NH18310 31600. If Allt Taige in spate continue up E bank of stream for 750m to bridge NH17922 32012.
8. Head W up well-defined ridge to Mullach a' Ghlas-thuill (792m) NH16362 31855.
9. Continue Nalong ridge to Braigh a' Choire Bhig (1011m) NH15685 33429. Loch a' Choire Bhig can be seen from near here.
10. Continue to follow ridge NE to Sgurr nan Clachan Geala (1095m). Loch Thuill Bhearnaich can be seen from near here.
11. Continue N to Sgurr na Lapaich (1150m) NH16092 35108.
11. Return by route of ascent.

Dogs: goats on Braigh a' Choire Bhig.

KELLAN MACINNES

To Swim Loch Thuill Bhearnaich and Loch a'Choire Bhig:
1. Follow steps 1-5 of previous route as far as the small windbreak of trees.
2. From trees walk 750m along lochside to next major stream, the Allt Taige and take footpath marked on map on E bank of stream NH18767 31114.
3. Follow footpath (noting but not crossing footbridge) til it ends near 600m contour NH17735 33096 then continue along E bank of Allt Taige for 1km to Loch Thuill Bhearnaich (760m) NH16885 34191.
4. Head S retracing your steps for 2.5km and then cross Allt Taige at bridge NH17922 32012.
5. Follow E bank of Allt Loch a' Choire Bhig for 2km over very rough ground to Loch a' Choire Bhig (750m) NH16205 33196. Some scrambling involved.
6. Return by same route.

Carn Eige Hill Lochs

Loch a'Choire Domhain and Coire Lochan
Grade: ***
Map: OS Sheet 25
Distance/Ascent: 14km/1033m
Starting Height: 250m
Time: 7h+breaks (+3h if swimming hill lochs)
Start/Finish: Mullardoch Dam near Cannich
1. Drive to car park at head of Glen Cannich where road ends at Mullardoch dam. Continue on foot to dam.
2. Take Mullardoch ferry and ask Angus to drop you at bay where Allt a' Choire Dhomhain empties into Loch Mullardoch NH15585 30140 (marked as Waterfall on OS sheet 25.)
3. Follow track on W bank Allt a' Choire Dhomhain for 100m past shed.
4. Turn R onto footpath NH15555 30065 (marked on map) heading SW

up shoulder of Carn Eige. Path is faint and hard to find in long grass at start.

5. Follow path as it zig zags NE up steep hillside heading for Bealach na h-Eige.

6. To swim in Coire Lochan (770m) NH12520 27820 descend W from Bealach na h-Eige for 2.5km. Allow 2h+ for lengthy diversion over rough ground. Alternatively enjoy excellent views of Coire Lochan from summit Carn Eige.

7. Continue along ridge to Creag na h-Eige where you can drop down into upper Coire Domhain to swim Loch a'Choire Domhain (880m) NH13995 26755 (allow 30mins+).

8. Path fades on flat ground above 880m. Continue to follow NE ridge to summit Carn Eige NH12370 26195 (1183m).

10. Return by route of ascent.

Mullardoch Ferry: Runs March-early August www.loch-mullardoch-ferry.co.uk

APPENDIX IV

Macrow's List of the Hill Lochs of Kintail

Name	Meaning	Location/ Altitude	Grid Reference
Loch a' Choire Dhomhain	*The loch of the deep corrie*	Below Munro Carn Eige 927m/3,041ft	OS Sheet 25 NH13995 26755
An Gorm-Lochan	*The green lochan*	Below Munro Sgurr nan Ceathramhnan 890m/2,919ft	OS Sheet 25 & 33 NH05769 23381
Coire Lochan	*The lochan of the corrie*	Below Munro Sgurr nan Ceathramhnan 777m/2,549ft	OS Sheet 25 & 33 NH04619 23538
Loch Tuill Bhearnach	*The loch of the notched hollow*	Below Munro Sgurr na Lapaich 758m/2,486ft	OS Sheet 25 NH16885 34191
Loch an Fraoich-choire	*The loch of the heather corrie*	Below Munro Sgurr nan Ceathramhnan 757m/2,483ft	OS Sheet 25 & 33 NH05690 24950
Loch a' Chlèirich	*The loch of the cleric*	Below Munro A'Ghlas-bheinn 747m/2,450ft	OS Sheet 25 & 33 NH00603 22662
Loch a' Choire Bhig	*The loch of the little corrie*	Below Munro Sgurr na Lapaich 747m/2,450ft	OS Sheet 25 NH16205 33196
Loch Coire nan Dearcag	*The loch of the corrie of the berries*	Below Munro Sgurr nan Ceathramhnan 736m/2,414ft	OS Sheet 25& 33 NH07140 22965
Coire Lochan	*The lochan of the corrie*	Below Munro Carn Eige 667m/2,166ft	OS Sheet 25 NH12520 27820
Loch Sgurr na h-Eige	*The loch of the notched peak*	South of Glen Elchaig 625m/2,050ft	OS Sheet 25 & 33 NH04882 27176

THE WILD SWIMMER OF KINTAIL

Loch Bhuic Mhòir	*The loch of the big buck deer*	North side of Loch Duich 536m/1,758ft	OS Sheet 25 & 33 NG92244 26056
Loch nan Eun	*The loch of the birds*	Between Loch Duich and Glen Elchaig 484m/1,587ft	OS Sheet 25 & 33 NG94735 26300
Loch na Craoibhe-caoruinn	*The loch of the rowan tree*	North side of Loch Duich 477m/1,564ft	OS Sheet 25 & 33 NG90750 25795
Loch an t-Sabhail	*The loch of the barn*	Between Loch Duich and Glen Elchaig 468m/1,535ft	OS Sheet 25 & 33 NG95815 25552
Loch na Faolaig	*The loch of the seagull*	North side of Loch Duich 457m/1,499ft	OS Sheet 25 & 33 NG90564 25641
Loch Gorm Mor	*The big blue loch*	North side of Loch Duich 449m/1,473ft	OS Sheet 25 & 33 NG91314 25361
Loch a' Mhuillin	*The loch of the mill*	North side of Loch Duich 443m/1,453ft	OS Sheet 25 & 33 NG90795 25110
Loch Mhoicean	(meaning obscure)	North-west of Loch Mullardoch 426m/1,397ft	OS Sheet 25 NH07099 31512
Loch nan Ealachan	*The loch of the swans*	North of Glen Elchaig 403m/1,322ft	OS Sheet 25 & 33 NG99701 28375
Loch a' Bhealaich	*The loch of the pass*	Between Glen Affric and Glen Elchaig 378m/1,240ft	OS Sheet 25 & 33 NH02490 20703
Loch Gaorsaic	*The loch of horror*	Between Glen Affric and Glen Elchaig 376m/1,233ft	OS Sheet 25 & 33 NH02265 22383

KELLAN MACINNES

Loch Lòn Mhurchaidh	*The loch of Murdoch's meadow*	South of Glen Elchaig 376m/1,233ft	OS Sheet 25 & 33 NH03296 26403
Loch na Maoile Buidhe	*The loch of the yellow rounded top*	North-west of Loch Mullardoch 375m/1,230ft	OS Sheet 25 NH04357 34425
Loch Thuill Easaich	*The loch of the corrie of the waterfall*	Between Glen Affric and Glen Elchaig 374m/1,227	OS Sheet 25 & 33 NH02760 23178
Loch Dubhach	*The dark lochan*	South shore of Loch Long 334m/1,0195ft	OS Sheet 25 & 33 NG91629 28471
Loch an Droma	*The loch of the long ridge*	Between Glen Elchaig and Loch Mullardoch 307m/1,007ft	OS Sheet 25 & 33 NH05899 28711
Loch Beinn a' Mheadhoin	*The loch of the middle mountain*	South shore of Loch Long 307m/1,007ft	OS Sheet 25 & 33 NG92065 28585
Loch Cruoshie	(meaning obscure)	North-west of Loch Mullardoch 254m/833ft	OS Sheet 25 NH05529 36266

NB Gaelic names are taken from the Ordnance Survey names book or are as translated for Macrow by local people in Kintail in 1946

RYMOUR BOOKS

poetry • history • debate

ALSO AVAILABLE FROM RYMOUR BOOKS
www.rymour.co.uk

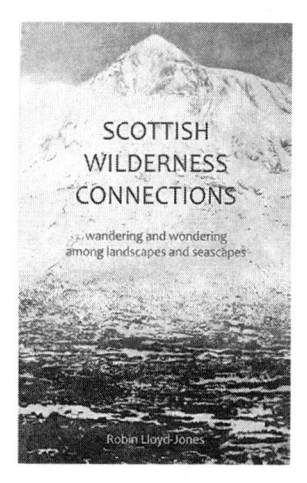

Robin Lloyd-Jones, *Scottish Wilderness Connections*,
148pp, illustrated

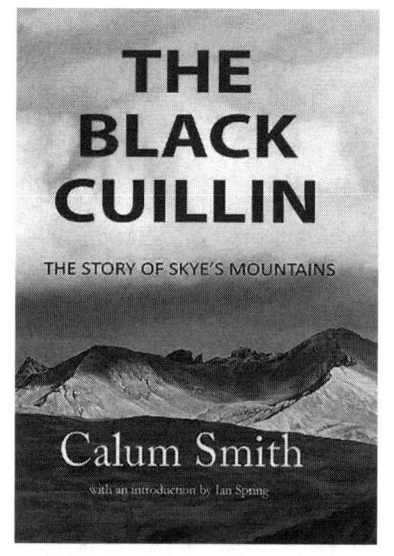

Calum Smith, *The Black Cuillin*,
340pp, illustrated